Great Musicians Series

Music Appreciation
for the Elementary Grades

Paganini

Haydn

Mozart

Bach

Handel

Schubert

Beethoven

Music Appreciation for the Elementary Grades: Book 1

Written by Elisabeth Tanner and Judy Wilcox

Layout design by Christi Gifford
www.TheGraphicLady.com

ISBN 978-1-61006-113-1
Copyright © 2013 by Zeezok Publishing, LLC
Printed in the United States of America

Zeezok Publishing, LLC
PO Box 1960 • Elyria, OH 44036
info@Zeezok.com

www.Zeezok.com

Table of Contents

Introduction

Dear Parents and Teachers,

Do you have a favorite musical composer? Can you hum along with popular classical pieces like Beethoven's *Fur Elise*, Handel's *Messiah* or Bach's *Minuet in G*? It has been said that "A love of classical music is only partially a natural response to hearing the works performed, it also must come about by a decision to listen carefully, [and] to pay close attention..."[1] The heart of this series is to introduce children to classical music and begin to instill within them a love and appreciation for this unique genre. We desire not only to encourage children to appreciate music, but to also motivate them to pursue music for themselves. Throughout this study, your student will meet the men who devoted their lives to composing and performing amazing pieces of music. They will be introduced to multiple songs by each composer and learn to recognize these well-loved pieces. This two-year series is structured to be a thorough music appreciation program, with an introduction to music theory. It has been written to meet all of the national benchmarks required for music appreciation for kindergarten through sixth grade. It not only meets the national academic requirements, but it also opens up a new world of art and entertainment for your students.

Components of *Music Appreciation for the Elementary Grades: Book 1*

Music Appreciation for the Elementary Grades: Book 1 will introduce children to seven different composers, dating from 1685-1828 (Bach, Handel, Haydn, Mozart, Beethoven, Paganini, and Schubert). Each composer's childhood and adult life are vividly described in individual biographies. Every important incident is mentioned and every detail of the stories is true. Each book contains written music and delightful pictures throughout. It is more than the human side of these books that will make them live, for in the music the great masters breathe.

In order to best meet the needs of each student, this program has been designed to be flexible and easily arranged. Each composer has been allotted four weeks, with the various activities being divided amongst those weeks. Please feel free to adjust this suggested layout any way that you see fit for your schedule and the student's needs. You may also omit some activities if time does not permit for them. (Please Note: The activities marked with an asterisk [*] are required in order to meet national music appreciation standards.)

Please be aware that most of the activities suggested in the *Student Activity Book* can be adjusted to each grade level by simply adapting the adult involvement. Older children, who can read, write, and follow multi-step directions will be able to work through the majority of the material on their own. Children who are younger will need an adult to help them read the biographies, discuss the questions orally, and work through the hands-on activities. There are a few instances where activities are specifically designated for the older grades, but otherwise the activities are able to be easily understood by a wide range of ages.

---

[1] Charles Rosen, Brainyquote.com http://www.brainyquote.com/quotes/authors/c/charles_rosen.html

Required Components:

Music Appreciation Student Activity Book

This book includes a variety of hands-on activities such as geography lessons, history lessons, recipes, instrument studies, music vocabulary, handwriting, musical facts of the Classical period, timelines, character trait studies, and so much more. Geared for a variety of learners—auditory, kinesthetic, visual, and just plain "active"—the *Student Activity Book* is an excellent companion to your reading experience.

Music Appreciation Music CDs

The Music CDs provide all of the supplemental music that corresponds with the weekly activities. On these CDs you will find all of the music that is included in the books (exactly as written), an additional thirty-five professionally recorded pieces, plus an explanation and demonstration of each of the instruments in the orchestra from Benjamin Britten's *Young Person's Guide to the Orchestra*. This music will enhance your child's understanding of the music concepts being taught each week.

Music Appreciation Lapbook CDs

The Lapbook CD provides seven lapbook templates. Students will create a lapbook for each composer, allowing them to connect with the music and the lives of these musicians in a hands-on way. These easy-to-assemble lapbooks will help solidify in your child's mind musical concepts, character traits, world geography, and information on the composers' lives.

The *Great Musician Series*

Available in print, Audio Book, and eBook editions, the following seven *Great Musician Series* biographies, by Opal Wheeler and Sybil Deucher, are the core of this course:
- *Sebastian Bach, The Boy from Thuringia*
- *Handel at the Court of Kings*
- *Joseph Haydn, The Merry Little Peasant*
- *Mozart, The Wonder Boy*
- *Ludwig Beethoven and the Chiming Tower Bells*
- *Paganini, Master of Strings*
- *Franz Schubert and His Merry Friends*

Optional Components:

Music Appreciation Coloring Pages

For the younger student, we also offer coloring pages for each biography in the *Great Musician Series*. Sold separately, this package of coloring pages includes over 60 professionally drawn illustrations. The coloring pages are directly related to scenes from the chapter being read.

Music Appreciation Bingo Game

This is easy to play and lots of fun too! The game features 45 informative cards on composers, instruments, and elements of music. The object is to match the cards to the picture on your board, and be the first to yell "Encore!" Recommended for all ages.

Scope and Sequence

Music Appreciation Standards	Bach	Handel	Haydn	Mozart	Beethoven	Paganini	Schubert
History:							
Compare music examples from different periods.	✓	✓	✓	✓	✓	✓	✓
Identify music examples from music literature; respond to the style of that period of music.	✓	✓	✓	✓	✓	✓	✓
Sing and listen to music from various historical periods.	✓	✓	✓	✓	✓	✓	✓
Identify, listen, and respond to music of different composers (compare/contrast).	✓	✓	✓	✓	✓	✓	✓
Discuss the lives and times of composers from different periods.	✓	✓	✓	✓	✓	✓	✓
Recognize and demonstrate theme variations in classical music.	✓	✓	✓	✓	✓	✓	✓
Research and identify musical instruments from different historical periods.	✓	✓	✓	✓	✓	✓	✓
Identify certain composers and place them in the right time period.	✓	✓	✓	✓	✓	✓	✓
Classify by composer (time, place, event) and a varied body of exemplary musical works.	✓	✓	✓	✓	✓	✓	✓
Identify major periods or genres in development of world music.	✓	✓	✓	✓	✓	✓	✓
Discuss the purpose of music from selected historical periods.	✓	✓	✓	✓	✓	✓	✓

Music Appreciation Standards	Bach	Handel	Haydn	Mozart	Beethoven	Paganini	Schubert
Music in Everyday Life:							
Communicate ideas about the importance of music in everyday life.	✓	✓	✓	✓	✓	✓	✓
Recognize how sounds and music are used in our daily lives.	✓			✓	✓	✓	
Listen to, identify, discuss, and respond to music written for specific purposes.	✓			✓	✓		
Recognize and describe how songs are used for a variety of occasions.	✓			✓	✓		
Music Styles in American History:							
Contrast opera and music theatre.				✓			
Music in Different Cultures:							
Sing and listen to music from world cultures.			✓	✓			
Recognize and describe how music serves as an expression in various cultures.		✓	✓	✓			
Recognize the interaction of people in music.			✓	✓		✓	
Research individual musical instruments from world cultures.			✓	✓			
Describe conditions under which music is created and performed in various cultures.			✓	✓			
Discuss how culture influences music.				✓			

Music Appreciation Standards	Bach	Handel	Haydn	Mozart	Beethoven	Paganini	Schubert
Music Style:							
Listen and respond to a variety of music styles.		✓	✓	✓	✓	✓	
Demonstrate how elements of music are used to create music style .		✓				✓	
Identify how elements of music communicate ideas or moods.		✓				✓	
Identify and describe contrasting music styles (march vs. lullaby…).		✓				✓	
Examine the chronological development of various music styles.		✓					
Types of Music:							
Identify mass, concerto, symphony…		✓		✓		✓	✓
How Music Is Created:							
Recognize and identify contextual elements that shape the development of music (time, location, culture, current events, social and political climate).					✓		
Recognize and identify the historical and cultural contexts that have influenced music (time, place, event).					✓		
Discuss how current developments in music reflect society in reference to themselves, community, and the world around them.					✓		
Demonstrate how music communicates meaning of text, feelings, moods, and images and how that influences personal preferences.					✓		
Describe the emotional connection to the musical experience.					✓	✓	

Music Appreciation Standards	Bach	Handel	Haydn	Mozart	Beethoven	Paganini	Schubert
Describe how music preferences reflect people's values, and how people respond to music.					✓	✓	
Describe how events during various historical periods have influenced the development of music.	✓	✓	✓	✓	✓	✓	✓
Developing Personal Musical Style:							
Develop and apply (use) criteria to determine personal preferences for specific musical works.						✓	
Identify personal preferences for specific music.	✓				✓	✓	
Justify one's personal preferences of music choice using music vocabulary.						✓	
Reflect on why others may have different music preferences.					✓	✓	
Express how characteristics of the music of their choice affects/are applicable to their daily experiences.					✓	✓	
Identify various uses of music in their daily experiences.						✓	

Music Theory Standards	Bach	Handel	Haydn	Mozart	Beethoven	Paganini	Schubert
Learning about Instruments:							
Identify instruments visually and aurally (tambourine, maracas, rhythm sticks, triangle, woodblock, finger cymbals).			✓				
Identify instruments visually and aurally (orchestra).		✓	✓				✓

Music Theory Standards	Bach	Handel	Haydn	Mozart	Beethoven	Paganini	Schubert
Classify the four families of orchestral instruments.			✓				
Identify instruments visually and aurally (band).			✓				
Identify selected electronic and world music instruments (guitar, violin, sitar, congas, bagpipes, synthesizer).			✓			✓	
Written Music and Vocabulary:							
Written music vocabulary (meter, Al Fine, DC al Coda, DC dal seno, tonality).							✓
1/8 notes and rests, 1/4 notes and rests, 1/2 and notes and rests, quarter notes and rests, 1/16 notes and rests, and dotted notes and rests.							✓
Analyze a piece of music using music vocabulary.							✓
Explore melody vs. harmony.						✓	✓
Recognize, identify, and use the key signatures.							✓
Identify elements of music (vocabulary, terms, rhythm, syllables, solfege, piano, forte).	✓	✓		✓	✓	✓	✓
Recognize clef, key signature, meter signature, tempo, note values, dynamic markings.							✓
Discuss how these elements determine the quality of a song in expressive music.		✓					✓
Read and notate music in the bass clef and the treble clef.							✓

Music Disc Track List

Music Disc 1

1. Bach p 43 Minuet
2. Bach p 47 March
3. Bach p 60 Gavotte
4. Bach p 66 Polonaise
5. Bach p 71 Chorale
6. Bach p 75 Gavotte
7. Bach p 81 Musette
8. Bach p 92 Minuet
9. Pomp & Circumstance
10. Mendelssohn Wedding March
11. Taps
12. Now Let Us to the Bagpipes Sound
13. Stars and Strips Forever
14. Joy to the World
15. Bach p 102 Gigue
16. Bach p 107 Bouree
17. Bach p 108 Musette
18. Bach p 112 Beside Thy Cradle Here I Stand
19. Bach p 114 Air on G String
20. Bach p 118 My Heart Ever Faithful
21. Bach p 122 Now Let Us to the Bagpipe's Sound
22. Handel p 37 Minuet
23. Handel p 58 Minuet
24. Handel p 64 Gavotte
25. Handel p 65 Passepied
26. Handel p 76 Gavotte with Variations
27. Handel p 83 Gavotte
28. Handel p 89 Gigue
29. Handel p 94 Vivace
30. 1812 Overture
31. Wiegenlied
32. Overture The Marriage of Figaro
33. Oh Susanna

Music Disc 2

1. Music for the Royal Fireworks
2. Arrival of the Queen of Sheba
3. Overture The Magic Flute
4. The Nutcracker Suite Dance of the Sugar Plum Fairy
5. Bach Toccata
6. Bach Aria
7. Handel p 112 Graceful Dance
8. Handel p 118 The Harmonious Blacksmith
9. Handel p 130 Hallelujah Chorus
10. Handel p 137 Minuet
11. Handel p 138 Bouree
12. Handel p 140 Courante
13. Handel p 143 Minuet
14. Handel p 145 Passepied
15. Handel p 146 Minuet
16. Handel p 147 Prelude
17. Handel p 148 Minuet
18. Handel p 150 Fugue
19. Handel p 152 Hornpipe
20. Handel p 154 Chaconne
21. Handel p 157 Bourree
22. Handel p 158 Intermezzo
23. Handel p 160 Gavotte
24. Handel p 162 Fughetta
25. Handel p 163 Sonatina
26. Handel p 166 Largo
27. Haydn p 43 Minuet in D
28. Haydn p 47 Andantino
29. Haydn p 58 Minuet in C
30. Haydn p 64 Sonata

Music Disc 3

1. Violin
2. Viola
3. Cello
4. Double Bass
5. Harp
6. Flute
7. Clarinet
8. Oboe
9. Bassoon
10. Piccolo
11. French Horn
12. Tuba
13. Trombone
14. Trumpet
15. Snare Drum & Cymbals
16. Bass Drum
17. Timpani

Music Disc 4

1. Haydn p 77 Minuet in E
2. Haydn p 80 La Roxelane
3. Haydn p 83 Allegro

4. Haydn p 85 Farewell Symphony
5. Haydn p 89 Serenata
6. Haydn p 91 Symphony in C
7. Haydn p 92 Toy Symphony
8. Country Gardens Marine Band
9. Allegro for Acoustic Guitar
10. Elements
11. Seeking
12. Haydn p 101 Scherzo
13. Haydn p 105 Andante from the Surprise Symphony
14. Haydn p 106 Andante from the Clock Symphony
15. Haydn p 112 Gypsy Rondo
16. Haydn p 115 Austrian Hymn
17. Rag Saraswati
18. Jarawali
19. No 2 Allegro for Harpsichord
20. Panpipe Recital
21. Grass Dance Theme Song
22. Indonesian Gong
23. Scottish Bagpipe Band
24. Jowelbinna Didgeridoo
25. Mozart p 21 Minuet in G
26. Mozart p 33 Minuet in F
27. Mozart p 52 Allegro
28. Mozart p 69 Theme from the Sonata in A
29. Mozart p 71 A Little Waltz
30. Mozart p 80 Wiegenlied
31. Mozart p 84 Longing for Spring
32. Mozart p 90 Song from the Magic Flute
33. Mozart p 93 Sonatina
34. Mozart p 94 A French Melody with Variation
35. Mozart p 96 Andante
36. Mozart p 97 Rondo
37. Mozart p 98 Bagatelle
38. Mozart p 100 Presto
39. Mozart p 101 Sonata
40. Mozart p 102 Minuet
41. Mozart p 103 Andante
42. Mozart p 104 Presto
43. Mozart p 105 Andante
44. Mozart p 106 Rondo
45. Mozart p 107 Allegretto
46. Mozart p 108 Sonata
47. Mozart p 109 Rondo

48. Mozart p 111 Sonata
49. Mozart p 114 A Little Minuet
50. Mozart p 116 Landler Secondo
51. Mozart p 117 Landler Primo
52. Mozart Landler Primo & Secondo Duet
53. Mozart p 120 Minuetto Secondo
54. Mozart p 121 Minuetto Primo
55. Mozart Minuette Primo & Secondo Duet
56. Mozart p 122 Country Dance (1) Secondo
57. Mozart p 123 Country Dance (1) Primo
58. Mozart Country Dance (1) Primo & Secondo Duet
59. Mozart p 124 Country Dance (2) Secondo
60. Mozart p 125 Country Dance (2) Primo
61. Mozart Country Dance (2) Primo & Secondo Duet

Music Disc 5

1. Battle Cry of Freedom
2. Beethoven p 50 Sonatina
3. Beethoven p 54 Ecossaise I
4. Beethoven p 56 Ecossaise II
5. Beethoven p 60 Romance
6. Beethoven p 74 Anger Over a Lost Penny
7. Beethoven p 80 Andantino
8. Beethoven p 83 Rondo
9. Beethoven p 89 Minuetto
10. Beethoven p 93 Rondo
11. Moonlight Sonata
12. Beethoven p 105 Thundering Tones
13. Beethoven p 106 Andante Melody
14. Beethoven p 108 Minuet in G
15. Beethoven p 111 Country Dance
16. Beethoven p 112 Country Dance
17. Beethoven p 113 Wistful Tune
18. Beethoven p 116 Pastoral Symphony
19. Beethoven p 122 Turkish March Secondo
20. Beethoven p 123 Turkish March Primo
21. Beethoven Turkish March Secondo & Primo Duet
22. Beethoven p 130 Minuet
23. Beethoven p 138 Allegretto
24. Beethoven p 142 Ninth Symphony
25. Beethoven p 147 Rondo
26. Beethoven p 148 Minuetto
27. Beethoven p 149 Andante

Weekly Lesson Outline

Bach

(Activities marked with an * are required in order to meet national music appreciation standards.)

Week One:

- 📕 Read Chapter 1*
- 📋 Answer Comprehension Questions
- 💜 Character Qualities
- 📚 Tidbits of Interest
- 🗒 Assemble Lapbook Folder
- ✋ Bach Family Facts (LB)
- 🌐 Places that Bach Visited Map Activity
- 🎼 Learning About Stringed Instruments Activity*

Week Two:

- 📕 Read Chapter 2 & 3*
- 📋 Answer Comprehension Questions
- 🎧 Listen to Music Disc 1, tracks 1-7*
- 💜 Character Qualities
- 📚 Tidbits of Interest
- ✋ Recipe for German Rye Bread
- 🎚 Oxidation Experiment (LB)
- ✍ Glory to God Copy Work
- 🎼 Music of the Baroque Period (LB)*
- 🎼 "What's that Song?" Vocabulary (LB)*
- 🎼 Name that Tune (LB)

Week Three:

- 📕 Read Chapter 4*
- 📋 Answer Comprehension Questions
- 🎧 Listen to Music Disc 1, track 8*
- 💜 Character Qualities
- 📚 Tidbits of Interest
- 🎼 Music in Everyday Life*
- 🎼 Music for Special Occasions and Purposes*

Week Four:

- 📕 Read Chapter 5*
- 📋 Answer Comprehension Questions
- 🎧 Listen to Music Disc 1, tracks 15-21*
- 💜 Character Qualities
- 📚 Tidbits of Interest
- 🎚 The Voyager (LB)
- ✋ Timeline Game (LB)*

Additional activity required for national music standards:

- ☐ Sing songs representing the child's culture

 ## Chapter One Comprehension Questions

1. What talent did nearly all members of the Bach family seem to share? _____

_____

2. Sebastian's father taught him about his great-great-grandfather, Veit Bach, who took his lute with him to work. Do you remember what his occupation was? _____

_____

3. The Bach family did something annually. What was it, and why did the whole village of Eisen-ach enjoy it? _____

_____

4. Sebastian sang in a scholars' choir that sang the same songs as an important Reformation leader in church history. Can you think of his name? _____

_____

5. What sad events changed Sebastian's life when he was a young boy? _____

_____

6. Sebastian went to live with his brother Christoph, but Christoph was very strict about some-thing. What were his rules and how did Sebastian respond to them?_____

_____

_____

7. In spite of Christoph's confiscation of Sebastian's copy of the music, Sebastian had done some-thing remarkable in the six month process. What was it?_____

_____

8. As the chapter ends, where is Sebastian preparing to go? _____

_____

1685	**Johann Sebastian Bach**	1750
1685	George Frederic Handel	1759
	1732 Franz Joseph Haydn	1809
	1756 Wolfgang A. Mozart	1791
	1770 Ludwig van Beethoven	1827
	1782 Nicolò Paganini	1840
	1797 Franz Schubert	1828

Character Qualities

Hospitality *(pp. 14,15, 121, 126)* – The Bach family was known as a hospitable family. Hospitality means being friendly and generous in entertaining guests and visitors. The family reunion was just one example of the Bach hospitality in action. It was a quality that Sebastian maintained throughout his life. His home was recognized as one of graciousness, friendship, and love.

Sense of Humor and Wit *(pp. 15, 16, 52)* – Sebastian himself was known as "a merry and companionable fellow."[1] In this chapter, the portion about the quodlibet of the fat cow that would not go to pasture and the quiet flowing river hints at Sebastian's love for laughter and merry songs. You have to admit that finding gold coins in herrings' mouths is somewhat humorous (providentially so). Anyone who likes coffee will be delighted to learn that Bach also loved coffee and even wrote a cantata about

Character Qualities
• Hospitality
• Sense of Humor and Wit

it (*The Coffee Cantata*)! That's good caffeinated humor in its richest sense. Once when Bach was praised for his skill as an organist, he replied, "There is nothing wonderful about it. You have only to hit the right notes at the right moment and the instrument does the rest."[2]

Tidbits of Interest

Chapter 1:

Pages 9–11: Eisenach (pronounced \eye-zen-ahk\), the village, nestles on the edge of the Thuringian forest. It is also the location of Wartburg Castle, where Martin Luther (1483–1546) once sought refuge from Pope Leo X and other critics from the Roman Catholic Church. Wartburg Castle is where Luther translated the New Testament into German, making it available to the common man for study and meditation. Remember that Luther emphasized having a personal, living, Bible-based faith in Jesus Christ. He was himself a musician, declaring that music was second unto the Gospel itself,

so that many of the hymns from the Lutheran hymnal became a source of stimulation for Bach's works.[3]

In Eisenach, Bach sang in the scholars' choir, an all-boy choir in which boys sang even the soprano parts. Often, they sang chorales, which were German Lutheran hymn-tunes, many composed or arranged by Luther himself.

Page 11: Sebastian is the name Bach is called most frequently in Wheeler and Deucher's book. There were 53 individuals in the Bach family who were named Johann.[4] Oh, and five of his own sons were named Johann, and two of his daughters were named Johanna![5] So you can see why children were often called by their middle names to eliminate some confusion.

Pages 14,15: The Bach family was wonderfully musical. In fact, one author says that Bach's "is the largest family tree in music."[6] There are more than 50 musicians with the name of Bach who are recognized by musicologists. It is interesting that the word *bach* in German means *brook*. Ludwig Beethoven once exclaimed, "His name ought not to be Bach, but ocean, because of his infinite and inexhaustible wealth of combinations and harmonies."[7]

Page 20: Johann Christoph Bach, Sebastian's older brother by fourteen years, was the church organist in Ohrdruff who gave Sebastian his

first keyboard lessons and took responsibility for him in 1695, after their father's death. Christoph had been a student of the composer Johann Pachelbel.[8] His library of music contained French and Italian manuscripts by the best Italian and French composers of the time.[9] It is believed that the copying of the works of the masters by moonlight may have contributed to Sebastian's blindness by age 65.

Learning About the Bach Family

Using the *Bach Family Facts* lapbook pages, follow the directions to cut out and assemble the pieces. Adhere this activity to section #5 & 6 in your Bach lapbook.

"Bach has the largest family tree in music."[6]

Bach Family Facts

Places that Bach Visited

Using the following clues, complete the map of places that Bach visited.

1. Frankfurt is the southernmost city on this map.
2. Ohrdruff is due west of Arnstadt.
3. Berlin is found in the northeast corner of this map.
4. Celle is the northernmost city on this map.
5. Jena is located southeast of Weimar.
6. Hanover is southwest of Celle.
7. Leipzig is almost halfway between Dresden and Cöthen.
8. The state of Brandenburg is south of Berlin.
9. Erfurt is situated west of Weimar and north of Arnstadt.
10. Muhlhausen is located northwest of Erfurt.

Learning About Stringed Instruments

Many of these instruments were popular during the Baroque Period. Bach composed and performed much of his music for these types of instruments.

Directions: Cut out the boxes on the next page and glue the descriptions under the appropriate instruments.

Keyboard Instruments

Clavichord	Harpsichord	Spinet	Virginal

Organ	Upright Piano	Grand Piano	Keyboard

The Violin Family

Violin	Viola	Cello	Double Bass
		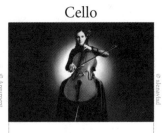	

The clavichord is one of the simplest of the keyboard family. Pressing a key causes a hammer action that strikes the strings. The volume is very soft.

The virginal is a member of the harpsichord family and uses the same mechanism. It only has one keyboard. The virginal's strings run parallel to the keyboard.

The harpsichord was very popular during the Baroque period. Even though it looks like a piano, it sounds different. It only has a range of about four octaves and the keys cause a mechanism (using quills) to pluck the strings.

Sometimes called the king of instruments, the organ can have several keyboards, as well as many pedals. A pipe organ can produce many sounds that imitate other instruments, depending on the shape of the pipes.

A spinet has keys that work a mechanism that pluck the strings. It only has one keyboard, and the strings in a spinet run diagonal to the keyboard. It is similar to the virginal and harpsichord.

The electronic keyboard can be played like an organ or a piano. It can imitate many other instruments and produce non-instrument sounds. The electronic keyboard is also called a synthesizer.

Upright pianos are the most common type of piano. They take up less space and cost less than the grands. Piano keys raise a hammer to strike the strings and can be played loudly or softly. The piano was invented around 1709.

The grand piano represents its name in sound quality and size. There are actually different sizes of grand pianos – a baby grand is about five feet long, while the concert grand is around nine feet long.

The violin is held and played under the player's chin. It is the smallest and highest pitched of the violin family. The violin has four strings and no frets. There are more violins in the symphony orchestra than any other instrument.

The largest member of the sting family, the double bass is about six feet tall. It rests on the ground and the player stands behind it to play. The double bass is usually played rhythmically.

The cello is a lot bigger than the viola and its range is one octave lower than the viola. It has a very mellow tone. The cello rests on the ground and the cellist sits behind it to play. It has four strings and no frets.

The viola is held by the musician to play and is a little bigger and deeper than the violin. This instrument plays in the tenor range. It has four strings and no frets.

Chapter Two Comprehension Questions

Comprehension

Bach

1. List some ways that people showed kindness or helpfulness to Sebastian and Erdmann in the beginning of this chapter. _____

   _____

   _____

2. The boys were excited about studying music to their heart's content. Initially, what was Sebastian's favorite instrument to play, and how did he improve the playing of it?

   _____

3. Sebastian was then allowed to play on another instrument and received lessons from Herr Böhm of St. John's Church. What was the instrument? _____

   _____

4. After three years at the school, Sebastian's high soprano voice changed, and he was not needed in the choir. How did he pay for his lodging at school? _____

   _____

5. Why did Sebastian walk to Hamburg? _____

   _____

6. After the concert and on his journey back to Lüneburg, Sebastian's mind was filled with thoughts of what? _____

   _____

7. How did Sebastian receive money to buy his dinner on his trip back to Lüneburg?_____

   _____

   _____

8. Sebastian received an invitation from the Duke of Weimar. What was he to do? _____

   _____

   _____

   _____

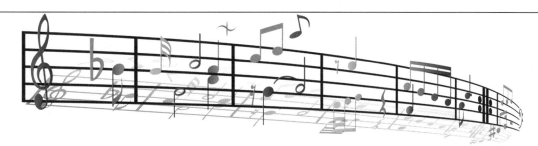

Chapter Three Comprehension Questions

1. What instrument did Sebastian play in the Duke's orchestra? _____
   _____

2. Sebastian visited family in Arnstadt. While there, he was invited to try a new item in the church. What was it? _____
   _____

3. After the organ concert at the church, what did the church leaders ask him to do? _____
   _____

4. Do you remember some of the elements of Sebastian's vow to the church leaders before beginning his duties there? _____
   _____
   _____
   _____

5. Sebastian loved that there was time to compose organ music at the church in Arnstadt, but how did the church leaders respond to his works? _____
   _____
   _____

6. Sebastian asked permission to see the great organist, Buxtehude, in Lübeck – but only for four weeks. How long did Sebastian end up staying? _____
   _____

7. What did the Duke of Weimar ask Sebastian to do? _____
   _____

8. Who was considered the only other German composer equal to Bach? _____
   _____

9. What competition had been arranged at the end of this chapter? _____
   _____
   _____

Character Qualities

Family-Oriented *(pp. 12, 14, 15, 104–106, 110, 111)* – The reunion attests to the importance of family in the Bach household. The very fact that Ambrosius took time to teach Sebastian how to play the violin also shows the significance of family unity and activity. This trait is something that Sebastian learned well from his father because he acted in the same manner with his own family. Doesn't the fact that he had twenty children speak volumes? He played with his children, cuddled them when they were crying, wrote music for them, and led them in their prayers.

Integrity *(pp. 70, 104)* – Bach asked the Duke of Weimar for permission to leave his role in the court orchestra before taking the position of organist at New Church in Arnstadt. Bach agreed to take certain vows regarding his duties in New Church, and he lived up to those vows for four years, even though he sometimes found the responsibilities constricting and suffocating. For the sake of his sons' educations, he chose the position of cantor over staying in a relative life of luxury with the Prince.

Page 40: Sebastian spent hours practicing on the clavier and experimenting with new fingering techniques. He is said to have had large hands that could stretch across 12 notes while performing running passages with his three middle fingers.[10] This was "an almost unheard of departure from the conventional way of playing scales. And with what amazing results!"[11]

Pages 41, 42: The organ is a keyboard instrument in which sound is produced by air passing through pipes of various size and construction to give a wide variety of pitches and timbres. In Bach's time, bellows attached to foot pedals were the means of forcing air through the pipes of the organ. It seems that all the miles of walking that Sebastian did helped build up his leg muscles, allowing him to pump the organ pedals all the more effectively. He also used a stick in his mouth to allow him to reach certain notes he couldn't have otherwise reached with his hands.[12] The organ is sometimes referred to as "the king of instruments." Bach was actually better known in his day as an *organist* than *as a composer*! Only ten of his compositions were published in his lifetime, though he wrote more than one thousand works (three-quarters of which were for Christian worship services).

Page 43: A minuet is a triple-meter (three beats per measure) French dance that was popular from the mid-17th century to the end of the 18th century. It also appears as an occasional element of the baroque instrumental suite.

Page 52: God's providential care for Bach on his return trip to Lüneburg is remarkable. The two gold ducats in the two herring heads were gold coins used in various European countries; these were apparently Danish coins.[13] According to one anecdotal telling of this event, Bach "had hardly started to tear [the herring heads] apart when he found a Danish ducat hidden in each head. This find enabled him not only to add a portion of roast meat to his meal but also at the first opportunity to make another pilgrimage, in greater comfort, to Mr. Reinecke [Reinken] in Hamburg."[14]

Page 63 – Both men and women wore wigs during

this time. It was apparently a sign of maturing from boyhood to manhood, as well as an accessory of fashion.[15] Manufactured head coverings were typically made of real hair during the 17th and 18th centuries, and men's wigs became common in those centuries. Bach still wore plain clothing, but he is often seen with a white wig in portraits and paintings from that time.

Pages 68, 69 – During holiday from responsibilities at the Duke's court, Bach visited family in Arnstadt (pronounced \arn-shtat\), a town known as "the Gateway to the Thuringian Forest." While he was there, his family invited him to try the new organ at New Church in Arnstadt. Bach loved to "test the lungs" of new organs by pulling out all the stops—giving full air to all the pipes.[16] An organist at that time would provide accompaniment for church services, improvise preludes and other needed incidental music, and test new organs as needed. Bach accepted the position and began composing in earnest—particularly works that led others in glorifying God. In fact, biographers consistently note that the "focus of his emotional life was undoubtedly in religion, and in the service of religion through music."[17]

Page 80 – When the Duke of Weimar extended another opportunity to play for his court, Bach accepted the invitation and moved his new wife, Maria Barbara, to the Duke's palace. He served the Duke for nine years—not only as musician, but also as footman (the servant in the livery, attending a rider or running in front of his master's carriage, or serving at the table, tending the door, and running errands) and as a huntsman (managing a hunt and looking after the hounds).

Page 82 – In the early 18th century, Germany was divided into hundreds of small states and imperial districts. There were over 300 such regions during Bach's lifetime. Prussia was the powerful state and former kingdom in northeast Germany, bordering the Baltic Sea, which was ruled by the Hohenzollern family. When Germany became a single country, the Prussian royal family ruled as emperors.[18] It continued as a state within the German nation until 1977.

Hands-on

Making German Rye Bread

In chapter two, Sebastian and Erdmann take a break from their journey to stop and rest. They eat a small lunch of black bread and sausage under a great fir tree.

You may want to try the following recipe for rye or black bread. It will help bring the story to life and fill your belly with a healthy, warm, chocolaty food.

German Rye Bread

3 c. all-purpose flour
¼ c. unsweetened cocoa powder
2 pkg. active dry yeast
1 tbsp. caraway seed
1 tbsp. salt

⅓ c. molasses
2 tbsp. butter
1 tbsp. sugar
3-½ c. rye flour
Cooking oil

In a large bowl, combine all-purpose flour, cocoa, yeast, and caraway seed. Heat and stir molasses, butter, sugar, 2 c. water, and 2 tbsp. oil until warm. Add to dry mixture. Beat at low speed with electric mixer for 1 to 2 minutes, scraping the bowl. Beat 3 minutes at high speed. Then by hand, stir in enough rye flour to make a soft dough. Turn out onto lightly floured surface; knead till smooth (about 5 minutes). Cover; let rest 20 minutes. Punch down. Divide in half. Shape into 2 round loaves on greased baking sheets or in 2 greased, 8-inch pie plates. Brush with a small amount of cooking oil. Slash tops with knife. Cover; let rise until double (45 to 60 minutes). Bake at 400 degrees for 25 to 30 minutes. Remove from pans; cool. Makes 2 loaves.

Oxidation Experiment

Do you know why the cap and lantern of the church at St. Michael's is of green copper? It is caused by oxidation, which is a reaction in which oxygen combines chemically with another substance. Copper almost always turns green or greenish-blue when it is exposed to the outside elements, such as rain and snow. It is the nature of copper and bronze to form this greenish "patina" which prevents rusting and corrosion. You can see the same process by putting a copper penny outside for a while. Oxidation also explains the greenish-blue color of the metal on the Statue of Liberty, for example.

Using the *Oxidation Experiment* lapbook pages, follow the directions to cut out and assemble the pieces. Adhere this activity to section #7 in your Bach lapbook.

Experiment

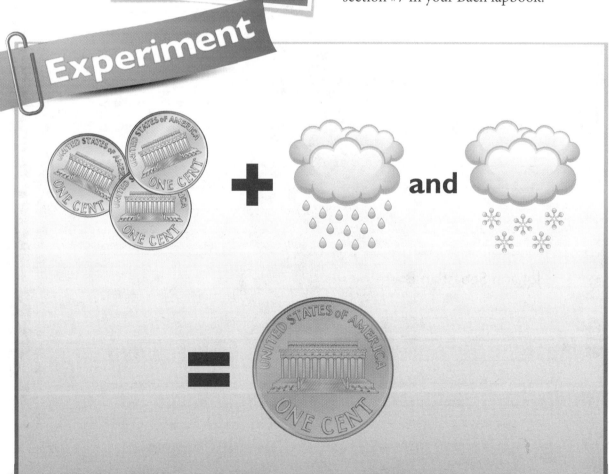

Glory To God Copy Work

Bach's months at St. Blasius Church in Mühlhausen (pronounced \myool-haw-zcn\) were pleasant. It was there that Bach solidified his purpose for music. In 1708 he wrote that he desired to create "well-regulated church music to the glory of God."[19] Bach often initialed blank manuscript pages with the letters "J.J." meaning Jesu Juva ("Help me, Jesus") or "I.N.J." meaning In Nomine Jesu ("In the name of Jesus"). Frequently his compositions were initialed at the end with the letters "S.D.G." representing Soli Deo Gloria or "To God alone, the glory."[14] Once he wrote, "Where there is devotional music, God is always at hand with His gracious presence."[15] (This comment was written in response to his reading of 2 Chronicles 5:13.)

Copy Work for Kindergarten - Third Graders

Directions: In your best handwriting, copy these phrases onto the lines below.

Jesu Juva

Soli Deo Gloria

In Nomine Jesu

Johann Sebastian Bach

Writing

Copy Work for Fourth – Sixth Graders

Directions: In your best handwriting, copy these phrases onto the lines below.

Bach

"Where there is devotional music, God is always at hand with His gracious presence." – Bach

_____

_____

_____

_____

_____

"Soli Deo Gloria" means "To God alone, the glory."

_____

_____

_____

_____

"Jesu Juva" is Latin for "Help me, Jesus."

_____

_____

_____

In Latin, "In Nomine Jesu" means "In the name of Jesus."

_____

_____

_____

_____

Music of the Baroque Period

The time period in which Bach composed his music has been categorized as the **Baroque period** of classical music. Bach had no compunction about composing works that followed the established "rules" of music from the Baroque period. In fact, he preferred the traditional ways of composing, not changing the music fashions of the time.[20]

Baroque music is contrapuntal in style; that is, several independent voices are used to weave a tapestry of sound. Some writers claim that the Baroque period was in response to the wars of the Renaissance and Reformation that had devastated much of Europe (1450–1600). Artists, architects, and musicians were attempting to escape the harsh realities by creating an ideal world through their arts. Other Baroque contemporaries of Bach's were the composers Vivaldi, Rameau, and Handel. Artists from this period included masters such as Rembrandt, Rubens, Velázquez, and Bernini.

Using the *Baroque Period Graduate Book* lapbook pages, follow the directions to cut out and assemble the pieces. Adhere this activity to section #2 in your Bach lapbook.

Thoughts About Baroque Music

What is your reaction to the music of this time period?
Think about the music you have listened to thus far from the book.
Complete these sentences.

1. When I listen to Bach's music I feel… (circle any that apply)

   relaxed and happy.   like stomping.   serene.

   like dancing.   bored.   fierce.

   sleepy.   like sighing.   agitated.

2. The music of the Baroque period is_____.

3. Kindergarten to Third Grade: Draw a picture of a scene from nature that comes to your mind when you listen to the music of Johann Sebastian Bach. (i.e. a flowing river, birds flying, majestic mountains, horses running, flowers swaying in the breeze…)

4. Fourth to Sixth Grade: Write a descriptive paragraph explaining a scene from nature that comes to your mind when you listen to the music of Johann Sebastian Bach. (i.e. a flowing river, birds flying, majestic mountains, horses running, flowers swaying in the breeze…)

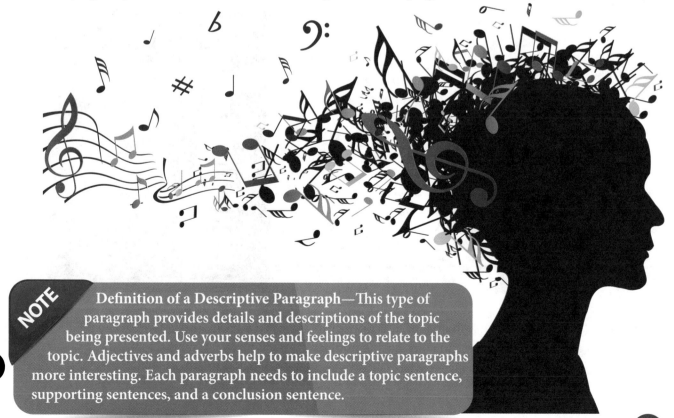

NOTE

Definition of a Descriptive Paragraph—This type of paragraph provides details and descriptions of the topic being presented. Use your senses and feelings to relate to the topic. Adjectives and adverbs help to make descriptive paragraphs more interesting. Each paragraph needs to include a topic sentence, supporting sentences, and a conclusion sentence.

"What's that Song?" Vocabulary

Using the *What's that Song?* lapbook pages, follow the directions to cut out and assemble the pieces. Adhere this activity to section #8 in your Bach lapbook.

Name that Tune

Even the letters of Sebastian's surname—B-A-C-H—spells out a melodic succession.[21] In German, the musical note B actually represents B-flat, while B natural was indicated occasionally by the letter H. So Bach's name in musical notes was B-flat, A, C, and B natural.[22]

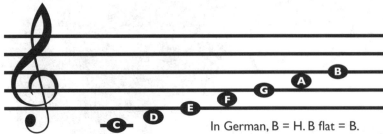

In German, B = H. B flat = B.

Using the *Name that Tune* lapbook pages, follow the directions to cut out and assemble the pieces. Adhere this activity to section #1 in your Bach lapbook.

Bach

Chapter Four Comprehension Questions

1. How do Marchand and Sebastian seem to be different in this chapter, and can you provide some examples that show these differences? _____

_____

_____

_____

_____

2. On the day of the competition, when it was Marchand's turn to perform, what announcement was made? _____

_____

3. Who asked Bach to become his court organist and violinist, and why did Bach agree to come?

_____

_____

Industriousness *(pp. 23, 24, 40, 46, 72, 80)* – Sebastian was not afraid of being constantly or regularly occupied, of keeping busy. On these pages, we see that busyness at an early age when Sebastian was willing to sacrifice sleep for the sake of copying Christoph's manuscripts by moonlight. Sebastian was also unafraid of a two-hundred mile hike to St. Michael's in Lüneburg in order to attend choir school. Now if that's not industriousness, then it is at least a fantastic exercise routine! Bach's development of new fingering techniques for the clavier and his willingness to walk all the way to Hamburg for an organ concert both attest to his willingness to work and sacrifice for his music. Again, Bach was willing to walk many miles to hear music by a master when he walked two hundred miles to Lübeck to hear Buxtehude. He served for nine years under the Duke, and not just in a musical capacity. That he would be willing to work as a footman and a huntsman says something about Bach's work ethic. In his lifetime, Bach wrote three hundred cantatas (only two hundred of which survived), five passions, several masses, three oratorios, and instrumental music primarily for church worship. In his own words, he believed that any "devout man could do as much as I have done, if he worked as hard."[23]

Humility *(pp. 36, 45, 49, 88, 90)* – Sebastian was willing to sleep in a hayloft in order to make it to St. Michael's, and in a cattle stall in order to hear Reinken play the organ in Hamburg. He also recognized the need to change his service at the school when his soprano voice changed, so he began playing in the church orchestra and accompanying singers as needed. Bach came to the competition dressed in a plain black suit. He did not mock Marchand for leaving before the contest was completed.

Chapter 4:

Page 85: Jean-Baptiste Volumier was the Kapellmeister for Dresden, and he was the one who coordinated the contest between Bach and Marchand. Jean Louis Marchand (pronounced \ zhan loo-ee mar-shawn\ – with a very nasal ending) was the private organist of the King of France (King Louis XV). Marchand was apparently applying for the post of organist at the court of Dresden. Volumier was not thrilled with the prospect of Marchand getting the job, so he arranged for his German friend to challenge the Frenchman. A contemporary of Bach's wrote in a letter in 1788 regarding this competition: "Perhaps it will be concluded that Bach was a challenging musical braggart…No, Bach was anything but proud of his qualities and never let anyone feel his superiority. On the contrary, he was uncommonly modest, tolerant, and very polite to other musicians. The affair with Marchand became known mainly through others; he himself told the story but seldom, and then only when he was urged."[24]

Page 86: A fugue (pronounced \fewg\) is a musical piece that uses certain rules to dictate the structure of the interaction of polyphonic voices, yet skill allows the exhibition of creative invention. This "freedom within an ordered world" concept mirrors Bach's lifestyle in the midst of the Baroque period, doesn't it?

Page 87: The Marshal, Count Flemming, provided the home for the contest. He is also referred

Bach was uncommonly modest, tolerant, and very polite to other musicians.

to as the Prime Minister who so loved music that he supported his own orchestra in his private residence.[25] He even bought a new harpsichord for the contest. The Crown Prince mentioned in this chapter is Frederick II, who later became the greatest King of Prussia (even calling himself such: Frederick the Great). While "the Soldier King" Frederick William I was not fond of music, science, or anything French, his oldest son was exactly the opposite—enjoying music, admiring French styles and architecture, and pursuing studies beyond mere military concerns.

Wheeler and Deucher make no mention of this event in Bach's life, but Bach was imprisoned for a time. Bach's most important duty in the Duke's court remained writing music, which was played and sung in the court chapel. Yet, when the position of Kapellmeister for the Duke became available, the Duke appointed a less qualified individual, and Bach was upset.[26] He determined to accept Prince Leopold's request to play at his court in Cöthen. However, the Duke was angered by Bach's move to a higher position, so the Duke put Bach in prison for a month. Bach made good use of his time, nonetheless. He wrote 46 pieces of music,[27] and composed a substantial portion of his Orgelbüchlein ("Little Book for the Organ") during that month.[28]

Music in Everyday Life

Music is all around us every day. Even if we do not intentionally play music ourselves, we are constantly presented with many different styles of music. Music can be entertaining. It can be used to get our attention. It can even be used to influence us to buy a certain brand or product. TV and radio commercials are a perfect example of this. A jingle is a short, catchy tune that promotes a particular product. While we are drawn to the music, we are also thinking about the brand it represents. Another example of how music affects us in daily life is how it is used in restaurants. Research has proven that people will chew their food more quickly when faster music is playing. Restaurants will often play fast tempo music during their busiest hours, so that people will finish their meals sooner and open up their table for other customers.

List at least five ways that music is used in daily life, for reasons other than simply enjoying it as entertainment. (Hint: Think about all the places you hear music when you are not at home.)

1.
2.
3.
4.
5.

Music for Special Occasions and Purposes

Johann Sebastian Bach composed music for many different reasons. He wrote church music, medleys for dancing, and lively marches. Oftentimes music is written with specific events or purposes in mind. The music provides an atmosphere that enhances whatever is happening.

Listen to Music Disc 1, tracks 9-14.

As you listen, match the number of the song track you are listening to with the picture it represents.

Track # ☐   Track # ☐   Track # ☐

Track # ☐   Track # ☐   Track # ☐

Discuss: How do these various songs make you feel? Happy or sad? Is it because of the musical notes and tempo of the music or because of the events with which we associate the music? Could both answers be true?

_____

_____

_____

_____

_____

Bach

Chapter Five Comprehension Questions

1. How did Bach sometimes help Prince Leopold in matters beyond music?_____

_____

_____

2. In Hamburg, after Sebastian had given an organ concert, the organ master Reinken told Bach that he alone had "the power to make it speak." Was this high praise? Why or why not?

_____

_____

_____

3. What was the advantage for the Bach family having Sebastian become cantor at St. Thomas' School in Leipzig (instead of remaining with Prince Leopold)? _____

_____

_____

_____

4. Bach's family experienced tragedy in this chapter (though it was only given one sentence), followed by a new joy. What were those events?_____

_____

_____

_____

_____

5. If asked to prove that Bach loved children, what evidence could you supply? _____

_____

_____

_____

_____

6. For whom did Emanuel become the Court Musician? *Hint: He was the same character for whom "Old Bach" played on seven harpsichords and composed a fugue on the spur of the moment.* _____

_____

_____

Character Qualities

Faith *(p. 76)* – He was willing to serve in the church, even taking part of his pay in the form of corn, wood, and fish. A substantial portion of his musical works focused on biblical themes. In some regards, Bach desired a position as a church organist so that he could spend more time composing, because he believed that the "object of all music should be the glory of God."[29] His cantatas emphasize the words and the message of the gospel.[30] His last work, dictated from his bed, was a chorale entitled *Before Thy Throne I Come.*

Creativity *(p. 86)* – He asked the King for a melody, and from that tune he improvised an entire fugue, weaving the melody in and out. Moreover, he accomplished such a feat in front of a live and musically critical audience!

Questions to ask yourself:
1. Which character trait(s) do I already show?
2. Which character trait(s) do I need to develop in my life?

Things that Bach Always Carried with Him

A Review of the Character Qualities of Johann Sebastian Bach

Draw a line to match the character quality with the correct definition.

1. Family- oriented

2. Hospitality

3. Humor and wit

4. Creativity

5. Industriousness

6. Humility

7. Integrity

8. Generosity

9. Faith

a. Complete sincerity and honest; always wanting to be truthful and do the right things.

b. When you use your imagination to make new and original things

c. Not bragging and acting proud or arrogant; down to earth

d. devotion and loyalty; believing and trusting in something, even when there is no proof

e. Family is very important to you; you want to spend time with and do things with your family.

f. Being friendly and generous in entertaining guests and visitors

g. Someone who can make quick remarks and tell great jokes

h. Kindness and graciousness in giving; ready to give as much as is needed without asking for anything in return

i. Constantly and eagerly working; a diligent worker; you don't mind giving up your free time to get something done and done right.

Chapter 5:

Page 99: Prince Leopold was himself a gifted musician of the viola, violin, and harpsichord, so he enjoyed having his music master travel with him. In 1720, Bach returned from a musical tour with the Prince to discover that Maria Barbara had died and was already buried. He "had left her hale and hearty on his departure. The news that she had been ill and died reached him only when he entered his own house."[31] Unfortunately, or perhaps providentially, Prince Leopold married Frederica Henrietta, a woman who was not interested in music. She resented her husband's practicing and made life difficult for Bach.[32] Her actions may have encouraged his decision to take the role of cantor for St. Thomas' School in Leipzig in 1723.

Page 104: As cantor at St. Thomas' School in Leipzig, Bach was responsible for the musical education of the students at the school, and often for all the other musical activities in the city. This role required him to produce a new composition for each service of the four largest churches in the city.[33] Moving away from the Prince's court lowered his social status and salary, but this new role allowed him to stay home so that he could focus on composing.[34] These were his crowning years of creativity, and he wrote vast numbers of vocal pieces and cantatas while in Leipzig.

Page 116: Bach had two eye operations shortly after visiting the King, but these operations weakened him and led to his total blindness before his death. He died in relative obscurity, even being buried in an unmarked grave at St. John's Cemetery in Leipzig. His body was exhumed in 1894, and again in 1950, at which time it was moved to a more esteemed grave at St. Thomas' Church.

Page 120: During his day, Bach was known as a master of the keyboard instruments—the organ, harpsichord, and clavichord. It wasn't until after his death that his overall musical power became more evident. Bach's compositions influenced later masters such as Mozart, Beethoven, Mendelssohn, Chopin, Schumann, and Brahms.[35] He has been called "The Father of Modern Music."

The Voyager

It seems appropriate that a musician who had such an impact on music and future composers should be known the world over—and even "the solar system over." In fact, in 1977 the Voyager spacecraft was launched into our solar system. On it was a gold-plated record on which—among other sounds and compositions—three of Bach's pieces are recorded. The first communication on the gold-plated record is Bach's Brandenburg Concerto No. 2. Granted, no space alien will ever encounter these compositions, but it is unique to think that the God of the Heavens is glorying in the music that Johann Sebastian Bach lovingly offered Him.

Using the *Voyager Program 1977* lapbook pages, follow the directions to cut out and assemble the pieces. Adhere the cutout to sections #3 & 4 in your lapbook.

Using the *Footprints Through Bach's Life Timeline Game* lapbook pages, assemble the game board cutouts as directed below.

Directions for Timeline Game:
Follow Sebastian on the footpath of his life, stopping to match the event cards with their correct year and picture on the game board.

To assemble:
- Cut out each round event card separately. (There are 22 event cards.)
- Print both pages of the game board.
- Paste the game board down on the back side of your lapbook folder sections #9-14. Adhere game pieces pocket to sections #15 & 16.

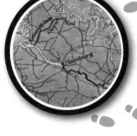

To play the game:
- Shuffle the event cards.
- Using the timeline on the next page, match the event to the year, starting at the first space on the game board.
- When completed, you will have a small, interactive timeline of the major events and influences in Bach's life.

1685-1699

1685: Bach is born in Eisenach, Germany (March 21, the first day of spring).[36] He is christened two days later on March 23. George Frideric Handel of Germany and Domenico Scarlatti of Italy are also born this year.

1686: Halley draws the first meteorological map.

1689: Peter the Great becomes Czar of Russia.

1691: Massachusetts absorbs Plymouth Colony and is given a new charter.

1694: Bach's mother, Elisabeth Lämmerhirt, dies.

1695: Bach's father, Johann Ambrosius, dies, and Sebastian moves in with Christoph (his brother) in Ohrdruff.

1696: Bach attends the Lyceum, a school in Ohrdruff.

1697: The Court of Versailles in France becomes the model for other European courts.

1698: Paper manufacturing begins in North America.

1700-1703

1700: A crown treaty is established between the Emperor Leopold I and Frederick III, Elector of Brandenburg. Unmarried women are taxed in Berlin. John Wesley, the preacher, is born.

1700 - 1702: Bach attends school at St. Michael's in Lüneburg. He learns musical composition and organ playing at St. Michael's.

1701: Sebastian walks to Hamburg to hear the organ master, Reinken, play at St. Katherine's church.

1702: William III dies in England and is succeeded by Queen Anne. She also gives royal approval to horseracing, and originates the sweepstakes idea.

1702: Bach plays violin in the Duke's court orchestra at Weimar.

1703: Isaac Newton is elected President of the Royal Society. Also, Peter the Great lays the foundations of St. Petersburg, Russia.

1703: Bach tests a new organ at New Church in Arnstadt and is offered the post of church organist almost immediately. He ministers there for four years.

1704-1717

1704: Bach writes his first cantata.

1705: Bach walks two hundred miles to Lübeck to hear Dietrich Buxtehude, the greatest organist of his generation.

1706: Bach returns to Arnstadt (after being away for several months in Lübeck). Benjamin Franklin is born this year. Johann Pachelbel, the German organist and composer, dies.

1707: Bach and his new wife, Maria, move to Mühlhausen, where he becomes the choir leader and organist at St. Blasius Church. The organist Dietrich Buxtehude dies. Handel meets Scarlatti in Venice. Mount Fuji erupts for the last time (so far). Scotland and England unite under the name Great Britain.

1708: Bach returns to the court of the Duke of Saxe-Weimar where he serves as chamber musician, concertmaster, and organist until 1717.

1708: Bach's first child, Catherina Dorothea, is born.

1709: The pianoforte (piano) is invented by the Italian harpsichord maker, Bartolomeo Cristofori.

1710: Bach's son, Wilhelm Friedemann, is born. Handel goes to England.

1711: A clarinet is used for the first time in an orchestra in an opera by J.A. Hasse.

1712: Future Frederick the Great, King of Prussia, is born. St. Petersburg becomes the capital of Russia (until 1922).

1713: King Frederick I of Prussia dies and is succeeded by Frederick William I (who rules until 1740).

1714: Bach's son, Carl Philipp Emanuel Bach, is born. Queen Anne dies and is succeeded by George Louis, elector of Hanover (for whom Handel is court music director); he becomes King George I.

1717: Bach participates in a contest in Dresden to see who is the best keyboard player: Marchand of France or Bach of Germany. Bach is temporarily arrested by the Duke but is grudgingly released to become the music director for Prince Leopold in Cöthen. Handel's Water Music is performed for the first time. Inoculation against smallpox is introduced in England by Lady Mary Montagu.

1717: Bach serves as court conductor for Prince Leopold until 1723.

1718-1750

1718: Peter the Great murders his son and heir, Alexis. England declares war on Spain.

1720: Bach's wife Maria Barbara dies.

1721: Bach marries Anna Magdalena Wülcken and composes the Brandenburg Concertos. Peter the Great is proclaimed Emperor of All the Russias.

1722: The first part of the Well-Tempered Clavier and Bach's first music book for Anna Magadalena are composed. Organ master Reinken dies.

1723: Bach becomes the cantor at St. Thomas's School in Leipzig.

1729: Bach's St. Matthew Passion is performed for the first time.

1732: Bach's son, Johann Christoph Friedrich, is born.

1735: Bach's youngest son, Johann Christian, is born.

1736: Bach is given the title of royal court composer by the Elector of Saxony, Frederick Augustus II, also known as Frederick the Great.

1737: Antonio Stradivari, of violin fame, dies.

1738: The future King George III is born.

1740: Bach's second son enters the service of Frederick II. Bach's eyesight is now very poor.

1741: Antonio Vivaldi of Italy dies.

1742: Bach composes the Goldberg Variations. Handel's *Messiah* is first performed in Dublin.

1745: Bach's first grandson, Johann August, son of C.P.E. Bach, is born.

1747: Bach visits Frederick the Great's court in Potsdam.

1750: Bach has two unsuccessful eye surgeries in March and April, leaving him almost blind. He dies in Leipzig on July 28 at age 65.

Sebastian Bach, The Boy from Thuringia Quiz

Name: _____ Date: _____

Multiple Choice:
Circle the correct answer.

1. Even though Sebastian's brother confiscated his copy of the music, what did Sebastian accomplish in six months?
    a. He memorized the music of the masters he was copying.
    b. He learned all the names of previous composers.
    c. He practiced the clavier for 15 hours a day.
    d. He wrote his own opera by the age of six.

2. How did Sebastian receive money to buy his dinner on his trip back to Lüneburg?
    a. He stole it.
    b. It was lying in a puddle on the road.
    c. It was inside two fish heads that dropped from a window.
    d. A friend gave it to him.

3. While visiting in Arnstadt, Sebastian was invited to try a new item in the church. What was it?
    a. The drums
    b. The organ
    c. The harpsichord
    d. The violin

4. Which country was Bach was born in?
    a. France
    b. Austria
    c. England
    d. Germany

5. In which musical time period did Bach compose his music?
    a. The Romantic Period
    b. The Baroque Period
    c. The Renaissance Period
    d. Classical Period

Match:

_____Organ

_____Upright Piano

_____Violin

_____Grand Piano

a.

b.

c.

d.

Answer these questions:

1. List two ways that music is used to influence us in everyday life.

_____

_____

2. What was aboard the Voyager spacecraft when it was launched into our solar system?

_____

_____

_____

_____

3. What was one character trait that Bach demonstrated?

_____

Week One: Chapter One Comprehension Questions

1. A talent for music, or musical ability, p. 11
2. A miller, p. 13
3. They had a family reunion, and it was a musical feast for the village as well as the family, pp. 14, 18.
4. Martin Luther, p. 20
5. His parents died, p. 20
6. His rules were to not practice on the clavier for more than an hour a day and to not use the music books

from his library. Sebastian responded by sneaking into the library, taking the book to his room, and copying the music for himself at night, pp. 21–24.
7. He had memorized the music of the masters he was copying, p. 28.
8. Choir school at St. Michael's in Lüneburg, p. 29

Week One: Major Cities that Bach Visited (Map Activity)

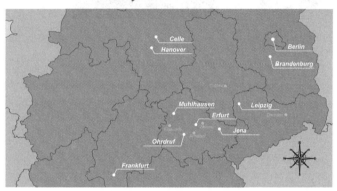

Week Two: Chapter Two & Three Comprehension Questions

Chapter Two

1. A man gave them a wagon ride, p. 35; others gave them directions to St. Michael's, p. 37; they received food from the monk, p. 38.
2. His favorite instrument was the clavier, and he improved the playing of it by using all five fingers, not just the three middle fingers, p. 40.
3. The organ, p. 42
4. He played in the church orchestra and accompanied singers, p. 45.
5. No, it wasn't for a hamburger. He went to hear the organ master Reinken, p. 46.
6. It was filled with thoughts of music, p. 51. I suppose thoughts of food would be an acceptable response, too, p. 52.
7. Two herrings' heads, each with a gold ducat, were dropped out a window right near Sebastian, p. 52.
8. He was invited to live at the Duke's palace and play in his orchestra, p. 55.

Chapter Three

1. Violin, p. 62
2. An organ, p. 68
3. He was asked to become the church organist and choir director, p. 69.
4. He promised to be a faithful servant of God, a good organist, to carry out all his duties, and to obey the church leaders' wishes, p. 70.
5. They complained that they were too long and not rehearsed enough. They were difficult to sing along with because they were sometimes improvisational, p. 72.
6. Three months, p. 74
7. The Duke asked him to live with him again and be the court organist, p. 79.
8. Handel, who had moved to England, p. 80.
9. A contest between Bach and Marchand to see who was the better keyboard player had been arranged, p. 82.

Week Three: Chapter Four Comprehension Questions

1. Marchand was from France, p. 85; he seemed proud, p. 85; he wore fancy clothes, p. 85; he focused on his own compositions, p. 85; he was somewhat cowardly, leaving the contest early, p. 89. Bach was from Germany, p. 85; he acted humbly and wore simple clothes, p. 88; he asked the king for a musical idea for

a fugue, p. 86; and he showed strength of character in not mocking Marchand for leaving, p. 90.
2. Marchand had left town in a carriage, p. 89.
3. Prince Leopold of Cöthen asked him, and Bach accepted because the Prince loved music too, pp. 90-91.

Week Three: Music in Everyday Life

(Possible Answers)

Background noise in stores
To get your attention (i.e. the ice cream truck, rides and games at the fair)
Alarm clock
Ringtones on cell phones
To create a mood

Week Three: Music for Special Occasions and Purposes

Track #___10___   Track #___14___   Track #___12___

Track #___13___   Track #___9___   Track #___11___

Week Four: Chapter Five Comprehension Questions

1. The Prince asked his advice on royal matters, p. 99.
2. Yes, it was coming from a great organist who appreciated the power and effectiveness of Bach's compositions, p. 101.
3. Friedemann and Emanuel, Bach's sons, would receive a fine education, p. 104.
4. Maria Barbara's death and Magdalena as Bach's new and musical wife, p. 105.
5. He had twenty of them! He taught them to play instruments and read music, p. 105. He wrote music for them, p. 106. He played with them — games, teasing, tickling, etc., p. 110. He took them with him on trips occasionally, p. 100. He led them in prayers, p. 110.
6. King Frederick the Great, p. 115

Week Four: Things that Bach Always Carried with Him

1. e
2. f
3. g
4. b
5. i
6. c
7. a
8. h
9. d

Sebastian Bach, The Boy from Thuringia Quiz

Multiple Choice:
1. a
2. c
3. b
4. d
5. b

Matching:
1. a
2. d
3. c
4. b

Questions:
1. (Two of these) In commercials, In restaurants, Background noise in stores, To get your attention (i.e. the ice cream truck, rides and games at the fair), Alarm clock, Ringtones on cell phones, To create a mood
2. Golden records with three musical pieces written by Bach
3. (One of these) Hospitality, family-oriented, humor and wit, industriousness, humility, integrity, faith, creativity, generosity

Weekly Lesson Outline

(Activities marked with an * are required in order to meet national music appreciation standards.)

Week One:

- Read Chapter 1*
- Answer Comprehension Questions
- Listen to Music Disc 1, track 22*
- Character Qualities
- Tidbits of Interest
- Assemble Lapbook Folder
- Halle, Germany - Then and Now (LB)
- Handel's Place in the World
- Who Am I?*
- The Spinet*
- The Oboe*

Week Two:

- Read Chapter 2*
- Answer Comprehension Questions
- Listen to Music Disc 1, tracks 23-25*
- Character Qualities
- Tidbits of Interest
- German Electors (LB)
- Elements of Music*

Week Three:

- Read Chapter 3*
- Answer Comprehension Questions
- Listen to Music Disc 1, track 26-29*
- Character Qualities
- Tidbits of Interest
- The Duel (LB)
- A Look at Venice (LB)
- Quoteworthy
- Identify Contrasting Music Styles*

Week Four:

- Read Chapter 4*
- Answer Comprehension Questions
- Listen to Music Disc 2, tracks 7-26*
- Character Qualities
- Tidbits of Interest
- A Taste of German Culture
- "Harmonious Blacksmith" (LB)*
- Water Music (LB)*
- Musical Compositions (LB)*
- Father of the Oratorio (LB)*
- Experiencing Blindness
- Handel's Messiah (LB)*
- The Life and Times of George Frederic Handel*

Additional activities on next page

Additional activities required for national music standards:

☐ Identify various uses of music in the United States.

☐ Describe how music is used in various cultures in the United States.

☐ Identify various uses of music in the child's culture.

☐ Identify similarities and differences in music of the United States and also in various cultures.

Chapter One Comprehension Questions

1. At the start of this chapter, who was missing, according to the town crier?

_____

2. When the "missing" George was found, where was he discovered?

_____

3. Do you recall what occupation or job Dr. Handel wanted George to undertake?

_____

4. Where did George and his aunt hide his birthday spinet so George could practice without an-gering his father? _____

_____

5. What did George do when his father refused to take him in the carriage to the Duke's palace at Saxe-Weissenfels? _____

_____

6. What were some ways that George worked to improve his musical skills?_____

_____

_____

1685	Johann Sebastian Bach	1750

| 1685 | **George Frederic Handel** | 1759 |

| 1732 | Franz Joseph Haydn | 1809 |

| 1756 | Wolfgang A. Mozart | 1791 |

| 1770 | Ludwig van Beethoven | 1827 |

| 1782 | Nicolò Paganini | 1840 |

| 1797 | Franz Schubert | 1828 |

Character Qualities

Focused *(pp. 12, 14, 39)* – George was very attentive to music, whether it was finishing the melody with the minstrels, going out early with his aunt to hear the town band at the market square, or practicing a mass for church until he had it memorized.

Diligence *(pp. 19, 23, 36, 38)* – George was diligent to improve his musical abilities by practicing during every spare moment. He practiced until a piece was mastered, and he spent hours copying master composers' works and writing his own pieces. George also stayed late at church to practice for services.

Humility *(pp. 16, 19, 26)* – Although George wanted to be a musician, he respected his father's wishes that he study to become a lawyer. George was humble enough to practice in a cold, dark attic for the sake of music. And he jogged a good portion of the way to the Duke's palace in his humble efforts to hear even more music.

Tidbits of Interest

Page 10: Doctor Handel, also named George Handel, was a barber-surgeon for the Duke of Saxe-Weissenfels.[1] Doctor Handel was married twice and was thirty years older than his second wife, Dorothea Taust Handel. He was actually sixty-three years old when his son George was born. Dorothea was the daughter of a Lutheran pastor, and she was known as a good and pious woman.[2] Dorothea's sister, Anna Taust (Tante Anna), lived with the Handel family and nurtured the young George's musical interests.

Pages 12-14: George's singing with the wandering minstrels mortified his father. Doctor Handel really wanted George to pursue an education in law, not in music. "[M]usicians at that period were regarded as a class of vagabonds, occupying a position even lower than that of servants. Most of the German servants, as Papa Handel pointed out, enjoyed the security of employment, while the vagabond musicians sang and starved their way over the gutters of Germany."[3]

Page 33: Young George was only eight or nine when the Duke heard him play the church postlude and commanded Dr. Handel to encourage such talent in his son.

Page 14: The market square where Tante Anna took George to hear the town band and the singers is looked over by four towers of the Liebfrauenkirche (the church where George later played the organ and took lessons from Zachau, p. 38). Immediately adjacent is the freestanding Rote Tower, or Red Tower, that soars 275 feet in the air. The Rote Tower has seventy-six bells chiming regularly throughout the day. Perhaps these are the chimes Tante Anna accompanied George to hear in the early mornings.

Pages 40, 41: Zachau convinced Dr. Handel that George needed to go to the royal court in Berlin to learn from the musical masters there. In fact, George was always indebted to Zachau for his encouragement and instruction. George began sending the music teacher's widow frequent gifts of money to help her out after Zachau's death in 1712.

Halle, Germany - Then and Now

Halle is a town in the Saxony-Anhalt state of Germany, just northwest of Leipzig. Its name actually comes from a Celtic word for salt. The city is closely connected with salt production from the nearby marshes along the Saale river—an important tributary of the Elbe river. Salt was called "white gold" and was used as a form of money for purchasing items during the Middle Ages. In Handel's time, the rich salt deposits still remained a major source of income for the residents of the area.

Using the *Halle (salt) and Present–day Halle* lapbook activity pages, follow the directions to cut out and assemble the pieces. Adhere the Halle (salt) portion to section #1 in your Handel lapbook. Place Present-day Halle on sections #3 & 4 and adhere in place.

Handel's Place in the World

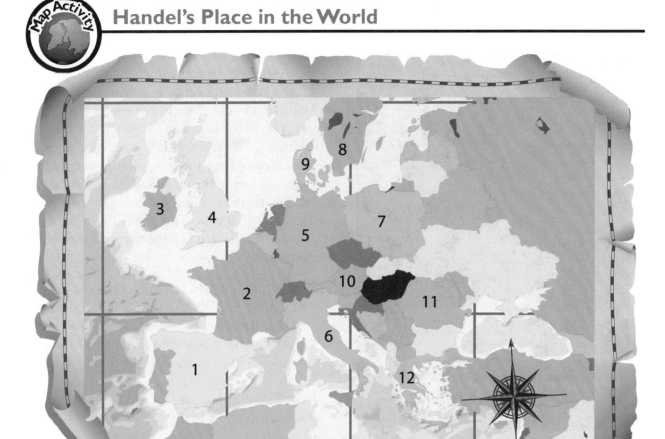

George Handel was born in Halle, Germany and later lived in Hanover and Hamburg. He also visited the German capital of Berlin. In 1706, he moved to Venice, Italy. After some time, Handel moved to London, England and became a naturalized English citizen. While in England, he also visited Dublin, Ireland for the first performance of the *Messiah*.

Using print and internet sources identify the twelve European countries indicated on the map above.

1. _____

2. _____

3. _____

4. _____

5. _____

6. _____

7. _____

8. _____

9. _____

10. _____

11. _____

12. _____

Who Am I?

George Handel was not the only famous musician born in 1685. In fact, there were several. **Using the information below, draw a line to match the fact with the musician it describes.**

1. I was born in Eisenach, Germany on March 21, 1685. I came from a whole family of musicians.

2. I was born on February 23, 1685 in Halle, Germany. My father was a doctor.

3. I was born on October 26, 1685 in Naples, Italy. My father was also a musician.

4. I am also known as the "Father of the Oratorio."

5. I walked to Halle to meet Handel.

6. I was a well-known harpsichord composer.

I am George Frederic Handel.

I am Johann Sebastian Bach.

I am Domenico Scarlatti.

Handel

NOTE

George Frederic Handel was born February 23, 1685. Johann Sebastian Bach was born eighty miles southwest of Halle in Eisenach, Germany, just twenty-six days after Handel's arrival, and Domenico Scarlatti (Italy's premier harpsichord composer) was born in Naples, Italy, in October of 1685. In October or November 1719, Handel, the "Father of the Oratorio," revisited his mother's home in Halle, Germany. The same day Handel left Halle, Johann Sebastian Bach arrived from Leipzig (a good twenty-five mile walk) to meet the renowned musician. Bach was known as a man unafraid of long walks, but it is interesting that he never once left the country of Germany. One can only imagine what a meeting between these two master composers might have produced. Handel wanted his music to have an "overall strong effect on his listeners, while Bach focused on perfection in each of his compositions."[4] In either case, the power and impact of each of these German composers is undeniable.

Writing The Spinet

A spinet is a smaller version of a harpsichord. It has one keyboard and one string per note. The strings in a spinet run diagonally to the keyboard. Pressing a key on the keyboard would cause a string to be plucked which makes the sound for that note.

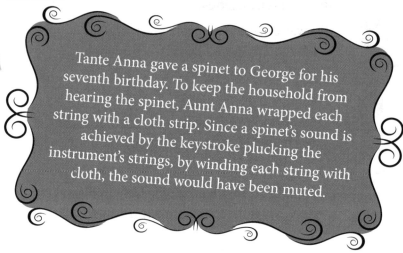

Tante Anna gave a spinet to George for his seventh birthday. To keep the household from hearing the spinet, Aunt Anna wrapped each string with a cloth strip. Since a spinet's sound is achieved by the keystroke plucking the instrument's strings, by winding each string with cloth, the sound would have been muted.

Referring to pages 18-23 in the book, *Handel at the Court of Kings*, fill in the missing adjectives and adverbs found in these phrases.

1. The sun shone _____…waking George from a _____ sleep.

2. Aunt Anna stealing _____ through the doorway, a _____ bundle under her arm…Placing it _____ beside the bed…

3. "_____ birthday, _____one," she whispered _____.

4. "the _____ _____ instrument and _____ put his hands on the battered keys…

5. _____ they carried the little instrument…and _____ wound each string with _____ strips of cloth.

6. …_____ seating himself…

7. George hurried away to the _____attic…to spend _____ hours at his _____ instrument.

8. …crept up the _____stairs…to play_____ melodies…

9. …the _____ musician in the _____ corner…struggled to read the notes of the _____ music.

10. …answered George _____…

11. Pulling her _____ shawl closer about her shoulders, Aunt Anna seated herself on the _____ stairs and listened…to the _____ melodies, the _____ _____ sounds

12. The _____ tones rand through the attic and the music stopped _____.

13. …looked at the _____ _____ figure…set the instrument on the _____ floor…

14. You shall keep the _____ thing…what _____ concerts he gave…

Grades 4-6: Identify the adjectives (ADJ) and adverbs (ADV) in these phrases by writing the correct abbreviation above each blank.

ADJ

describes nouns and pronouns; answers -

• What kind?
• Which one?
• How many?

ADV

describes verbs, adjectives, and other adverbs; answers -

• How?
• When?
• Where?
• How much?
(often ends in -ly)

The Oboe

Handel's first published work, in 1695, was written mainly for the oboe. What do you know about the oboe? **Using print and internet sources, answer the questions below.**

1. To what instrument family does the oboe belong?

2. How many reeds does an oboe use?

3. What special job does the oboe have in an orchestra?

4. What kind of sound does an oboe make?

Handel

Chapter Two Comprehension Questions

1. At the start of this chapter, to what city was George headed and why? _____

   _____

2. What kind of contest arose at the Elector's court for which George readily volunteered?

   _____

3. Why did George have to return rather suddenly to Halle? _____

   _____

4. Can you list at least two ways in which George kept himself occupied in Halle when he returned

   home? _____

   _____

5. At the end of this chapter, what evidence do we have that Mother Handel supported George's

   musical efforts and desires? _____

   _____

Character Qualities

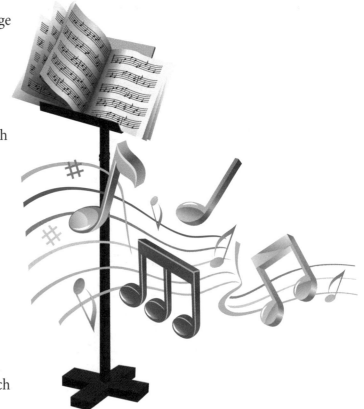

Undaunted *(pp. 45, 48)* – George was not intimidated or frightened by the prospect of leaving his parents in order to get to Berlin. He was eager to hear the music of the masters there. Moreover, he was not scared by Buononcini's musical challenge in the contest at the Court of the Elector, though George would have been years younger than Buononcini.

Leadership *(pp. 57, 59, 66)* – George took the responsibility of earning a living for his mother, aunt, and two little sisters when Dr. Handel died. George already demonstrated leadership in conducting musicians and singers even as a young man. He would compose new pieces and then strictly direct his classmates in the singing of those works. He also directed music for seven churches in Halle, providing special compositions for each house of worship.

Hard-working (*pp. 60, 62, 66*) – For a time, George provided income for his family after Dr. Handel's death *and* attended the university where he studied to become a lawyer. He would get up before sunrise to work at the cathedral where he had been hired as the choir director and organist. Supplying music and direction for seven churches in Halle also demanded an incredible amount of effort and diligence.

Tidbits of Interest

Pages 47, 48, 55: Buononcini and Ariosti were both Italian musicians befriended by the Elector's wife, Sophia Charlotte. There were some intriguing family ties among the acquaintances that George made in these youthful years. For example, Electress or Princess Charlotte was the daughter of the Elector of Hanover and the sister of Georg Ludwig, whom Handel later knew as King George I of England.[5] Princess Charlotte was a music lover who encouraged musicians within the royal court, and it is possible that her "encouragement" motivated the Elector to want to send Handel to study with the masters in Italy.

Pages 56, 57: George had to return to Halle (a ten-day coach ride from Berlin) before his dreams of studying in Italy could be fulfilled. Shortly after his return to Halle, just twelve days before his twelfth birthday, George's father died.

Page 60: In addition to providing a small income for his family, George attended school at a new Latin school in Halle. In February of 1702, he registered as a student at Halle University, studying to become a lawyer. A month later (March 1702), Handel became the organist at the Calvinist Domkirche Cathedral, which was somewhat ironic. He was a seventeen-year-old Lutheran receiving a salaried position at a Calvinist church. At the Domkirche (or Cathedral), George became "one of the foremost organists of the first half of the eighteenth century."[6] While he was there, George was responsible not only for performing on the organ, but also for caring for the organ and keeping it in perfect condition.

Page 64: In 1703 Handel quit the university, resigned from the Domkirche, and made plans to visit Hamburg, which was the cosmopolitan center of North German music at the time.

German Electors

At this point in time, Germany was made up of small states ruled by electors who lived like royalty. During the Middle Ages, groups of princes were chosen to elect the emperor of the country, and these electors had considerable power over their own courts or states. In 1696, when George went to visit Berlin, the elector was Elector Friedrich III, who was trying to build a palace that rivaled Louis XIV's palace at Versailles in France. Elector Friedrich also wished Emperor Leopold I of Germany to coronate him as King of Prussia (a larger kingdom or state within Germany). The coronation finally occurred in 1701.

The Electors of Germany

Using the *Electors* lapbook activity pages, follow the directions to cut out and assemble the pieces. Adhere the Electors portion to section #7 in your Handel lapbook.

Elements of Music

(How Music Communicates Ideas, Styles, and Moods)

Before the late 1920's, silent movies used music to communicate suspense, comedy, romance etc., even though no words were spoken. How was this possible? Many different styles of music were used to enhance the drama on the screen. The different elements of music communicated ideas and created a variety of moods. Moviegoers could experience a diverse range of emotions as the music filled the theater. In this lesson, we will learn about some elements of music and how they create style and affect the listener.

Main Elements of Music:

• **Melody and Harmony**—Melody is the part of a song that we can sing. It is a pattern of notes that creates a recognizable tune. Harmony is the combination of notes that produces new sounds called chords. (A chord is usually three notes played at the same time.) Harmony notes are played along with the melody notes. They help to support the melody and create a fuller sound. One way music style is created is though the various combinations of harmony and melody. These two elements can also influence the mood of the song. Dissonant chords in harmony are used to create feelings of drama, mystery, fear and surprise. These conflicting chords can also express pain, sadness, or strife.

• **Dynamics**—Dynamics indicate the correct volume throughout a piece of music. Crescendo (<) means slowly becoming louder. Decrescendo (>) means slowly becoming softer. The volume of a song greatly influences its style and intensity. (The abbreviations used to indicate dynamics are from Italian words.) Loud: (f) forte= loud, (mf) mezzo forte= medium loud, (ff) fortissimo= very loud Soft: (p) piano=soft, (mp) mezzo piano= medium soft, (pp) pianissimo= very soft

Mark the following sounds as loud or soft by circling the correct symbol.

Race cars on the race track (*ff* or *p*)

Elephants stomping (*f* or *pp*)

Wood crackling in the fireplace (*mf* or *pp*)

Going through a car wash (*mf* or *p*)

A marching band playing (*ff* or *f*)

Someone breathing hard after jogging (*p* or *mp*)

A phone ringing (*mf* or *ff*)

Water trickling over rocks (*mp* or *ff*)

A whisper (*f* or *p*)

A vacuum cleaner (*mf* or *pp*)

Fire sirens racing by (*f* or *p*)

Typing on computer keys (*f* or *mp*)

A fan blowing (*f* or *pp*)

A jet plane taking off (*ff* or *pp*)

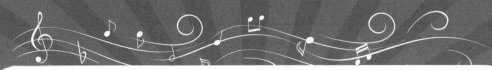

Main Elements of Music:

• **Rhythm**—Rhythm is the repetitive beat of music. Music is divided into certain sections that have a particular pattern of beats and is played in a specific amount of time. Turn on the radio and scan through various radio stations. As you hear songs played in different music styles, stop and listen to the rhythm. Begin to tap you foot or clap your hands to the beat of the music. You will begin to sense the rhythm of the song as you move to the music. The style of a song is determined in part by its rhythm and tempo.

• **Tempo**—Tempo refers to the how fast or slow the piece of music should be played or sung. (The words used to indicate tempo are also Italian.)

Draw a line from the tempo word to the animal that has a similar quality.

Lento
(slowly)

Andante
(moderately slow, a walking pace)

Allegro
(fast)

Vivace
(lively)

Presto
(very fast)

Main Elements of Music:

• **Timbre**—Timbre is the way one instrument (or voice) sounds different from another instrument. For instance, you can distinguish the sound of a trumpet from the sound of a flute, simply by hearing them played. This difference is often referred to as "musical color." Each instrument expresses its own mood or feeling. Many adjectives are used to describe the timbre of an instrument. Listed on the next page are some of those words.

Examples of musical instruments and how their timbre might be described:
(Note: This is very subjective because it depends on how the instrument is played, what song it is playing, and personal preference.)

| Brilliant
Trumpet | Harsh
Oboe | Sweet
Flute | Piercing
Piccolo | Dark
Tuba |

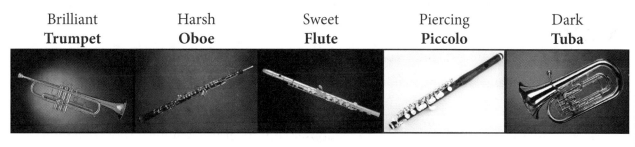

| Warm
French Horn | Muddy
Double Bass | Soothing
Clarinet | Heavy
Drum | Lonely
Violin |

Fill in each box with a color that reminds you of that word.

Brilliant	Harsh	Sweet	Piercing	Dark

Warm	Muddy	Soothing	Heavy	Lonely

Handel

Chapter Three Comprehension Questions

1. What was the first musical job George obtained when he arrived in Hamburg, and how did that position change in a single momentous day? _____

   _____

2. George and Johann Mattheson, a fellow composer and singer in Hamburg, both tried for a specific musical position in the city of Lübeck. What was the job, and why did neither man end up taking the post? _____

   _____

   _____

3. George met a couple of very important people from Italy—one while he was in Hamburg and one when he later moved to Venice. Do you recall who either of those men were?

   _____

   _____

4. What was George's nickname when he was in Italy? _____

   _____

5. At the end of this chapter, Handel agreed to take charge of the court music for what prince?

   _____

Character Qualities

George acknowledged the Prince's leadership over him . . . he knew his proper place and the proper protocol . . .

Humor *(pp. 72, 92, 93)* – George's sense of humor was evident in his practical joking in Director Keiser's orchestra. His teasing included: pretending to lose his place in the music, dropping his bow, and claiming the music was too difficult. George also later hid behind a mask at a masquerade ball in Venice and teased the revelers with his musical talent.

Respectful *(p. 98)* – When he joined the Prince of Hanover's court, George acknowledged the Prince's leadership over him. When he wished to visit England, he requested a leave of absence from the prince. He knew his proper place and the proper protocol in the elector's court.

Tidbits of Interest

Pages 69, 70: Hamburg is described as a city of adventure and music. Hamburg is located right along the Elbe River as it opens to the North Sea, making it Germany's largest port city. Moreover, in Handel's time Hamburg was a city in which opera was being produced widely (combining French, Italian, and German styles). Remember, it was considered "the city" of music in northern Germany.

Pages 70, 76: Director Reinhard Keiser was the principal composer and manager of the theater and opera house in Hamburg. Keiser often tried to incorporate three or four different languages, fireworks, and elegant processions into his operas.[7] The leading tenor at the opera house was Johann Mattheson who was himself a composer and singer. Handel became the second violinist in this opera's orchestra.

Page 72: Handel apparently enjoyed teasing others in a sober-faced manner. Mattheson stated, "He acted as though he could not count up to five...I know well how he will laugh up his sleeve when he reads this, though he laughs outwardly but little..."[8]

Page 81: Lübeck is about forty miles from Hamburg. The famous organist Dietrich Buxtehude (pronounced \boox-teh-hoo-deh\) was a Danish-German composer who remained the organist at Marienkirche (St. Mary's Church) for nearly forty years. To become the successor to Buxtehude would have been quite an honor, but the drawback to the position was that whoever inherited the post also "inherited" Buxtehude's unmarried, elderly daughter. Both Handel and Mattheson declined the offer. It's interesting to note that Johann Sebastian Bach turned down the same offer two years later.[9]

The Duel

Johann Mattheson was four years older than George.[10] He was a remarkable individual in his own right, able to play the organ, harp, bass, violin, flute, and oboe. He also studied law, sang in and wrote operas, and authored eighty-eight books on music, philosophy, and science.[11]

It appears that the friendship between Mattheson and Handel may have grown beyond their association at the opera house in that Handel became a non-paying boarder at Mattheson's father's house in 1704. In addition, Mattheson would sing in operas composed and directed by Handel.

There is a side story of these two composers' relationship that reveals Handel as an adventurous musician. Once, when Handel refused to allow Mattheson to conduct a part of Mat-

theson's *own* opera, Mattheson became so angry that he boxed Handel's ears. They instantly drew their swords and began dueling, but Mattheson's weapon broke against a large button on Handel's coat (thankfully preventing the sword from going through Handel's body).[12]

The button-and-broken-sword incident immediately released the tension from the situation, and their quarrel subsided nearly as rapidly as it had arisen.

Using *The Duel* lapbook activity matchbook pages, follow the directions to cut out and assemble the pieces. Adhere this activity to section #8 in your Handel lapbook.

A Look at Venice

Venice (known as Venezia in Italy) is a city built on over one hundred islets along the Adriatic Sea. Supported by millions of wooden stakes and canals linked together by some 400 bridges, it is the only city in the world built entirely on water. This certainly explains the need for riding in the unique Italian boat called a gondola (p. 91). During Carnival in Venice, a ten-day celebration before Lent, revelers and dancers experience a topsy-turvy life of giddiness, foolishness, and rebellion. Masks are worn by most partiers at Carnival to make everyone equal (ignoring class,

gender, occupation, and so forth). While in Venice, Handel became known as "*Il Caro Sassone*," or "the dear Saxon." It was also during this time in the city of canals that Handel became good friends with Italy's foremost harpsichord composer, Domenico Scarlatti.[13] Yes, this is the same Scarlatti that shared George's birth year. It is said that Scarlatti's regard for Handel's musical virtuosity "became so intense that at a somewhat later period he never mentioned his rival in several contests of improvisation at the harpsichord and organ without crossing himself."[14]

Using *Venezia* lapbook activity matchbook pages, follow the directions to cut out and assemble the pieces. Adhere it vertically to section #10 in your Handel lapbook.

"...I should be sorry if I only entertained them; I wished to make them better."[15]
—George Frederic Handel

"Handel is the only person I would wish to see before I die, and the only person I would wish to be, were I not Bach."
—Johann Sebastian Bach

Handel

"The very gates of heaven seemed to open above me and as the music went onto the paper, choirs of angels with glad eyes sang the 'Hallelujah Chorus.'"[16]
—George Frederic Handel

"Handel, to him I bow the knee."
—Ludwig van Beethoven

when asked to name the greatest composer ever

"It was Handel's ambition to make men think instead of relieving them from thinking."[17]
—Handel Biographer

Identify Contrasting Music Styles

Many different styles of music are enjoyed throughout the world. Remember how the various elements of music determine a song's style? Listen to these contrasting styles of music and identify the differences that you hear.

Using the Music Discs, follow the directions below.

Listen to Music Disc 1, tracks 30 & 31 (a march vs. a lullaby), then answer these questions.

Did these songs sound different? _____

Did they make you want to do different things? _____

Respond to this music by marching around the room and then lying down on the floor.

What would happen if you listened to a march while you were trying to go to sleep?_____

Can you march to a lullaby?_____

_____

Listen to Music Disc 1, tracks 32 & 33 (a classical song vs. a folk song). As you listen to these songs, think about the differences and similarities in the music. Write a short description comparing and contrasting classical and folk music. (Print or internet sources may also be helpful.)

_____

_____

_____

_____

_____

_____

_____

_____

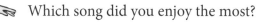

Listen to Music Disc 2, tracks 1 & 2 (slow music vs. fast music).

Draw continuous lines and circles on a separate sheet of paper while the music is playing. As you listen to the slow song, draw your lines slowly. When you hear the fast song, draw the lines and circles quickly. Try to stay in time with the music while you draw.

Which song did you enjoy the most?

_____

_____

Listen to Music Disc 2, tracks 3 & 4 (music from a symphony orchestra vs. music played by a solo piano). Label each of the words below with SO (symphony orchestra) or SP (solo piano) based on how each song sounded.

_____Complex   _____Subdued   _____Thin

_____Loud   _____Simple   _____Overflowing

Listen to Music Disc 2, tracks 5 and 6 (suspenseful music vs. calm music).

Even today, movies and radio dramas use music to communicate feeling. Think about your favorite movie or radio program. How do you know when something important or suspenseful is about to happen? How does the music sound when someone is relaxed or quietly talking? Draw a picture of your favorite part of the story. Then make a border around the picture with words related to the music from that scene or part of the drama. (i.e. scary, dangerous, sleepy, quiet…)

Chapter Four Comprehension Questions

1. The Queen of England asked Handel to write a special composition. What was this composition celebrating in England? _____

    _____

2. Why was Handel nervous about the Prince of Hanover's arrival in England?

    _____

    _____

3. Why did Handel compose the work entitled *Water Music*? _____

    _____

    _____

4. Do you recall how Handel became inspired to compose "The Harmonious Blacksmith?"

    _____

    _____

    _____

    _____

5. What fellow German composer did Handel just miss meeting at his mother's home in Halle?

    _____

6. What is perhaps Handel's most famous work—or at least his most famous oratorio? And where was it first performed? _____

    _____

    _____

7. What were audience members asked to do at the Music Hall in Dublin in order to make more room for additional guests? _____

    _____

    _____

8. What physical struggle did Handel face as he grew older? _____

9. Handel is known as one of the greatest composers and organists in the world. He is also known as the Father of the_____.

Character Qualities

Creativity *(pp. 106, 109, 124)* – It required incredible creativity to compose an opera (*Rinaldo*) in only two weeks' time upon arriving in England. Handel then went on to imagine soothing melodies that would serenade the new King aboard his barge on the Thames. Finally, to compose a masterpiece like *Messiah* in only twenty-four days is nothing less than inspired.

Intentional *(pp. 107, 109, 125, 126, 131)* – Handel used his time deliberately—whether composing new works or training new singers while he was delayed from crossing the channel to Ireland. He also composed certain pieces for specific purposes: to celebrate the treaty in England, to appease the new King, and to make its listeners better people, not merely to entertain the audience.

Generous *(pp. 128, 130, 133)* – In spite of being away from England for a year, and in spite of some negative publicity about his works,

Handel graciously agreed to come back to England to perform his oratorio *Messiah*. Moreover, he conducted this famous composition for charitable causes such as the homeless children of the Foundling Hospital. He also gave numerous concerts near the end of his life even though he was suffering from aging and blindness. Only a generous heart could give so much physically *and* musically.

Character Qualities of George Handel

(Character Qualities Review)

George Handel demonstrated many admirable character traits throughout his life. Cut out the strips on the following page and glue the definitions under the correct trait.

Focused

Diligent

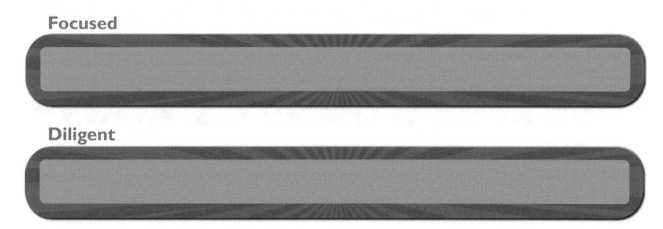

Humble

Undaunted

Strong Leadership

Hardworking

Humorous

Respectful

Creative

Intentional

Generous

Cut out these strips and glue them under the correct character trait.

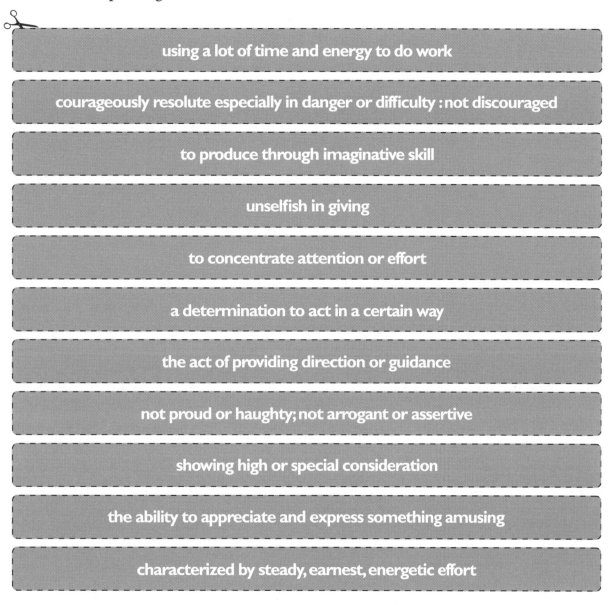

using a lot of time and energy to do work

courageously resolute especially in danger or difficulty : not discouraged

to produce through imaginative skill

unselfish in giving

to concentrate attention or effort

a determination to act in a certain way

the act of providing direction or guidance

not proud or haughty; not arrogant or assertive

showing high or special consideration

the ability to appreciate and express something amusing

characterized by steady, earnest, energetic effort

On another piece of paper, write a short story detailing a time when someone demonstrated one of the character traits above. Your story may be fiction or nonfiction. (Fiction: a story you create in your imagination. Non-Fiction: a story about something that actually happened.)

Tidbits of Interest

Page 106: Handel was only twenty-five when he arrived in London, but his good reputation was well known in the musical world of that city. Aaron Hill, the director of the London Opera, for example, begged Handel for a new opera, and eleven days later that opera (*Rinaldo*) was ready for preliminary production.[18] It was performed at Queen's Theatre or Queen's Hall the day after Handel's twenty-sixth birthday, and it was called, "the first real operatic success in English history," which had been dominated by Italian opera up to that point.[19]

Page 120: Handel returned to London, where he helped manage the Royal Academy of Music for the next seventeen years and invested his life savings in a new London opera house.[20] Handel even traveled to Dresden, Germany, in order to obtain singers for these operas. (Unfortunately for Handel, several unsuccessful opera seasons cost him his $50,000 of savings.[21])

Page 125: The Lord-Lieutenant of Ireland was William Cavendish, the Duke of Devonshire. This invitation from Dublin restored Handel's spirits, which had been deflated by financial failures, jealous contemporaries, piracy of his works, and poor health.[22]

Page 128: Fishamble Street was a market or "fish shambles" from the medieval period. The Charitable Music Society's Hall, where *Messiah* was performed, asked women to eliminate the hoops from under their dresses, and the men to leave their swords at home, and it is believed that the managers of the Hall increased the capacity from the usual six hundred persons to seven hundred by making such a request.[23] In 1743, Handel returned to England and staged *Messiah* in London.

A Taste of German Culture

In honor of the final supper Handel enjoyed at the inn near the North Sea, it seems only appropriate to eat sausages for supper while reading this chapter! There are several different types of sausage that can be readily found in most grocery stores, and that are fairly accurate ethnically to this story. You may wish to try any of the following sausage varieties:

• Bratwurst is a pale, smoked sausage made of finely minced veal, pork, ginger, nutmeg, and other spices.

• Frankfurters that are of the genuine German variety (which are not the same as American frankfurters) contain finely chopped lean pork with salted bacon fat, and are smoked.

• Knockwurst or knackwurst, which are short, plump smoked sausages that contain finely minced lean pork, beef, spices, and garlic, are often served with sauerkraut.

• Wienerwurst is made of beef and pork flavored with coriander and garlic, and it is believed to be the origin of the American frankfurter. (Yes, even just a hot dog will do.)

(NOTE: *These meats are often acquired tastes, but they will add some depth to your study by giving your children a true flavor of German culture.*)

"The Harmonious Blacksmith"

Handel stayed at the mansion of the Duke of Chandos from 1718 to 1720 and was master of the duke's chapel along Edgeware Road.[24] The duke had been the paymaster-general of the English armies during the War of the Spanish Succession.[25] He planned to build an elaborate palace that included a private road from his mansion to a nearby village called Cannons, nearly ten miles away.

Perhaps Handel was exploring the new, private road up to Cannons when the thunderstorm let loose. Handel supposedly sought shelter at a smithy's shop in Whitchurch, which is another village closely connected to Cannons. A reporter in 1835 researched this story behind "The Harmonious Blacksmith" and discovered an anvil at a forge near Whitchurch "that, when struck, gave out first a B and then an E, important notes in the key of E, in which 'The Harmonious Blacksmith' is composed."[26]

Using *The Harmonious Blacksmith* lapbook activity pages, follow the directions to cut out and assemble the pieces. Adhere this activity to section #11 in your Handel lapbook.

Water Music

Handel obtained leave of the elector to visit England, promising a quick return. He was actually absent from Hanover for almost exactly a year. He set foot on English soil in the autumn of 1710.[27]

The Prince of Hanover was coming to London, then, to be crowned King of England. Because Handel had been away from Hanover longer than he had anticipated, he decided to write a special work to appease the new king while he sailed along the river Thames. The Thames is the main artery around which the city of London grew. By sailing its length, the new king could see and be seen by the residents of London. Ironically, while George Handel embraced English life and culture, King George Ludwig never really learned the English language and customs, preferring to leave England to its own devices and choosing to live in Hanover as much as possible.

The barges on which the royal court rode docked at Chelsea, which is a village outside

the sprawl of central London. Handel's special composition, *Water Music*, was "superbly conceived for outdoor performance, and particularly for sounding over the wide, echoing spaces of a river."[28] The king was indeed pleased by the composition and pardoned his court composer for being away for so long.

Using the *Water Music* lapbook activity matchbook pages, follow the directions to cut out and assemble the pieces. Adhere this activity to sections #5 & 6 in your Handel lapbook.

Handel—Week 4 Activity Pages

Musical Compositions

When the Handels returned to Halle, George began taking lessons from Friedrich Wilhelm Zachau (sometimes spelled Zachow), who was the organist of Liebfrauenkirche (Church of Our Lady) in Halle. George trained with Zachau for three years, and Zachau instilled in the young musician a lifelong intellectual curiosity. Zachau's method was practical (not just theoretical), and he required George to compose a complete motet or cantata each week, in addition to his regular exercises.

There are many different types of musical compositions. Many musical pieces were written for use in church services, while others were written for entertainment.

Cut out the information below. Adhere them to sections #12, 14, 15 & 16 in your Handel lapbook.

A Mass is...
a choral piece of music that celebrates the Eucharist during a Catholic Mass by setting certain parts of the service to music.

A Motet is...
a choral piece of church music. Sometimes an organ would accompany the vocals, but usually it was only written for voices.

A Cantata is...
a work of music that could be religious or secular. The voices of the choir are accompanied by instruments.

A Concerto is...
a musical piece where a solo instrument is accompanied by an orchestra; usually written in three parts.

A Symphony is...
a composition written for the instruments of an orchestra. It is usually varied and involves many elements of music.

"Father of the Oratorio"

After 1717, Handel began composing oratorios, which blend the "solemnity of the cantata with the lightness of the opera—a Biblical drama in which the poem relates the story and the music supplies the scenery."[29]

Handel's use of Biblical themes for his oratorios was often misunderstood by church people because the productions were performed in theaters—a revolutionary use of theater and a revolutionary way of presenting religious

Using the *Father of the Oratorio* lapbook activity pages, follow the directions to cut out and assemble the pieces. Adhere this activity vertically to section #2 in your Handel lapbook.

messages.[30] For example, among those who spoke out against theatrical performances of *Messiah* was John Newton, composer of "Amazing Grace."[31] Yet, Handel refused to respond to such attacks and apparently had good relations with other church "pillars" like Charles Wesley, for whom he supplied the music for the hymn "Rejoice, the Lord is King."[32]

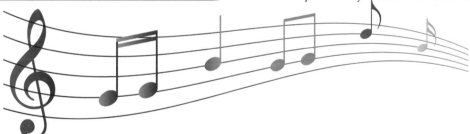

Experiencing Blindness

In 1751, during the composing of a chorus for his newest oratorio, *Jephtha*, Handel stopped and noted at the bottom of the page that he was experiencing a relaxation of the sight in his left eye.[33] By 1752, as Handel entered his mid-sixties, his eyesight was weakened enough that he sought treatment from John Taylor, an "opthalmiater" whom some call a quack doctor. Taylor had operated unsuccessfully on Bach's eyes just two years before, yet Handel was determined to be able to continue composing, and he needed his sight to do that well.[34] By the end of writing *Jephtha*, he could hardly see the notes with a magnifying glass. While Handel said he didn't fear darkness, he dreaded ending his work, so he endured painful treatments on the apparent cataracts in his eyes. According to reports, these treatments were done without anesthesia and consisted of "piercing the balls of his eyes with a needle."[35]

Handel's impending blindness curtailed some of his composing abilities in the last years of his life, but he still sought music and his faith for comfort and encouragement. He would practice the harpsichord for hours each day, and then he organized performances to share that music with the public. He also continued regularly in his church worship at St. George's in Hanover Square in London.[36]

In order to sense what Handel must have experienced as he lost his sight, complete the five instructions below.

1. Close your eyes and write your name, address, and phone number on a piece of paper.
2. Have someone talk to you while your eyes are closed.
3. Cover your eyes with a blindfold, and try to tie your shoes and zip your coat.
4. While having your eyes tightly shut, watch a few minutes of TV or a movie.
5. Hold onto someone's arm as you maneuver up and down stairs, keeping your eyes closed the whole time.

On the lines below, describe the feelings you experienced as you attempted to perform these tasks without your sight. Now think about why you are thankful for your eyes, and list five reasons here.

_____

_____

_____

_____

_____

_____

_____

_____

_____

_____

Handel's *Messiah*

Perhaps George Frederic Handel's greatest work was his oratorio *Messiah*, which he began composing on August 22, 1741 and completed on September 14, some twenty-four days later. That's 260 pages of manuscript filled in less than a month![37] Moreover, even though he was fifty-six when he finished *Messiah*, Handel announced that he was not tired and immediately began composing another biblical oratorio entitled *Samson*. Remarkably, Handel placed *Messiah* in a drawer where it was ignored for almost a year.

Handel traveled to Ireland on November 18, 1741 for the first production of the *Messiah*. All of the proceeds from that first performance went to three charitable undertakings, including a debtor's prison and the Foundling Hospital. After that introductory performance, anytime *Messiah* was presented, almost all the proceeds went to benefit charities.[38] While Handel never married or had a family of his own, he was always known as a charitable man who generously cared for widows and orphans.

Following royal protocol, the entire audience at a later *Messiah* presentation stood to their feet when the king rose, and this initiated the tradition of standing during the "Hallelujah Chorus"—a tradition that has lasted for more than two centuries.

Lord George Henry Kinnoul praised *Messiah* as "fine entertainment," to which Handel replied in exasperation, "My lord, I should be sorry if I only entertained them; I wished to make them better."[39]

In the spring of 1759, Handel organized a series of ten concerts that he would conduct, ending with the *Messiah* shortly before Easter. He had expressed to his friends a desire to die on Good Friday, "in the hope of rejoining the good God, my sweet Lord and Savior, on the day of His resurrection."[40] Only eight days after his final conducting of *Messiah*, and on Good Friday, April 14, he said farewell to his friends and asked his servant to leave him. "I have now done with the world,"[41] he said, and with that "the singer and his Messiah met face to face."[42]

Over three thousand people attended Handel's funeral, and he was honored by the royal court when he was buried in Poet's Corner in Westminster Abbey. A monument of George F. Handel in Westminster Abbey shows the "Father of the Oratorio" holding a manuscript for the solo start of *Messiah's* third part, appropriately entitled 'I Know That My Redeemer Liveth.' " Handel was honored to serve most of his life at the court of kings—but how much more glorious to be serving now in the Court of the King of Kings!

Using the *Handel's Messiah* lapbook activity pages, follow the directions to cut out and assemble the pieces. Adhere this activity to section #13 in your Handel lapbook.

The Life and Times of George Frederic Handel

Using the timeline, describe what happened to the following people/places. (Listed in chronological order)

1. William and Mary _____

_____

2. Handel (1696) _____

_____

3. Mayan Civilizations _____

_____

4. Jonathan Edwards and John Wesley _____

_____

5. Deerfield, Connecticut _____

_____

6. Edmund Halley _____

_____

7. Handel (1706) _____

_____

8. Handel (1711) _____

_____

9. D.G. Fahrenheit _____

_____

10. Lady Montagu _____

_____

11. New Orleans _____

_____

12. Texas _____

13. Brazil _____

14. Ben Franklin _____

_____

15. Handel (1759) _____

1685-1695

1685 - George F. Handel is born in Halle, Germany, on February 23. Johann S. Bach and Domenico Scarlatti, also composers, are born.

1689 - William and Mary are proclaimed King and Queen of England and Scotland for life. Peter the Great becomes the Russian Czar.

1694 - Handel visits the Duke of Saxe-Weissenfels in Saxony, Germany. He begins taking lessons from Zachau, organist in Halle. The University of Halle is founded.

1695 - Handel writes his first published music, primarily for the oboe. Nehemiah Grew, an English botanist, isolates Epsom salts (magnesium sulfate).

1696-1703

1696 - George F. Handel is sent to Berlin to make an impression on the court. Peter the Great sends fifty young Russians to study shipbuilding and fortifications in Venice, Holland, and England.

1697 - Handel's father dies twelve days before George's twelfth birthday. The last remains of Mayan civilization are destroyed by the Spanish in Yucatan. The Court of Versailles becomes a model for European courts.

1701- War of the Spanish Succession begins (and continues until 1714).

1702 - Handel enters the University of Halle as a law student.

1703 - Handel quits at the university and resigns from Domkirche to move to Hamburg. Peter the Great lays the foundations of St. Petersburg. Revivalists Jonathan Edwards and John Wesley are both born.

1703-1710

1703 - George Handel arrives in Hamburg, Germany, and works under Director Keiser in the opera orchestra.

1704 - Handel fights a duel with his friend Johann Mattheson. (A providentially placed button saves his life.) J.S. Bach writes his first cantata. French soldiers and Indians massacre settlers in Deerfield, Connecticut.

1705 - Handel's first opera, *Almira*, is performed in Hamburg. Joseph I becomes the Holy Roman Emperor. Edmund Halley predicts the return in 1758 of a comet seen in 1682.

1706 - Handel moves to Italy, where he lives until 1710. Benjamin Franklin is born. Johann Pachelbel, German composer and organist, dies.

1709 - Handel's opera, *Agrippina*, is successful in Venice, Italy. Bartolomeo Cristofori of Italy invents the pianoforte.

1710 - Handel becomes the music master to Elector Prince George of Hanover. German engraver Jakob LeBlon invents three-color printing.

1711-1759

1711 - Handel's first London opera, *Rinaldo*, is completed in fourteen days and is performed in Queen's Hall. The clarinet is used for the first time in an orchestra. And English trumpeter John Shore invents the tuning fork.

1713 - Peace Treaty of Utrecht ending War of the Spanish Succession is signed. Handel composes "Utrecht Te Deum" in honor of treaty's signing.

1714 - Queen Anne dies and Elector George of Hanover becomes English monarch. D.G. Fahrenheit constructs mercury thermometer with temperature scale.

1717 - Handel's *Water Music* is first given on the Thames. Future Empress Maria Theresa of Austria is born. Inoculation against smallpox is introduced in England by Lady Montagu.

1718 - Handel acts as music mastor for the Duke of Chandos. William Penn dies. New Orleans is founded by the Mississippi Company.

1719 - Handel returns to Germany briefly and misses visit with J.S. Bach by hours. Handel becomes director of London's Royal Academy of Music.

1720 - Handel writes the Harpsichord Suite No. 5 with "The Harmonious Blacksmith." Spain occupies Texas. Wallpaper becomes fashionable in England.

1723 - Handel purchases residence in London on Brook Street. Antony van Leeuwenhoek, Dutch scientist, credited with inventing the microscope, dies.

1721 - Handel becomes a naturalized English citizen. George I dies, succeeded by son George II. Quakers demand abolition of slavery. Coffee is first planted in Brazil.

1741 - Handel composes the *Messiah* in twenty-four days and visits Dublin, Ireland, for its first performance. (Some sources list 1742 as its first performance.) Maria Theresa accepts crown of Hungary, and future Emperor Joseph II is born. Antonio Vivaldi dies.

1743 - *Messiah* first staged in London, England. Thomas Jefferson is born. French explorers reach the Rocky Mountains.

1752 - Handel receives treatments on eyes from John Taylor. Ben Franklin invents lightning conductor. Great Britain adopts Gregorian calendar on September 14.

1759 - Handel finishes series of ten concerts, dies on Good Friday, April 14, and is buried in Westminster Abbey.

Handel

Handel at the Court of Kings Quiz

Name: _____ Date: _____

Matching:
Match these musical terms with the correct definition.

1. _____ Lento		a. Loud
2. _____ Andante		b. Very fast
3. _____ Presto		c. Soft
4. _____ (*f*) forte		d. Very soft
5. _____ (*mf*) mezzo forte		e. Slow
6. _____ (*ff*) fortissimo		f. Medium loud
7. _____ (*p*) piano		g. Very loud
8. _____ (*mp*) mezzo piano		h. Moderately slow
9. _____ (*pp*) pianissimo		i. Medium soft

Multiple Choice:
Circle the correct answer.

10. How did George improve his musical skills?
    a. He played his spinet during any spare moment.
    b. He listened to other musicians.
    c. He copied compositions of German and Italian composers.
    d. All of the above.

11. Which other famous musicians were born in 1685?
    a. Beethoven and Haydn
    b. Bach and Scarlatti
    c. Paganini and Schubert
    d. Chopin and Mozart

12. Why did Handel write *Water Music*?
    a. To celebrate Prince Hanover's coronation as the King of England
    b. To entertain travelers aboard a ship bound for Germany
    c. To appease Prince Hanover since Handel had been away from Germany for so long
    d. a. and c.

13. What is Handel's most famous oratorio?
    a. *Jeptha*
    b. *Samson*
    c. *The Messiah*
    d. *The Occasional Oratorio*

14. What physical struggle did Handel experience later in life?
    a. Stomach ulcers
    b. Blindness
    c. Loss of hearing
    d. Arthritis

15. What was Handel known as?
    a. "Father of the Oratorio"
    b. "Father of the Cantata"
    c. "Father of the Symphony"
    d. "Father of the Mass"

Week One: Chapter One Comprehension Questions

1. George, Doctor Handel's son was missing, p. 10.
2. George was in the streets, holding the torch for and singing with the wandering singers of Halle, pp. 11, 12.
3. He wanted George to become a lawyer — not a minstrel, pp. 13, 14.
4. It was hidden in the attic, p. 19.
5. George chased after the carriage on foot until noonday, pp. 25, 26.
6. He played his spinet during any spare moments (even during bedtime), p. 19. George listened to other musicians, pp. 14, 28, 30. He practiced until he mastered pieces, pp 23, 39. George copied compositions of German and Italian composers, p. 36. He also worked on his own compositions for various instruments, pp. 34, 36.

Week One: Handel's Place in the World Map activity

1. Spain
2. France
3. Ireland
4. United Kingdom (Great Britain)
5. Germany
6. Italy
7. Poland
8. Sweden
9. Denmark
10. Austria
11. Romania
12. Greece

Week One: Handel and His Contemporaries Who Am I?

1. Johann Sebastian Bach
2. George Frederic Handel
3. Domenico Scarlatti
4. George Frederic Handel
5. Johann Sebastian Bach
6. Domenico Scarlatti

Week One: The Spinet and Oboe
(The correct answers are in bold)

1. The sun shone **brightly (ADV)**…waking George from a **sound (ADJ)** sleep.
2. Aunt Anna stealing **softly (ADV)** through the doorway, a **heavy (ADJ)** bundle under her arm…placing it **carefully (ADV)** beside the bed
3. "**Joyous (ADJ)** birthday, **little (ADJ)** one", she whispered **smilingly (ADV)**.
4. the **old (ADJ), worn (ADJ)** instrument and **quickly (ADV)** put his hands on the battered keys
5. **Quietly (ADV)** they carried the little instrument… and **carefully (AVD)** wound each string with **thin (ADJ)** strips of cloth
6. … **breathlessly (ADV)** seating himself …
7. George hurried away to the **dusty (ADJ)** attic… to spend **happy (ADJ)** hours at his **beloved (ADJ)** instrument.
8. … crept up the **steep (ADJ)** stairs to play **beautiful (ADJ)** melodies …
9. … the **young (ADJ)** musician in the **dim (ADJ)** corner… struggled to read the notes of the **difficult (ADJ)** music.
10. … answered George **softly (ADV)** …
11. Pulling her **warm (ADJ)** shawl closer about her shoulders, Aunt Anna seated herself on the **cold (ADJ)** stairs and listened… to the **lovely (ADJ)**

melodies, the **delicate (ADJ)**, **tinkling (ADJ)** sounds.

12. The **stern (ADJ)** tones rand through the attic and the music stopped **suddenly (ADV)**

13. … looked at the **trembling (ADJ)**, **little (ADJ)**

figure…set the instrument on the **rough (ADJ)** floor …

14. You shall keep the **tinkling (ADJ)** thing…what **fine (ADJ)** concerts he gave …

Week One: The Oboe

1. It is a woodwind instrument.
2. It uses a double reed.
3. The oboe gives the note to which the orchestra tunes before concerts.
4. The oboe has a clear and piercing sound. Some also describe it as nasally sounding.

Week Two: Chapter Two Comprehension Questions

1. George headed to Berlin, for the Elector's Court, where he could hear the music of masters like Ariosti and Buononcini, p. 45.

2. A musical contest arose in which Ariosti would provide a theme, and George and Buononcini would then compose a piece from that theme, p. 48.

3. George's father demanded it, p. 56. When he got home, George learned that his father was very ill, p. 57.

4. He continued attending Latin school, p. 59. He later began attending the University to study law, p. 60. George composed new songs, gave concerts, and continued playing for the church when Zachau was out of town, pp. 60, 66. He became the organist and choir director for the churches in Halle, pp. 60, 66.

5. She gave George a small purse of money to help him get to Hamburg to study more music and make a living there, p. 67.

Week Two: Elements of Music

Race cars on the race track *ff*
Elephants stomping *f*
Wood crackling in the fireplace *pp*
Going through a car wash *mf*
A marching band playing *ff*
Someone breathing hard after jogging *mp*
A phone ringing *mf*

Water trickling over rocks *mp*
A whisper *p*
A vacuum cleaner *mf*
Fire sirens racing by *f*
Typing on computer keys *mp*
A fan blowing *pp*
A jet plane taking off *ff*

Lento – turtle
Andante – cow
Allegro- horse

Vivace- squirrel
Presto- cheetah

Week Three: Chapter Three Comprehension Questions

1. Handel became a violinist for an orchestra under Conductor Keiser at the opera house, p. 70. One day Handel directed the orchestra and musicians when Keiser was ill, p. 73. The directors of the opera house promptly offered Handel a position as leader for a year of the opera in Hamburg, p. 75.
2. The position was church organist at Marien-kirche in Lübeck, a post the famous German organist Buxtehude was giving up because of his age. Neither man chose the post, however, because the arrangement required the new organist to marry Buxtehude's daughter, p. 82.
3. George met Prince Medici while he was in Hamburg, p. 86, and later met the Italian composer Scarlatti when he lived in Venice, p. 93.
4. George's nickname was "The Saxon," p. 93.
5. George took charge of court music for The Prince of Hanover, pp. 96, 97.

Week Three: Identify Contrasting Music Styles
All answers are subjective.

Possible answers for Cassical vs. Folk Music

Contrast: Classical music follows more specific rules of composition. Folk music is freely written and differs greatly based upon the geographic region where is originates. Classical music is typically written for instruments of the orchestra, whereas folk music incorporates many different instruments (many of which are common to a specific local.) Classical music is usually performed in a formal setting, with a conductor and a seated audience. Folk music is generally viewed as a casual expression of culture and is often performed in small groups or for one's own pleasure.

Compare: Both of these music styles can be fast or slow in tempo. They include instrumental and lyrical pieces and can be written for one or more instruments.

SO Complex	**SP** Subdued	**SP** Thin
SO Loud	**SP** Simple	**SO** Overflowing

Week Four: Chapter Four Comprehension Questions

1. It celebrated the new treaty England had signed, p. 107.
2. Handel had been away from Hanover's court for so long, he feared the Prince would be angry with him, p. 108.
3. He intended it to be played for the Prince/King while he floated down the river Thames on his way to a celebration of the King's coronation, p. 109.
4. During a thunderstorm, Handel sought shelter in a blacksmith's shop and listened to the blacksmith singing an old folk melody while he hammered on the anvil, p. 117.
5. Handel missed Johann Sebastian Bach, who had walked from Leipzig to meet him, p. 121.
6. *Messiah*, p. 123. It was performed first in Dublin, Ireland, p. 128.
7. The women were asked not to wear hoops under their dresses, and men were to come without swords, p. 128.
8. Handel struggled with blindness, p. 131.
9. He is known as the "Father of the Oratorio", p. 133.

Week Four: Character Traits

Focused - to concentrate attention or effort
Diligent - characterized by steady, earnest, energetic effort
Humble - not proud or haughty; not arrogant or assertive
Undaunted - courageously resolute especially in danger or difficulty: not discouraged
Leadership - the act of providing direction or guidance
Hardworking - using a lot of time and energy to do work
Humor - the ability to appreciate and express something amusing

continued

Respectful - showing high or special consideration
Creative - to produce through imaginative skill
Intentional - a determination to act in a certain way
Generous - unselfish in giving

Week Four: The Life and Times of George Frederic Handel
(The answers are in bold.)

1. William and Mary–**William and Mary are proclaimed King and Queen of England and Scotland for life**
2. Handel (1696)–**George F. Handel is sent to Berlin to make an impression on the court.**
3. Mayan Civilizations–**The last remains of Mayan civilization are destroyed by the Spanish in Yucatan.**
4. Jonathan Edwards and John Wesley–**Revivalists Jonathan Edwards and John Wesley are born.**
5. Deerfield, Connecticut–**French soldiers and Indians massacre settlers in Deerfield, Connecticut.**
6. Edmund Halley–**Edmund Halley predicts the return in 1758 of a comet seen in 1682.**
7. Handel (1706)–**Handel moves to Italy where he lives until 1710.**
8. Handel (1711)–**Handel's first London opera, *Rinaldo*, is completed in fourteen days and is performed in Queen's Hall.**
9. D.G. Fahrenheit–**D.G. Fahrenheit constructs mercury thermometer with temperature scale.**
10. Lady Montagu–**Inoculation against smallpox is introduced in England by Lady Montagu.**
11. New Orleans–**New Orleans is founded by the Mississippi Company.**
12. Texas–**Spain occupies Texas.**
13. Brazil–**Coffee is first planted in Brazil.**
14. Ben Franklin–**Ben Franklin invents lightning conductor.**
15. Handel (1759)–**Handel finishes series of ten concerts, dies on Good Friday, April 14, and is buried in Westminster Abbey.**

Handel at the Court of Kings Quiz

1. Lento–slow (e.)
2. Andante–moderately slow (h.)
3. Presto–very fast (b.)
4. (*f*) forte–loud (a.)
5. (*mf*) mezzo forte–medium loud (f.)
6. (*ff*) fortissimo–very loud (g.)
7. (*p*) piano–soft (c.)
8. (*mp*) mezzo piano–medium soft (i.)
9. (*pp*) pianissimo–very soft (d.)

Multiple Choice:

10. d.
11. b.
12. d.
13. c.
14. b.
15. a.

Handel

Weekly Lesson Outline

Haydn

(Activities marked with an * are required in order to meet national music appreciation standards.)

Week One:

📕 Read Chapter 1*

📋 Answer Comprehension Questions

❤️ Character Qualities

📚 Tidbits of Interest

🌐 Joseph Haydn's Travels

📁 Assemble Lapbook Folder

✏️ Haydn Family Facts

✋ What's in a Nickname? (LB)

✋ The Life of a Wheelwright (LB)

🎼 Rhythm Instruments*

Week Two:

📕 Read Chapter 2 & 3*

📋 Answer Comprehension Questions

🎧 Listen to Music Disc 2, tracks 27-30*

❤️ Character Qualities

📚 Tidbits of Interest

✋ A Tourist's Guide to St. Stephen's Cathedral (LB)

✋ Enjoying a Taste of Austria

✋ A Look at Vienna's Society (LB)

✋ Apartment Living in Vienna (LB)

🎼 The Orchestra*

Week Three:

📕 Read Chapter 4*

📋 Answer Comprehension Questions

🎧 Listen to Music Disc 4, tracks 1-7*

❤️ Character Qualities

📚 Tidbits of Interest

✋ Papa Haydn's Symphony Fun Matching Game (LB)*

✏️ Three Great Composers, One Small City*

✋ Supper with Joseph Haydn

✋ Joseph Haydn Puzzle Activity

🎼 Band Music and Instruments*

Week Four:

📕 Read Chapter 5*

📋 Answer Comprehension Questions

🎧 Listen to Music Disc 4, tracks 12-16*

❤️ Character Qualities

📚 Tidbits of Interest

🎼 Tell Me About the Symphony (LB)*

🎼 An Introduction to World Instruments*

✋ World Events Timeline (LB)*

Chapter One Comprehension Questions

1. What did Matthias Haydn (Joseph's father) do for a living? _____

_____

2. Who came to visit the Haydn family in Rohrau? And what instrument did he bring? _____

_____

3. What did Sepperl (Joseph) use for his make-believe violin? _____

_____

4. What did Cousin Frankh offer to do for the Haydn family—especially for Joseph? _____

_____

5. What did Cousin Frankh teach six-year-old Joseph to play for a big procession in Hainburg?

_____

6. Why did Herr Reutter come from Vienna to Cousin Frankh's house? _____

_____

7. What was Joseph's reward from Herr Reutter for learning to trill when he sang? _____

_____

1685	Johann Sebastian Bach	1750
1685	George Frederic Handel	1759
1732	**Franz Joseph Haydn**	1809
1756	Wolfgang A. Mozart	1791
1770	Ludwig van Beethoven	1827
1782	Nicolò Paganini	1840
1797	Franz Schubert	1828

Character Qualities

Attentiveness *(pp. 10, 11, 13, 16, 19, 20, 22, 23, 25)* – Joseph listened attentively to many things: Herr Kreutter's market stories at the fruit stall, his father's singing, the rhythm of the music at the impromptu concerts at home, his mother's advice, the masses that the older boys sang in church, Herr Frankh's drum training, and Herr Reutter's trilling instructions.

Neatness *(pp. 16, 20)* – Yes, this is an admirable character quality…believe it or not! Perhaps Joseph's obedience to his mother's advice to keep clean and neat is as admirable as his attempts to keep clean. It's also significant that Joseph had already learned this quality at only six years of age.

Fearlessness *(pp. 18, 27)* – Although he was only six years old, Joseph was not afraid to leave home (on his parents' counsel and instruction, mind you) for the sake of learning music. He later approached the move to Vienna with the same boldness, readying himself with hard work and practice so he could become a Viennese choir boy.

Humility *(pp. 16, 20)* – Joseph was reared in a simple thatched roof cottage. His father was a hard-working wagonmaker and repairman, not a high-paying job. Joseph learned how to sing masses at Cousin Frankh's church, humbly taking his share of punishments for missed notes.

Chapter 1:

Page 9: Franz Joseph Haydn was born on March 31 or April 1, 1732. Haydn claimed that his "brother Michael preferred to claim that I was born on 31 March because he did not want people to say I had come into the world as an April fool."[1]

Page 20: Cousin Frankh was a demanding instructor, and Haydn later admitted, "I shall be grateful to that man as long as I live for keeping me so hard at work."[2] Frankh's wife did not wash or repair young Joseph's clothes to the same standard his mother had upheld. "I could not help perceiving, much to my distress, that I was gradually getting very dirty, and though I thought a good deal of my little person, was not always able to avoid spots of dirt on my clothes, of which I was dreadfully ashamed; in fact I was a regular little urchin."[3]

Page 21-23: Haydn learned to play the drum for a procession during the Week of the Cross (May 11–18).[4] The drum he played for the procession is still preserved in the church in Hainburg.[5]

Page 24-26: In 1740, Karl Georg Reutter, the newly appointed choir master at St. Stephen's Cathedral in Vienna, came to Hainburg in search of new choristers. When Reutter asked Haydn why he could not "shake" or trill, a contemporary of Haydn records that the young boy replied, "How can you expect me to shake when my cousin [Frankh] does not know how to himself?"[6] Reutter then took Haydn between his knees and showed him how to produce the notes in rapid succession in a "good shake" or trill. Reutter immediately rewarded the lad with a plate of fine cherries when Joseph trilled for him. Haydn said he still thought of those lovely cherries whenever he happened to trill.[7]

To trill (or shake) is when an instrument or voice produces a series of notes in fast succession. This musical technique is usually created with a principal note, plus the note above or below it.

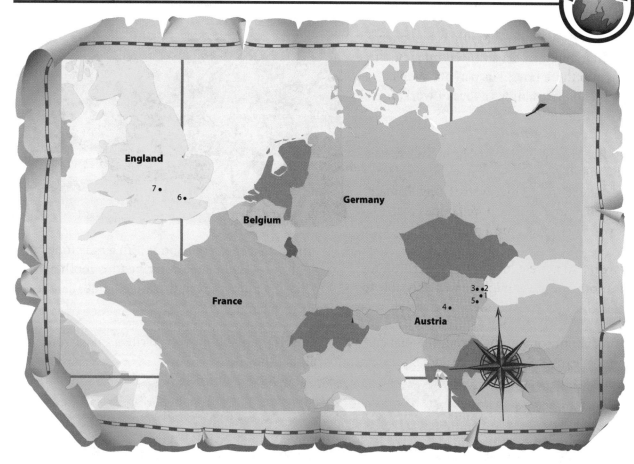

Haydn

Joseph Haydn left home when he was six years old. He spent much of his life in his beloved Austria, but also traveled to England where his music was greatly appreciated. Follow the dot-to-dot above to map out Haydn's early travels. In his later years, Joseph Haydn returned to his little house in Vienna where he composed and performed music until his death in 1809.

The numbers listed below correspond with the numbers in the dot-to-dot. Using the pages listed from the book, *Joseph Haydn, The Merry Little Peasant*, identify the cities where Haydn lived or visited.

1. _____ (p. 9)   5. _____ (p. 66)

2. _____ (p. 17)   6. _____ (p. 100)

3. _____ (p. 31)   7. _____ (p. 107)

4. _____ (p. 53)

Haydn Family Facts

Maria and Matthias had twelve children, but only six survived infancy: three girls and three boys. His parents instilled in Joseph and his siblings a love of work, method, and cleanliness.[8]

Mother Haydn, formerly Maria Koller, was reluctant to let her six-year-old leave. However, she and Matthias were strong Roman Catholics, and she harbored hopes that Haydn would become a priest.[9]

Haydn had a great love and appreciation for his mother, even though he was only able to spend his early childhood with her. (He recognized that she cared about him as she took care of him.) Haydn later described his mother as "having always given the most tender care to his welfare."[10]

Think about somebody in your life that cares for you **AND** cares about you. Write a thank you note to them expressing your love and appreciation for all that they do.

What's In a Nickname?

Sepperl was a nickname given to young Joseph in Austrian fashion, just as it was the custom to call children by their second names rather than their first.[11]

Using the pages for *What's In a Nickname,* follow the directions to cut out and assemble the pieces. Adhere this activity to section #1 in your Haydn lapbook.

The Life of a Wheelwright Wheel Book

Matthias Haydn was a master wheelwright who made wheels for wagons, repaired wagons, and even made wagons. He learned to play the harp while traveling through Germany and Austria as a journeyman wheelwright (after his apprenticeship).

Using the pages for *The Life of a Wheelwright Wheel Book,* follow the directions to cut out and assemble the pieces. Adhere this activity to section #5 & 6 in your Haydn lapbook.

Rhythm Instruments

There are many different places you can purchase rhythm instruments, but they can also easily be made with inexpensive materials. Below are some suggestions on how to create a variety of instruments.

- ♪ **Rhythm sticks:** Purchase a 1" dowel rod and cut it into 12" sections. Sand the ends smooth and paint each stick.
- ♪ **Sandpaper blocks:** These blocks can be created with a 1"x4" piece of wood cut into 4-5" lengths. Staple medium grade sandpaper to one side of each block.
- ♪ **Maracas:** Select a small plastic bowl with a lid. Fill the bowl with a small amount of dry rice. (You may want to seal the lid with glue or tape.)
- ♪ **Tambourines:** This instrument can be made with either disposable paper plates (the heavy duty ones work the best) or embroidery hoops. If you choose to use the paper plates, decorate the bottom of each plate and glue the plates together. (The tops face each other.) Using a hole punch, punch holes along the edge of the plates, about 2" apart. Tie jingle bells to each hole with ribbon or yarn. If you use the embroidery hoop, you can simply tie the jingle bells around the hoop with ribbon or yarn. It would be helpful to tie the string onto one part of the hoop first, and then insert the other part tightly to secure the bells.

Discuss the various rhythm instruments listed above and the sounds they make. Look up pictures of these instruments, and think of ways you could make other musical instruments.

After making the instrument(s) of your choice, choose from the following list of activities and have **fun making music!**

- ♪ Use your instrument while quoting common nursery rhymes. Shake, strike, or rub the instrument as you say each word, then as you say each syllable.
- ♪ March around the room, playing your instrument, while you sing your favorite song. Keep time by following the beat of the song.
- ♪ Listen to music on the radio or a recording. Try to follow the rhythm of the song with your instruments. Listen closely for rests (pauses) and tempo changes (fast or slow).

Chapter Two Comprehension Questions

1. What were the choir boys' duties in the great St. Stephen's Cathedral?

   _____

   _____

2. Why did the boys enjoy singing at the homes of noblemen? _____

   _____

   _____

3. When the choir boys sang at Schönbrunn, the royal palace, what mischief did Haydn become involved in twice? And what was his punishment for such mischief?

   _____

   _____

   _____

4. What did Joseph do to improve his musical abilities? (There are several possible answers from this chapter.) _____

   _____

5. Who else became a choir boy at St. Stephen's and became Joseph's responsibility?

   _____

   _____

6. What two things happened that brought an end to Joseph's time at St. Stephen's?

   _____

Chapter Three Comprehension Questions

1. When chapter three opened, who helped out young Joseph by giving him food and a place to

    stay? _____

    _____

2. How was Joseph later able to get his own room? _____

    _____

3. What else did that money allow Joseph to do besides get his own place? _____

    _____

    _____

    _____

4. Joseph began working with music master Porpora. What were some of Joseph's responsibilities?

    _____

    _____

    _____

5. How did Joseph's attitude or nature affect his boss Porpora? _____

    _____

6. What royal family member requested Joseph to become his Kapellmeister, or music director, at

    his palace? _____

Character Qualities

Studiousness – *(pp. 59, 60, 61, 63)* Joseph practiced many hours each day to improve his skills and his music. He tried to learn as much as possible from the music masters he was around. And he listened to the teaching of Porpora, the compositions of Gluck and Wagenseil, and the ideas of other artists like Kurz. His diligence paid off in learning to write quartets and symphonies, and finally being invited to the prince's palace.

Creative *(pp. 32, 41, 42)* – Haydn's creative interests were evident in his willingness to give up play time so he could listen to the organ at the cathedral and in his efforts to write music in twelve parts, though he had little training in composition. Joseph's persistence and diligence were also evident in his purchase of two books, on the rules of writing music, and in his staying up late to study composition.

Adventurous *(p. 37)* – Joseph was ready and willing to explore the palace grounds at Schönbrunn. Moreover, he was at the very top of the boards surrounding the new construction, climbing frighteningly higher and higher.

Frugality *(pp. 52, 56, 57, 59)* – Joseph worked hard to earn money to survive in Vienna. He rented a cold attic room and used a worm-eaten harpsichord to save money so he could focus on composing and practicing.

Mischievousness *(pp. 44, 45)* – Maybe Haydn's mischievous spirit in snipping the pigtail is not admirable or worthy of imitation, but his fun-loving spirit helped make his music what it became. Joseph's love for laughter, humor, and joyous things affected his compositions, his friendships, and his opportunities in life.

Leadership *(pp. 38, 39)* – Joseph helped care for the younger choir members. Joseph especially worked hard at making life easier for his brother Michael at the cathedral and school. Haydn was also a leader in the gymnastic antics at Schönbrunn, much to the empress's chagrin.

Cheerfulness *(pp. 57, 62)* – Haydn was happy in spite of his difficult circumstances. He considered himself as fortunate as a king in a palace when he had time to compose, though he was composing in a chilly room with little light. Joseph's cheerful disposition even changed his master Porpora's attitude.

Empress Maria Theresa

Hungary, and wife of Franz I. She ruled the Hapsburg family from 1740–1780. During that time she began many financial, agricultural, and educational reforms that strengthened Austria's economy and resources. Schönbrunn Palace was the Hapsburg showcase for wealth and architectural greatness, rivaling that of the French royal family at Versailles. Haydn also soon learned that Empress Maria's commands were not to be ignored.

Page 42: Haydn always found composition to be a labor, but even as a young man he set for himself regular hours to compose.[14]

Pages 45, 46: With only three ragged shirts, a worn coat, and no money or recommendation, Haydn was dismissed from St. Stephen's at age seventeen on a cold day in November of 1749.[15]

Chapter 2:

Pages 32, 33: Haydn studied music for the church services very carefully, and he claimed that he acquired his practical knowledge of musical techniques by listening to those works. Later in his life, Haydn asserted, "I listened more than I studied. I listened attentively and tried to turn to good account what most impressed me. In this way my knowledge and ability were developed."[13]

Pages 36, 38: Empress Maria Theresa was the Empress of Austria, Queen of Bohemia and

Chapter 3:

Page 55: The director at the chapel in Mariazell was Florian Wrastil, a former singer at St. Stephen's. Haydn's perfect sight-reading of a difficult solo part earned him the privilege of staying at the chapel for a week. He received good meals for the first time in months, and the singers even took up a small collection for Haydn's return to Vienna.

Page 57: Wheeler and Deucher comment that Joseph "never could be sad about anything for very long." Haydn wanted to make people smile and ease their hardships and troubles.[16] His mu-

> **"I listened more than I studied. I listened attentively and tried to turn to good account what most impressed me. In this way my knowledge and ability were developed."**
>
> **—Joseph Haydn**

sic was usually joyful and light in style—a style that caused some puritanical church members to criticize his compositions. Haydn's reply was, "Since God has given me a cheerful heart, He will forgive me for serving him cheerfully."[17]

Page 65: In 1758 Haydn obtained a salaried position with some security as a musician at Count Ferdinand Maximilian von Morzin's home. Morzin's summer residence is where Haydn's first symphony was performed, with Haydn directing the orchestra from his harpsichord. Prince Paul Anton Esterhazy was present at the symphony, and in 1761 the prince offered Joseph a musical position at his palace in Eisenstadt [pronounced I´zunshtAt] in eastern Austria.

Page 66: Wheeler and Deucher make no mention of Haydn's marriage, perhaps because most biographers record it as an unhappy union. Joseph married Maria Anna Keller, the sister of a violinist from St. Stephen's at the same time that Joseph was a choir boy. Maria was three years older than Joseph and was unable to provide him with children. She seemed indifferent to music, as well. She even lined her pastry tins with his manuscripts, or used his compositions as hair curlers! Nevertheless, Haydn remained faithful to her and supported her for the rest of her life. They lived separate lives, with Haydn focusing on his music and Maria devoting her time to the church.[18]

A Tourist's Guide to St. Stephen's Cathedral

The splendor of Vienna was at its height in the 1740s, when Haydn was a choir boy at St. Stephen's. St. Stephen's Cathedral has been in the heart of Vienna for centuries. It was built in A.D. 1147, and for many years it was the highest building in Europe, measuring almost 137 meters tall. The Roman Catholic cathedral exemplifies Gothic style, including the gigantic roof, the narrow south tower, and the tall stained-glass windows.

The educational system at St. Stephen's was conducted on a monitorial basis—meaning that the older boys taught the younger ones. Joseph taught his brother Michael. His other younger brother, Johann Evangelist, later became a choir boy at St. Stephen's as well.

Joseph's musical training at St. Stephen's included singing, violin, and clavier, but not instruction in music theory or composition. Haydn later claimed that he only received two lessons in musical theory from Herr Reutter in his nine years with the choir.[19]

Using the *A Tourist's Guide to St. Stephen's Cathedral* pages, follow the directions to cut out and assemble the pieces. Adhere this activity to section #2 in your Haydn lapbook.

Enjoying a Taste of Austria: Making Kugelhopf

While Joseph was a choir boy at St. Stephen's, Baker Hermann invited him to get warm in his kitchen and served him a "nice fat cake with raisins and a thick sugar icing on top" (page 34). Your family will certainly enjoy tasting this traditional Austrian cake called Kugelhopf.

Recipe for Kugelhopf
from the kitchen of Baker Hermann

½ c. raisins
¾ c. almonds, chopped (optional)
1-½ tsp. grated lemon rind
6 c. flour, sifted
¼ c. lukewarm water
1 tsp. salt
Confectioners' sugar or icing

1 c. sugar
2 tsp. yeast
2 c. milk
2 eggs, well beaten
⅓ c. melted butter
1 tsp. vanilla extract

Combine raisins, almonds, and lemon rind with ½ cup flour; toss until well coated. Combine sugar, salt, and 2½ cups flour in large mixing bowl. Sprinkle yeast over water; stir until well mixed. Add yeast mixture to ingredients in large mixing bowl; beat with spoon until smooth. Beat in eggs thoroughly. Add butter gradually beating constantly. Stir in milk and vanilla extract. Add remaining flour; beat until smooth and satiny. Add raisin mixture; mix thoroughly. Cover with towel and let rise in warm place for 1½ hours or until double in bulk. Stir down dough and turn into large, buttered fluted cake pan. Cover with towel and let rise for another hour. Bake in preheated 350-degree oven for about 50 minutes or until cake tester comes out clean. Remove from pan; cool on wire rack. Cover and let stand one day. Sprinkle with confectioners' sugar before slicing, or add thick sugar icing as would Baker Hermann.

A Look at Vienna's Society

Joseph Haydn spent many of his early years in Vienna, Austria. The culture of that day was based on distinct classes of society. This distinction determined where a person could live, income, and social standing. Musicians could move from one class to another, depending on their skill, popularity, and social connections.

Using *A Look at Vienna's Society* pages, follow the directions to cut out and assemble the pieces. Adhere this activity to sections #15 in your Haydn lapbook.

Vienna, Austria 1745

Apartment Living in Vienna

Interesting Notes:

Pietro Metastasio brought Haydn a promising young piano pupil who was then ten years old. Marianne Martinez was the daughter of a Spanish nobleman living in the same district of Michaelerhaus, and Joseph taught her for three years in exchange for free food.[22] Marianne became a leading musician in Vienna—equally talented as a singer, pianist, and composer. She even played duets with Wolfgang Mozart!

Haydn was also introduced to the famous Italian composer and singing teacher, Nicola Porpora, through the Martinez family. Porpora gave Haydn valuable criticism on his compositions and helped him improve his Italian. Haydn apparently helped Porpora improve his temperament. Porpora is described as a man then "sour beyond all that can be imagined,"[23] but Haydn patiently learned by observing Porpora's teaching methods and acting as his valet.

A merchant friend of Joseph's father, Anton Bucholz (or Buchholz, as it is spelled in some documents), lent Joseph 150 florins—interest free and without a date for repayment. Joseph apparently repaid the loan a year after he received it, which was a remarkable feat considering his job situation at the time.[20]

In Haydn's will from 1801, he gave to "Fraulein Anna Buchholz, one hundred florins, in as much as in my youth her grandfather lent me one hundred and fifty florins when I greatly needed them…"[21]

With this money, Haydn rented his own room at the top of a house in Michaelerhaus—a district of Vienna near the Church of St. Michael's (where Spangler sang). Pietro Metastasio lived in the same house as Haydn. He was an Italian poet and librettist who wrote words for operas, oratorios, and so forth.

Using the *Apartment Living in Vienna* pages, follow the directions to cut out and assemble the pieces. Adhere this activity horizontally to sections #11-14 in your Haydn lapbook.

Haydn

The Orchestra

An orchestra is typically divided into four sections or families. (Definitions are from Encarta® World English Dictionary.[24])

The String Family:

The Violin is a wooden musical instrument with four strings and an unfretted fingerboard. It is held under the player's chin and played with a bow. The violin has the highest range in the violin family. Listen to Music Disc 3, track 1.

The Viola is a stringed instrument slightly larger and lower in pitch than a violin. It is also held under the chin and played with a bow. The viola is tuned an octave above the cello and is the alto of the violin family. Listen to Music Disc 3, track 2.

The Cello is a large stringed instrument of the violin family that is held upright between a seated player's knees and played with a bow; the cello has a full deep sound. Listen to Music Disc 3, track 3.

The Double Bass is the largest and lowest in pitch of the instruments of the violin family, used in the modern symphony orchestra. (It is also commonly found in jazz and dance bands, where it is usually plucked rather than bowed.) Listen to Music Disc 3, track 4.

The Harp is a triangular-shaped instrument that has a curved neck and strings stretched between the neck and the body, at an angle to the sound box. The modern orchestral harp is large and played by a seated player. Listen to Music Disc 3, track 5.

The Conductor…
- directs the orchestra in tempo, dynamics, and style.
- must know the entire musical score.
- performs much of their work during rehearsals and individual practices.

The Woodwind Family:

Music is what *feelings* sound like.

—Author Unknown

The Flute is an instrument with a cylindrical narrow body, usually held out to the right of the player, who blows across a hole in the mouthpiece to generate a high-pitched sound. (The flute family includes the piccolo, the alto flute, and the bass flute.) Listen to Music Disc 3, track 6.

The Clarinet is a musical instrument with a straight body and a single reed. Listen to Music Disc 3, track 7.

The Oboe is an instrument that produces a penetrating high sound and consists of a slim tubular body with a double reed and keys operated by the fingers. Listen to Music Disc 3, track 8.

The Bassoon is a low-pitched, double-reed instrument. Its wooden body is attached to the mouthpiece by means of a thin metal pipe. Listen to Music Disc 3, track 9.

The Piccolo is the smallest member of the flute family, with a range one octave higher than the standard flute. Listen to Music Disc 3, track 10.

The Brass Family:

The French Horn is a coiled brass orchestral instrument with a long looped pipe ending in a wide round bell, with other pipes and valves attached to it within the loop. French horns have a mellow, brassy tone and are usually played with one hand in the bell of the instrument to control its volume. Listen to Music Disc 3, track 11.

The Tuba is a low-pitched musical instrument held vertically with the bell pointing upward and the mouthpiece set horizontally; it has three to five valves. Listen to Music Disc 3, track 12.

The Trombone is an instrument of varying size with a U-shaped slide that is moved to produce different pitches. Listen to Music Disc 3, track 13.

The Trumpet is a musical instrument, either straight or coiled, with three valves and a flared bell; it has a brilliant tone and a middle to high register. Listen to Music Disc 3, track 14.

The Percussion Family:

The Cymbal is a circular brass instrument played with a stick or in pairs by striking them together. Listen to Music Disc 3, track 15.

The Bass Drum is a large drum that has a cylindrical body, two drumheads, and a low indefinite pitch. Listen to Music Disc 3, track 16.

The Snare Drum is a drum fitted with snares to produce a rattling effect. Listen to Music Disc 3, track 15.

The Kettle Drum, also called timpani, consists of large copper or brass drum covered with parchment skin that can be adjusted to alter the pitch. Pitch is altered by screws and pedals that increase or decrease the skin's tension. Listen to Music Disc 3, track 17.

The Orchestra

Lapbook Review Card:
Write the correct name of each instrument in the blank below the picture. Cut out the box along the dotted line and adhere this activity to section #9 in your Haydn lapbook.

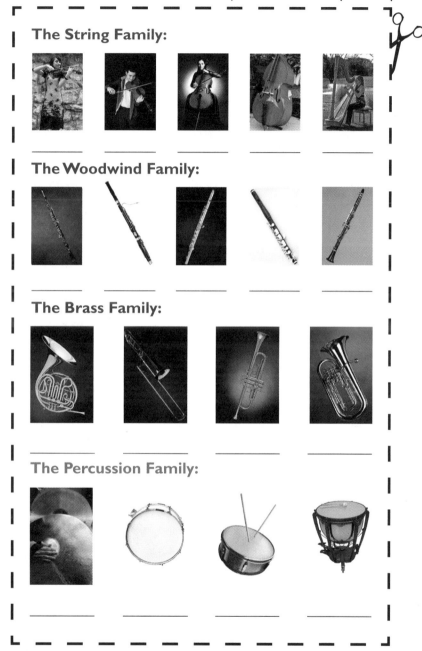

The String Family:

The Woodwind Family:

The Brass Family:

The Percussion Family:

Instruments of the Orchestra Memory Matching Game
Cut out the cards on the next six pages. Mix up the cards and lay them in rows, face down. On your turn, turn over two cards at a time. If you find the instrument and the correct name, keep the set. If the cards are not a match, turn them face down again. (Remember where each card is!) When all the cards are turned over, the person with the most matched sets wins.

Double Bass
String Family

Bassoon
Woodwind Family

Cymbals
Percussion Family

Violin
String Family

Kettle Drum
Percussion Family

Viola
String Family

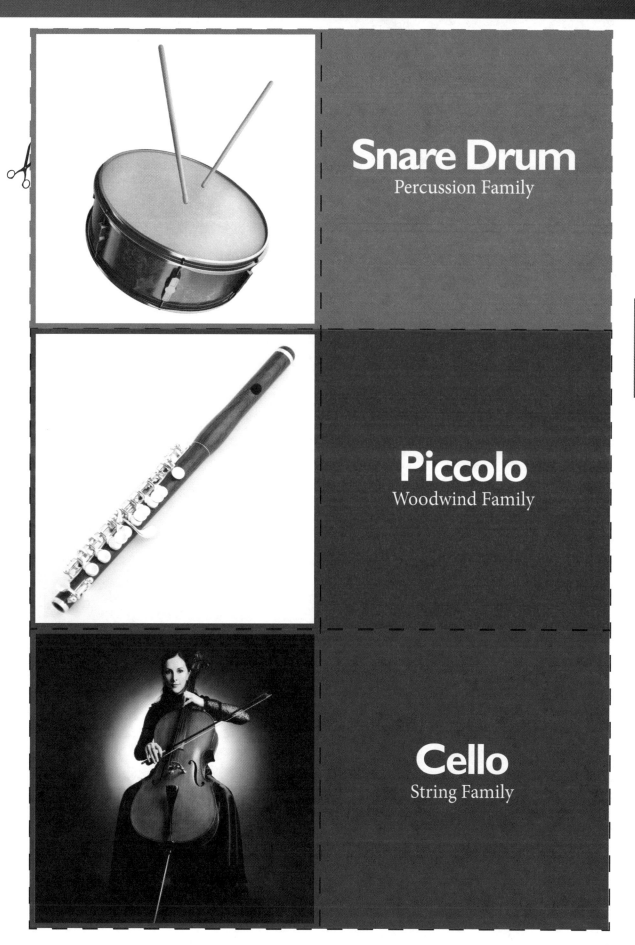

Snare Drum
Percussion Family

Piccolo
Woodwind Family

Cello
String Family

Haydn

French Horn
Brass Family

Flute
Woodwind Family

Bass Drum
Percussion Family

Haydn

Clarinet
Woodwind Family

Oboe
Woodwind Family

Harp
String Family

Haydn

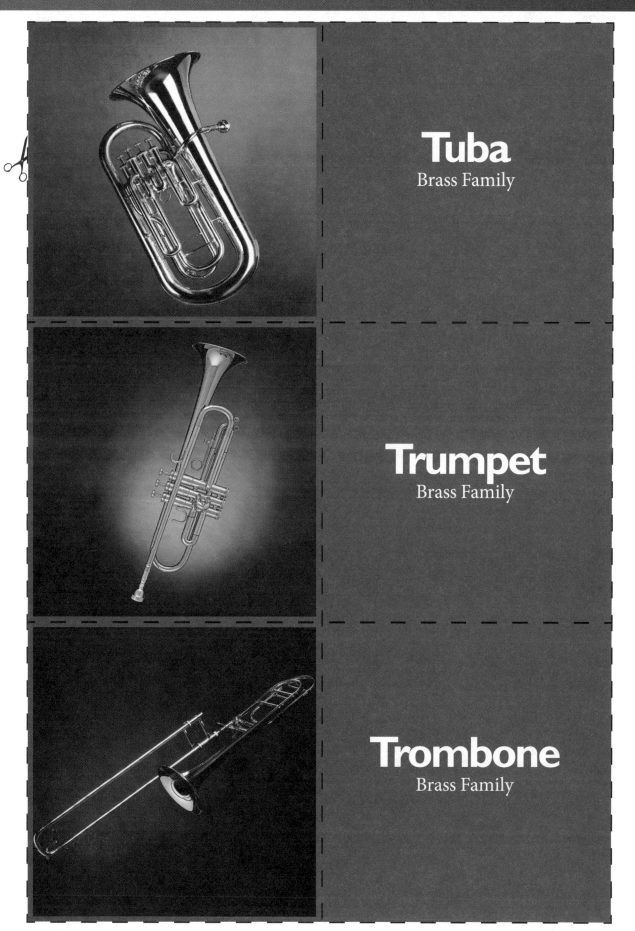

Tuba
Brass Family

Trumpet
Brass Family

Trombone
Brass Family

Haydn

The Orchestra

The instruments of the orchestra are arranged in a specific way. This placement aids in the projection of sound, allows the performers to hear each other's parts, and assists the conductor in his directing.

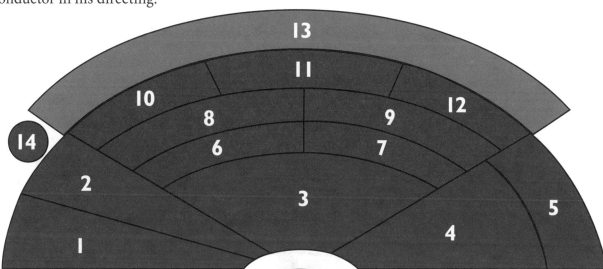

Section 1 **First Violins**

Section 2 **Second Violins**

Section 3 **Violas**

Section 4 **Cellos**

Section 5 **Double Basses**

Section 6 **Flutes**

Section 7 **Oboes**

Section 8 **Clarinets**

Section 9 **Bassoons**

Section 10 **French Horns**

Section 11 **Trumpets**

Section 12 **Trombones & Tubas**

Section 13 **Percussion**

Section 14 **Harp**

*Note for Parents: The music performed by a symphony orchestra is beautiful and powerful. It would be a wonderful experience to share with your child! Attending an orchestra concert will allow them to see, hear, and feel the instruments they have just studied.

Lapbook Activity:
Cut along the dotted line of both boxes. Adhere this activity vertically to section #17-20 in your Haydn lapbook.

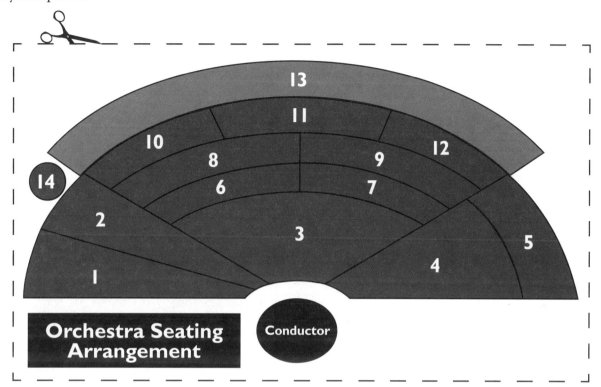

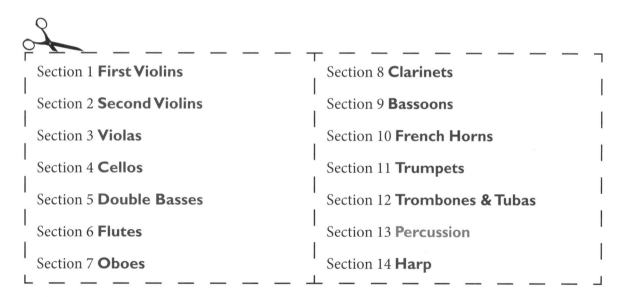

Section 1 **First Violins**

Section 2 **Second Violins**

Section 3 **Violas**

Section 4 **Cellos**

Section 5 **Double Basses**

Section 6 **Flutes**

Section 7 **Oboes**

Section 8 **Clarinets**

Section 9 **Bassoons**

Section 10 **French Horns**

Section 11 **Trumpets**

Section 12 **Trombones & Tubas**

Section 13 **Percussion**

Section 14 **Harp**

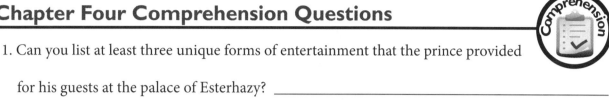

Chapter Four Comprehension Questions

1. Can you list at least three unique forms of entertainment that the prince provided

   for his guests at the palace of Esterhazy? _____

   _____

   _____

   _____

2. What did Joseph's orchestra fondly nickname him? _____

3. Why were the musicians in the orchestra becoming restless and dissatisfied with life at Ester-

   hazy? _____

   _____

4. How did Haydn finally convince the prince to let the musicians go? _____

   _____

5. With what famous young composer did Haydn become dear friends? _____

   _____

6. To what country was Haydn invited to direct an orchestra for a man named Salomon? _____

   _____

Character Qualities

Hard-working *(pp. 72, 73, 78, 79, 87)* – Haydn not only directed and performed with the Prince's orchestra far into the night, but he also woke at daybreak to begin writing new music for the day. He traveled with the orchestra when they were requested to play for the empress at Schönbrunn Castle. He received daily music orders from Prince Esterhazy, and he and his men rarely were allowed to leave the palace of Esterhazy. Haydn even played the organ at a nearby village chapel each Sunday.

Fun-loving *(pp. 84, 87, 92, 93)* – Joseph basically composed the *Farewell* Symphony as a joke to help the Prince realize that his men needed a vacation. He enjoyed vanilla ice cream, fresh fruit, and pastries. Now that's sweet fun! He spotted toy instruments at a country fair and incorporated them into a delightful symphony, the *Toy* Symphony. Haydn was obviously a man who enjoyed music and didn't take it seriously all the time.

Generous *(pp. 86, 87, 93, 94)* – Haydn encouraged a young composer named Wolfgang Mozart. Joseph played the organ for a small chapel every Sunday. And Haydn gave up time and energy to plan a trip to England in order to share his music with new people.

Tidbits of Interest

Pages 74, 76: Haydn's special diamond ring mentioned here was something of a good luck charm that he wore when he composed an important work. In fact, one contemporary biographer of Haydn declared, "that when the master forgot to put on the ring no ideas came to him."[25] Please note, however, that Haydn prayed daily before beginning to compose, which one would consider a much more effective approach to writing quality music than wearing a diamond ring.[26]

Page 84: While Esterhazá was intended to be a summer residence, it soon became the prince's permanent home. Because it was built on a plot that flooded, the climate at Esterhazá was frequently poor. The musicians (including Haydn) were often sick because of the swampy dampness. Moreover, Esterhazá was farther from Vienna than Eisenstadt had been. Most of the musicians' families had to live in Vienna because the housing at Esterhazá was not large enough for their families. In 1772, when the prince did not make his customary visit to Vienna, and the musicians had been separated from their families for nearly a year, they became restless and asked Haydn to convey their displeasure to the prince in some musical manner. Thus was born Haydn's Symphony No. 45, nicknamed *Farewell*. The Prince took the hint, and preparations for a trip to Vienna were started the next day!

Pages 92, 93: Haydn wrote *Toy* Symphony in 1788 for different toy instruments and strings. It is proof that though Haydn had no children of his own, he had a deep understanding of little ones and a delightful sense of fun.

Pages 93, 94: Prince Nicholas died in September of 1790, and his son Anton succeeded him to the Esterhazy title, but Anton had no musical interests. In fact, the new prince disbanded the orchestra and choir (keeping only the military band) and kept Haydn on an annual pension. After serving the Esterhazy family for over twenty-nine years, Haydn finally had time to journey abroad. So when Johann Peter Salomon, a brilliant violinist and concert promoter from England, invited Haydn to give a series of concerts in London, the fifty-eight-year-old composer took the opportunity. Salomon's actual introduction to Haydn is recorded as, "My name is Salomon; I have come from London to fetch you."[27]

Papa Haydn's Symphony Fun Matching Game

Haydn's natural gift for dealing with disputes among his musicians and daily problems in the orchestra earned him their respect. His fatherly care gained him the nickname or title of Papa, a title that remained with him throughout his life.

Joseph Haydn was fun-loving and there are several stories in the book of clever and fun antics with Haydn's symphonies.

Miracle Symphony

***Farewell* Symphony** was composed as a joke to help the prince realize that his men needed a vacation. (p. 84)

***Clock* Symphony** is light cheerful music. (p. 106)

***Toy* Symphony** was written after Haydn spotted toy instruments at a county fair and incorporated them into a delightful symphony. (p. 92)

***Surprise* Symphony** was written to surprise napping concertgoers. (p. 103)

Using the *Papa Haydn's Symphony Fun Matching Game* pages, follow the directions to cut out and assemble the pieces. Adhere this activity to section #8 in your Haydn lapbook.

Three Great Composers, One Small City

Joseph Haydn and Wolfgang Mozart probably first met in Vienna in 1781. They became very close friends, and some believe Haydn's best symphonies were composed after this friendship developed.[28] There was absolutely no rivalry or envy between the two composers. They each respected the other's works, and Mozart valued Haydn's opinion above that of any other musician—even his father.[29] In 1785, Mozart played six new quartets he had dedicated to Haydn. Haydn told Mozart's father that Wolfgang was the greatest composer he had ever known "either in person or by reputation."[30] When Mozart and Haydn said good-bye before Haydn's trip to England, Mozart sobbed, "We shall never meet again."[31] They never did. Less than a year after Haydn's departure, Mozart died (in December 1791). At first Haydn refused to believe the news of Mozart's death because Haydn himself had been rumored as dead in 1778! Haydn was so deeply affected by Mozart's death that he was often moved to tears at the mere mention of Mozart's name.[32]

Haydn returned to Vienna in mid-summer of 1792. He passed through Bonn, Germany on his way home, and it was there that he met Ludwig van Beethoven. Haydn agreed to give the young composer lessons in composition. They returned "to the little house just outside Vienna [so Beethoven could] study with the master." (page 108) Their differing personalities and ages (Haydn was sixty; Beethoven was only twenty-two.) made a close friendship nearly impossible. Nevertheless, Beethoven respected Haydn immensely—even paying tribute to the aged composer at Haydn's last public appearance by stepping forward to kiss Haydn's hand.[33]

Vienna, Austria is unique in that these three great men lived, visited, and worked in this city. Not every town can claim such notoriety!

What about your town? Has anyone famous been born or lived in your town? What is the history of the area? Was something invented or produced there? Is it known for something special?

Do some research on your town, local area, or county.

Try to answer these questions:
- Has anyone famous been born or lived here?
- Did anybody famous (or infamous) visit here?
- What is the history of this area?
  - Why was the town started?
  - Who was the founder?
  - What year did it become a town?
  - What was the main industry in the area?
- Was something invented or produced here?
- Is our town known for something special?

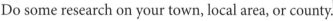

After you have compiled your research, choose one of the following options to share what you have learned.

1. Draw a picture depicting why your town is famous.
2. Write a short essay about the history and value of your town.
3. Create a tourist brochure for your town. Include the history you have learned. Promote anything that makes your town stand out. (People, places, events…)
4. Pretend you are a reporter for the local newspaper or television station. Write an eye witness report of the events you have researched.

Some suggestions for information include the …
- Local Historical Society
- Local Library
- Local Newspaper Office
- Local Senior Citizens Center
- Local Historical Markers
- Internet

(NOTE: Local festivals are often held in remembrance of an event associated with the town or to celebrate something the town is known for, i.e. "Corn capital of the world.")

Supper with Joseph Haydn

It would only be appropriate to serve a meal of macaroni and cheese with ice cream for dessert while reading this chapter of Joseph Haydn.

Macaroni and cheese actually became popular right around this time in Haydn's life. Thomas Jefferson returned home from a trip to Paris in 1789 with a macaroni mold, and he served macaroni in the White House in 1802. Macaroni and cheese was even considered fancy enough fare to appear on the tables of Italian and French royalty in 1798! And ice cream has been fashionable dessert since all the way back to the 4th century B.C., though it was perhaps more fruit sorbet than the ice and milk concoctions that King Tang developed in China during the Shang Dynasty (A.D. 618–697). Ice cream recipes were brought back to Europe, and creamed ice was very popular in French and Italian courts by the 1600s.

Joseph Haydn Puzzle

Using the *Joseph Haydn Puzzle* pages lapbook pages, follow the directions to cut out and assemble the pieces. Adhere this activity to section #3 in your Haydn lapbook. (Note: There is a simple and a difficult version.)

Haydn

This painting is said to represent Haydn crossing the English Channel during his second visit to London. This was around the time when he was composing *The Creation*.

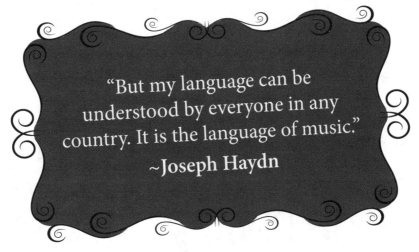

"But my language can be understood by everyone in any country. It is the language of music."

~Joseph Haydn

Band Music and Instruments

The term "band music" covers a wide genre of music. There are many different kinds of bands that showcase many different kinds of instruments. Throughout history, bands have communicated to every age group and have played a major role in expressing local culture and philosophy.

Read the following paragraphs about band music and band instruments. Then answer the questions.

1. A concert band (also known as a symphonic band or a wind band) is quite similar in makeup to the orchestra. One main difference is that the strings are not the dominant instrument. Although string instruments may be part of a concert band, they do not play the same key role as they do in an orchestra. The majority of members play woodwinds, brass, or percussion instruments. This allows for greater variety of instruments to be included in the band. The musical style of a symphonic band varies depending on the purpose of the performance, the instruments involved, and the director's style. Their repertoire can include jazz, blues, classical compositions, show tunes, big band music, marches, and other popular songs. If you have ever watched a local community band, a military band, or a marching band, you have heard a concert band perform. This band is quite entertaining and a delight to watch. Their music is energetic and exciting. Listen to Music Disc 4, track 8.

2. The guitar is a versatile instrument that is used in many bands. Depending on how it is played, it can be used in different genres of music including classical music, country western music, rock and roll and pop bands, big band music, jazz, and many others. There are two types of guitars, acoustic and electric. They produce distinctly different sounds and are played in a specific way. Guitar is a valuable instrument to learn because it is adaptable to so many different styles of music. Listen to Music Disc 4, track 9.

   Acoustic Guitar

3. Many bands use electric instruments which gives them a unique sound and style. Examples of this are rock bands or modern pop bands. Electrical instruments are defined as "musical instruments in which the use of electric devices determine or affect the sound produced by the instrument."[34] Familiar electronic instruments are the electric keyboard, the electric guitar, and the electric organ. These instruments are often connected to loudspeakers and amplifiers so that the music can be projected over large crowds. A synthesizer is another electric instrument "that can generate and modify sounds electronically."[35] It has keys like a piano, but has a very distinct sound that can be changed frequently throughout the song. New technology is constantly improving the capabilities of electronic instruments. It will be amazing to watch how these instruments continue to change. Listen to Music Disc 4, tracks 10-11.

   Electric Guitar

Electric Piano Keyboard

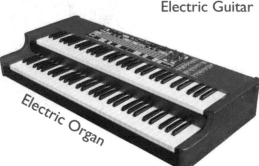
Electric Organ

1. Explain one difference between an orchestra and a concert band. _____

_____

_____

_____

2. Identify three styles of music performed by a concert band.

   •

   •

   •

3. Why is the guitar a valuable instrument to learn? _____

_____

_____

4. What are two types of guitars?

   •

   •

5. In your own words, define an electrical instrument. _____

_____

_____

_____

_____

6. Demonstrate why electric instruments are beneficial in large crowds. _____

_____

Haydn

Lapbook Review Card:

Write the correct name of each instrument in the blank below the picture. Cut out the box along the dotted line and adhere this activity to section #10 in your Haydn lapbook.

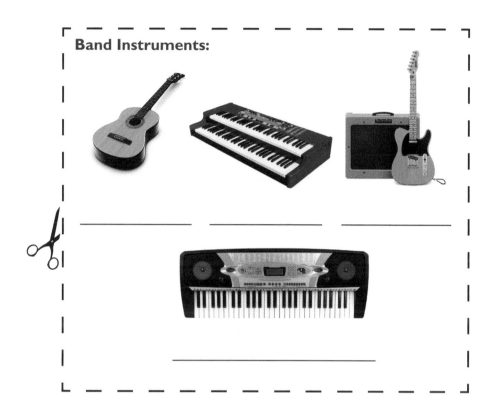

Band Instruments:

_____   _____   _____

_____

Week 4 Activity Pages

Haydn

Chapter Five Comprehension Questions

1. What was Joseph's emotional response to traveling to England? Was he terrified, excited, uncaring, or what? _____

2. What composer was honored by a special festival at Westminster Abbey? (Haydn considered him the "master of us all.") _____

   _____

3. Can you explain why Haydn wrote his *Surprise* Symphony? _____

   _____

   _____

4. What other famous composer (though he was a budding composer at this point) did Haydn

   meet in Bonn, Germany on his way home to Vienna? _____

5. What did Haydn's hometown of Rohrau do to honor him? _____

   _____

6. What was the English response to Haydn and his music during both of his visits?

   _____

   _____

   _____

7. What did Haydn do to help Emperor Francis celebrate his royal birthday?

   _____

   _____

8. Haydn has become known as the "Father of the _____."

Character Qualities

Fun-loving *(pp. 103, 106, 112)* – Again, Haydn's humor and love of fun is evident in his music. He wrote the *Surprise* Symphony to startle napping concertgoers. And his music is often light and cheerful, like his "Gypsy Rondo" and the *Clock* Symphony.

Grateful *(pp. 100, 107, 110)* – Haydn was appreciative of the mastery of other composers and musicians, as seen in his response to Handel's music at the London music festival. He showed his gratitude for a doctorate of music degree that Oxford University gave him by writing a special *Oxford* Symphony. And he was grateful to his parents for the humble home they provided for him and for the sacrifices they made to enable him to pursue music.

Loyal *(pp. 108, 113-115)* – While Haydn may have received more honor in England than in Austria, he remained loyal to his prince's requests to return to the Esterhazy home. Moreover, he continued writing music for the Esterhazy family gatherings. He even wrote a special hymn for Emperor Francis's birthday.

Joseph Haydn demonstrated many positive characteristics throughout his lifetime. He was an enjoyable man to be around and well-respected by those who knew him.

Listed below are several characteristics described throughout the book, *Joseph Haydn, The Merry Little Peasant*. Using a thesaurus, provide two synonyms and two antonyms for each word that is given.

	Synonyms	Antonyms
Humble		
	Synonyms	Antonyms
Attentive		
	Synonyms	Antonyms
Fearless		
	Synonyms	Antonyms
Neat		

	Synonyms	Antonyms
Adventurous		
Creative		
Leader-like		
Frugal		
Diligent		
Cheerful		
Industrious		
Playful		
Generous		
Grateful		
Loyal		

Haydn

Pages 100-101: By January 8, 1791, Haydn was already writing a friend to say, "My arrival caused a great sensation throughout the whole city [London] and I was mentioned in all the newspapers for three successive days... Everyone wants to know me...if I wish, I could dine out every evening...I wish I could fly for a time to Vienna to have some quiet in which to work, for the noise in the street is intolerable."[36]

Page 108: Windsor Castle is an official residence of England's royal family and is the largest occupied castle in the world. It is over 900 years old. Haydn played for the Prince of Wales (future King George IV) numerous times during his months in England. In fact, Haydn was invited to Carlton House, the prince's residence, twenty-six times and even wrote the prince's favorite punch recipe in his diary.[37]

Page 114-115: While he was in England, Haydn was impressed by the playing of the English anthem "God Save the King." Haydn believed the Viennese and Austrian people needed a morale boost during their struggles against Napoleon and the wars surrounding the French Revolution. He thought adopting a patriotic hymn as a national anthem would help, so in January of 1797 he composed his *Emperor* Quartet for a text called "God Save the Emperor Franz." Haydn's work was adopted at once by the people, and it remained the official Austrian national anthem for over a century. You may recognize it better as the hymn "Glorious Things of Thee Are Spoken" (words by John Newton). Emperor Franz was otherwise known as Emperor Francis, the grandson of Maria Theresa. Ironically, in spite of being defeated by Napoleon's armies, Emperor Francis emerged from the Congress of Vienna in 1815 as one of the most powerful of European monarchs. By early May of 1809, Napoleon's troops invaded Vienna, and the city surrendered to the French. Napoleon ordered a guard outside Haydn's home so that the invalid composer could be as comfortable as possible during their occupation of the city. As an act of defiance against the occupying French forces, Haydn played the new Austrian national anthem on his piano each day.

Pages 116-118: Haydn's last public appearance was on March 27, 1808, at a special performance of his oratorio *The Creation*. Haydn wrote of this work, "Never before was I so devout as when I composed The Creation. I knelt down each day to pray to God to give me strength for my work."[38] He explained that his goal was to inspire worship and adoration of the Creator, and to put the listener "in a frame of mind where he is most susceptible to the kindness and omnipotence of the Creator."[39] At this final concert, Haydn was seated next to Princess Esterhazy, "who wrapped the old man in her own shawl when she noticed him shivering a little. Many other ladies followed her example, and soon Haydn was covered with the costliest of garments."[40] When the performance ended and the audience applauded, Haydn lifted his hands to heaven and announced, "Not from me – from there, above, comes everything."[41]

Franz Joseph Haydn was a humble, merry little peasant who once stated, "I offer all my praises to Almighty God, for I owe them to Him alone."[42] In his lifetime, he composed over one hundred symphonies, seventy-six string quartets, oratorios, operas, concertos, masses, and dozens of chamber works. In his final days, Haydn expressed the hope "not wholly to die; but to live on in my music."[43] Though Haydn slipped into a coma and died on May 31, 1809, God answered his prayer to live on through his music. His merry music continues to cheer and refresh the weary world of today.

Tell Me About the Symphony

During Haydn's second trip to London (1794–1795), he took his servant and copyist, Johann Elssler, with him. It was during this visit that he wrote some of his final symphonies: Nos. 102–104. Yes, that means that he wrote over one hundred symphonies in his lifetime. No wonder he is called the "Father of the Symphony!"

Using the *Tell Me About the Symphony* pages, follow the directions to cut out and assemble the pieces. Adhere this activity to section #7 in your Haydn lapbook.

An Introduction to World Instruments

Music is used as a valuable expression of life in almost every culture around the world. Whether it is for religious practices, holiday celebrations, or entertainment, music is often a clear representation of a country's style and tradition.

One way that music communicates a variety of styles is through the use of different instruments. Many cultures use specific instruments in their music which leads to a distinct sound associated with their culture. Below are pictures of several instruments from around the world.

Using print and internet sources, answer three questions about each of the following musical instruments.

1. From what country did this instrument originate?
2. For what occasions is this instrument used?
3. What makes this instrument unique?

Examples:

Sitar:	Listen to Music Disc 4, track 17.

a South Asian stringed instrument with a rounded resonating body and a long fretted neck with several playing strings; used for Hindu classical music in India

Conga Drum:	Listen to Music Disc 4, track 18.

a tall tapering drum, played with both hands and used in Latin American and African music; used for dancing and religious music

Harpsichord:	Listen to Music Disc 4, track 19.

**Panpipes
(also called the pan flute):**   Listen to Music Disc 4, track 20.

Native American Drum: Listen to Music Disc 4, track 21.

Gong: Listen to Music Disc 4, track 22.

Great Highland Bagpipes: Listen to Music Disc 4, track 23.

Didgeridoo: Listen to Music Disc 4, track 24.

Haydn

Research: If you had the opportunity to visit any country in the world, where would you go? Using print and internet resources, research the local music style and instruments of that culture. Chose one type of instrument to study more thoroughly and write a short essay describing the look, sound, and use of that instrument.

Haydn

Lapbook Review Card:

Write the correct name of each instrument in the blank below the picture. Cut out the box along the dotted line and adhere this activity to section #16 in your Haydn lapbook.

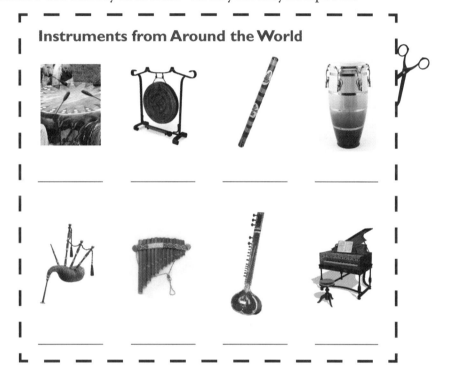

Instruments from Around the World

World Events Timeline

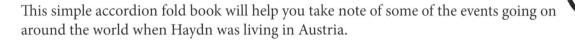

This simple accordion fold book will help you take note of some of the events going on around the world when Haydn was living in Austria.

Using the *World Events Timeline* lapbook pages, follow the directions to cut out and assemble the pieces. Adhere this activity to section #4 in your Haydn lapbook.

Haydn, The Merry Little Peasant Quiz

Name: _____ Date: _____

Matching:
Match each instrument to the correct family:

_____ Violin

_____ Flute

_____ Trombone

_____ Cello

_____ Cymbals

_____ Oboe

_____ Trumpet

_____ Kettle Drums

a. Brass Family

b. Percussion Family

c. String Family

d. Woodwind Family

Fill in the Blanks:
Using the Word box, fill in the blanks.

☐ six   ☐ Mozart   ☐ Papa Haydn

☐ Schubert   ☐ Herr Haydn   ☐ twelve

☐ versatile   ☐ eight   ☐ Handel

1. How old was Haydn when he left home? _____

2. What nickname did the orchestra members give Joseph Haydn? _____

3. With which young composer did Haydn become good friends? _____

4. The guitar is a valuable instrument to learn because it is…? _____

Week One: Chapter One Comprehension Questions

1. He was a wheelwright, pp. 9, 11.
2. Cousin Matthias Frankh from Hainburg brought his violin with him, p. 11.
3. He used two smooth pieces of wood, p. 13.
4. He offered to take Joseph to Hainburg to teach him music (the clavier, violin, and singing), p. 13.
5. He played the drum, p. 23.
6. He was looking for boys to sing in his choir at St. Stephen's Cathedral, p. 24.
7. He received a plateful of fresh cherries, and he was given the opportunity to become a choir boy at St. Stephen's, pp. 26, 27.

Week One: Map Activity

1. Rohrau, Austria (p. 9)
2. Hainburg, Austria (p. 17)
3. Vienna, Austria (p. 31)
4. Mariazell, Austria (p. 53)
5. Eisenstadt, Austria (p. 66)
6. London, England (p. 100)
7. Oxford, England (p. 107)

Week Two: Chapter Two Comprehension Questions

1. They sang in the processionals at the church services, p. 31. They also sang for special services, feast days, and processionals through the city, p. 33.
2. They could finally get warm and eat delicious food from the banquet hall, p. 35. Joseph also loved listening to the music, pp. 39, 40.
3. Joseph climbed the boards and supplies around the new construction on the palace, p. 37. After the Empress had scolded him for doing it, and he dared to do it again, Joseph received a caning from Herr Reutter, p. 38.
4. He listened to the orchestral instruments playing together at banquets, p. 40. He tried writing his own music in twelve parts, p. 41. Haydn purchased some books on composition and studied them to improve his skills, p. 41. He also worked late into the night trying to rewrite his melodies more beautifully, p. 42.
5. Michael, Joseph's younger brother also became a choir boy, p. 38.
6. First, his voice changed and it was not as pleasing to the Empress as it had been when he was younger, p. 44. Second, Joseph was caned and expelled from the choir when he snipped off another choir member's pigtail with his new scissors, p. 45.

Week Two: Chapter Three Comprehension Questions

1. A singer from another church, Spangler helped Joseph, p. 51.
2. A friendly merchant named Bucholz gave Joseph money (150 florins), p. 56.
3. He could spend time composing and practicing instead of playing at balls for pay, pp. 52, 56.
4. He played the accompaniment for Porpora's singing pupils, p. 61. He also became Porpora's valet: shining his shoes, brushing his clothes, and running his errands, pp. 61, 62.
5. His boss was cross and severe, but Joseph's cheerfulness about everything made Porpora more friendly, p. 62.
6. Prince Esterhazy at Eisenstadt requested Joseph come, p. 65.

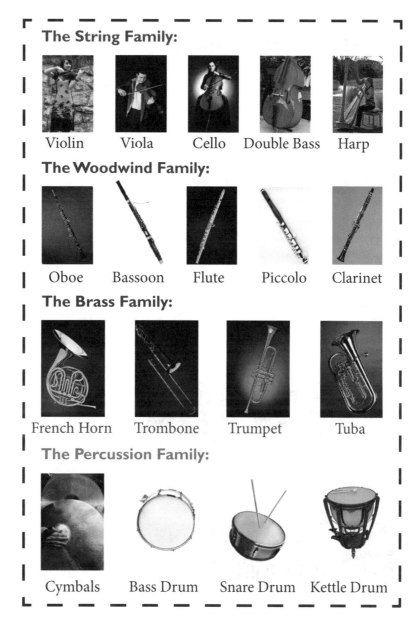

The String Family:

Violin   Viola   Cello   Double Bass   Harp

The Woodwind Family:

Oboe   Bassoon   Flute   Piccolo   Clarinet

The Brass Family:

French Horn   Trombone   Trumpet   Tuba

The Percussion Family:

Cymbals   Bass Drum   Snare Drum   Kettle Drum

Week Three: Chapter Four Comprehension Questions

1. The prince provided plays and operettas, including some for a marionette theatre, p. 69; fireworks, p. 72; hunting activities, p. 72; food delicacies, p. 72; and new music from Haydn, p. 73.
2. Joseph was called Papa Haydn, p. 74.
3. They needed a vacation, p. 84. They were kept so busy rehearsing and playing concerts that they had no time to visit families or rest, p. 82.
4. Haydn wrote a symphony, now known as the *Farewell* Symphony, in which each instrument gradually dropped out and the musician left the stage, until the final musician walked off the platform, pp. 84, 85. The prince got the joke and let the men go home.
5. Wolfgang Mozart became his friend, pp. 86, 95.
6. He was invited to England, p. 94.

Week Three: Band Music and Instruments

1. Strings are not the dominant instrument in a concert band; the majority of members play woodwinds, brass, or percussion.
2. There are several possible answers—jazz, blues, classical compositions, show tunes, big band music, marches, and other popular songs.
3. The guitar is a valuable instrument to learn because it is very versatile and is used in many styles of music.
4. Acoustic and electric

5. Define an electrical instrument: (Make sure the student uses their own words.) An electrical instrument is a musical instrument in which the use of electric devices determine or affect the sound produced by the instrument.
6. Electrical instruments are beneficial in large crowds because they are often connected to loudspeakers and amplifiers so that the music can be projected over large crowds.

Band Instruments:

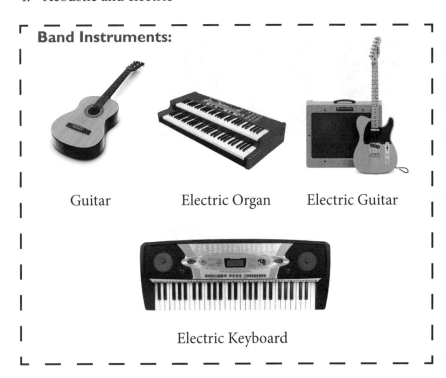

Guitar   Electric Organ   Electric Guitar

Electric Keyboard

Week Four: Chapter Five Comprehension Questions

1. Haydn considered the trip a great adventure, p. 99.
2. George F. Handel was honored, p. 100.
3. Haydn wanted to startle the ladies who began to doze during his concerts, p. 103. By starting the music slowly and quietly, and then interrupting it suddenly with a crashing chord, he knew he could make the ladies jump and listen.
4. He met Ludwig Beethoven, p. 108.

5. They placed a monument in his honor in Rohrau, p. 109.
6. The English loved him and his music, cheering him loudly at concerts, p. 103. They did not want Haydn to leave and gave him many gifts at his departure, p. 113.
7. Haydn wrote a beautiful hymn that became the national anthem of Austria, pp. 114, 115.
8. Symphony, p. 118

Week Four: Character Traits

(Answers may vary.)

	Synonyms	Antonyms
Humble	lowly, meek, modest, unassuming, unpretentious	arrogant, egotistical, haughty, pompous, superior
Attentive	absorbed, engrossed, intent	absentminded, distracted, unfocused
Fearless	bold, courageous, gallant, heroic, valiant	cowardly, fainthearted
Neat	crisp, tidy, uncluttered	disheveled, disorderly, messy, unkempt
Adventurous	daring, nervy, gutsy	cautious, timid, wary
Creative	clever, inventive, original	unimaginative, uninspired
Leader	head, master, chief	follower, imitator
Frugal	economical, thrifty	spendthrift, wasteful
Diligent	engaged, industrious, working	inactive, idle
Cheerful	bright, upbeat	dour, gloomy, sulky

Haydn

	Synonyms	Antonyms
Industrious	employed, productive	inactive, unoccupied
	Synonyms	Antonyms
Playful	frisky, sportful	sober, serious-minded
	Synonyms	Antonyms
Generous	charitable, unselfish, big-hearted	cheap, miserly, stingy, tight-fisted
	Synonyms	Antonyms
Grateful	appreciative, indebted	rude, thankless
	Synonyms	Antonyms
Loyal	constant, devoted, steadfast	fickle, untrue, traitorous

Week Four: An Introduction to World Instruments

Harpsichord–It is a stringed instrument resembling a grand piano but usually has two keyboards and two or more strings for each note and produces tones by the plucking of strings with plectra. The harpsichord is used in the performance of older music.

Panpipes–It is a set of reeds of different lengths that are bound together in a row and played by blowing across the top of each pipe. Panpipes have been in use since ancient times. The pan flute is used for entertainment and is often associated with Peruvian music today.

Native American Drum–These drums are made of wood and leather, and are often decorated with drawings depicting nature as well as feathers and beads. These drums originated with the Native American people and are a vital part of their culture. The drums are used in religious ceremonies, celebrations, and for dancing and singing and storytelling.

Gong– It is a circular bronze plate that makes a resonant sound when struck with a mallet. It is used as an orchestral percussion instrument, to summon people to meals, and as an alarm. This instrument is of Asian origin.

Great Highland Bagpipes–It is a musical instrument having a flexible bag inflated either by a tube with valves or by bellows, a double-reed melody pipe, and from one to four drone pipes. Bagpipes originated in the ancient Middle East, but are now associated primarily with Great Britain (Ireland and Scotland). This instrument is used by the military, for funerals, and for various ceremonies. There are even bagpipe contests!

Didgeridoo–It is an Australian Aboriginal musical instrument with a long thick wooden pipe that is blown to create a deep reverberating humming sound. It is used for ceremonial dancing and singing.

(**Note:** These answers were derived from various dictionary definitions.)

Instruments from Around the World

Native American Drum — Gong — Didgeridoo — Conga Drum

Great Highland Bagpipes — Panpipes — Sitar — Harpsichord

Haydn, The Merry Little Peasant Quiz

Matching:
1. c.
2. d.
3. a.
4. c.
5. b.
6. d.
7. a.
8. b.

Fill in the Blanks:
1. six
2. Papa Haydn
3. Mozart
4. versatile

Weekly Lesson Outline

Mozart

(Activities marked with an * are required in order to meet national music appreciation standards.)

Week One:

- Read Chapter 1*
- Answer Comprehension Questions
- Listen to Music Disc 4, track 25*
- Character Qualities
- Tidbits of Interest
- Assemble Lapbook Folder
- Window to the World Tour (LB)
- The Mozart Family
- "Music Was Born in Him"
- German Words to Know

Week Two:

- Read Chapters 2 & 3*
- Answer Comprehension Questions
- Listen to Music Disc 4, tracks 26-27*
- Character Qualities
- Tidbits of Interest
- Musical Vocabulary Notes (LB)*
- Mozart's Favorite Instrument
- Music of the Classical Period (LB)*
- Instruments of the World (review)*
- Music In Your World*

Week Three:

- Read Chapter 4*
- Answer Comprehension Questions
- Listen to Music Disc 4, tracks 28-29*
- Character Qualities
- Tidbits of Interest
- Wunderkinder Concerts (LB)
- Mozart and Money (LB)
- Music of Mozart Cards (LB)*
- Music and Culture*

Week Four:

- Read Chapter 5*
- Answer Comprehension Questions
- Listen to Music Disc 4, tracks 30-61*
- Character Qualities
- Tidbits of Interest
- Fellow Composers Bookmark
- Learning About the Opera (LB)*
- Learning About the Opera Venn Diagram*
- Wunderkind Accomplishments (LB)
- Mozart's Life at a Glance (LB)

Additional activity required for national music standards:

- [ ] Attend live music performances and demonstrate audience behavior appropriate for the context and style of music performed.

Week 1 Activity Pages

Mozart

Chapter One Comprehension Questions

1. Why did Father Leopold come bounding up the stairs at the beginning of this chapter?

_____

_____

2. The baby was baptized as Johannes Chrysostomus Wolfgangus Theophilus Mozart, but what did his parents usually call him? _____

3. Can you name any of the Mozart family pets—by species or by name?

_____

4. What was Papa Leopold's occupation? _____

_____

5. What did Wolfgang learn to do just by watching his older sister, Nannerl? _____

_____

6. How did Wolfgang amuse himself for hours on end—to the harm of the wallpaper and table-cloths, unfortunately? _____

7. The Mozart family soon learned that there was one thing Wolfgang enjoyed doing more than anything else—even more than playing with toys. What was it? _____

_____

8. Whom did Wolfgang love most next to God? _____

1685	Johann Sebastian Bach	1750
1685	George Frederic Handel	1759
1732	Franz Joseph Haydn	1809
1756	**Wolfgang A. Mozart**	1791
1770	Ludwig van Beethoven	1827
1782	Nicolò Paganini	1840
1797	Franz Schubert	1828

Character Qualities

Family-Oriented *(pp. 13, 16, 17)* – Leopold was proud of his new son, and Marianne (Nannerl) was glad for a little brother. The parents were kind, attempting to do everything they could to make their home a cheerful one. Leopold took time to teach his children music, an activity that unified their home, making it a welcoming place.

Energetic Enthusiasm *(pp. 16, 17, 22)* – Wolfgang pounded his fists in time to the music, and they had a hard time keeping him away from the clavier. His first attempt at composing a concerto was covered with inkblots and smears in his enthusiasm to write down his musical ideas.

Eager Learner *(pp. 17, 19, 23)* – Wolfgang expressed an interest in learning the clavier just by observing his sister's lessons and experimenting with thirds. He hated stopping his lessons and was earnest in wanting to learn more. The young Mozart even attempted to write a concerto.

Sweet-tempered *(pp. 18, 19, 24)* – Wolfgang was described as sweet-tempered and patient. He sat to learn a new minuet and then cheerfully ran off to find his sister. He smiled merrily when Papa talked with him about the gift God had given him.

Character Qualities

Mozart

Creative *(p. 17, 21, 23)* – Finding thirds at the age of three, writing a minuet at age five and a concerto at five, all seem to show tremendous creative abilities. And God was praised for this musical gift and creative spirit.

Revered His Father *(p. 19, 20, 24)* – "Next to God comes Papa," young Wolferl announced. His love for his father was evident in how he enjoyed spending time with his father during music lessons, in his eagerness to have Leopold write his songs in a copybook, and in being unintimidated by his father—even sitting at his father's desk to write a concerto.

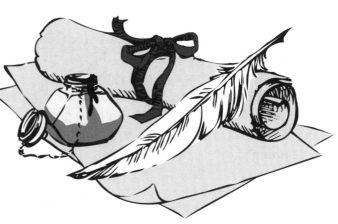

Tidbits of Interest

Page 14: The Mozarts were devout Catholics who had their new son baptized into the church just a few days after his birth on January 27, 1756. He was christened as Johannes Chrysostomus Wolfgangus Theophilus Mozart. The name *Theophilus* means "loved by God," which is translated in Latin as the name *Amadeus*.[1] His parents' religious influence and guidance seems to have developed within him a personal relationship with Christ and a deeply religious nature.[2] He once wrote his father, "Papa must not worry, for God is ever before my eyes. I realize His omnipotence, and I fear His anger; but I also recognize His love, His compassion, and His tenderness towards His creatures. He will never forsake His own. If it is according to His will, so let it be according to mine. Thus all will be well and I must needs be happy and contented."[3]

Page 15: Wolfgang loved animals. He even once broke off a concert to chase after a cat that had wandered into the hall. He also wrote his terrier, Bimperl, notes of affection from cities all over Europe.[4]

Page 20: Wolfgang would amuse himself with sums for hours on end. When he was thirteen, he wrote to Nannerl asking her to send a copy of her rules of arithmetic because he had lost his own and was forgetting his mathematical tables. He also asked for any other arithmetic "examples" she could send to entertain him.[5] Playing with figures remained a hobby all his life. He even took up the popular problem of "composing minuets 'mechanically,' by putting two-measure melodic fragments together in any order."[6]

Page 23: Herr Johann Andreas Schachtner was a trumpeter in the archbishop's court and a dear friend of the family. In 1792, Schachtner wrote Nannerl that Wolfgang's delicate and refined ear was horrified by the playing of a horn alone, so much so that "merely holding a horn toward him terrified him as much as if it had been a loaded pistol. His father wished to overcome this childish alarm, and ordered me once, in spite of his entreaties, to blow toward [Wolfgang]; but, oh! that I had not been induced to do it. Wolfgang no sooner heard the clanging sound than he turned pale and would have fallen into convulsions, had I not instantly desisted."[7]

Wolfgang Amadeus Mozart was born on January 27, in Salzburg, Austria. His family began to travel the world when Mozart was a very young age. Use the maps in this activity to get an overview of the places he visited.

Using the *Window to the World Concert Tour* lapbook pages, follow the directions to cut out and assemble the pieces. Adhere the shutter fold book to section #1 in your Mozart lapbook.

Major Cities Visited

- London -
- Paris -
- Brussels -
- Antwerp -
- Amsterdam -
- Bonn -
- Munich -
- Vienna -
- Salzburg -
- Zurich -
- Geneva -
- Berne -
- Rome -

Mozart

Countries Visited

- England -
- France -
- Belgium -
- Germany -
- Austria -
- Switzerland -
- Italy -

The Mozart Family

Read these paragraphs and answer the following questions.

The Mozarts lived on the third floor of the "Hagenauer House" for twenty-six years. Their home consisted of a kitchen, small chamber, living room, bedroom, and a study. Leopold Mozart and Anna Maria Mozart had six children, but only two survived to adulthood.

Marianne (or Maria Anna) was four years older than her little brother. Her nickname, Nannerl, is what German-speaking people call a "cozy name"—a name of affection and sweetness, such as Susie is a cozy name for Susan, or Danny for Daniel. In 1769, Nannerl retired from concert tours, but she and Wolfgang remained dear siblings their whole lives. "[I] am ever your unalterably attached and loving brother" is a sample of Wolfgang's farewells in his letters to her.[8] Marianne continued to teach music all her life. She married a magistrate in 1784, had three children, and lived until 1829.[9]

Leopold Mozart was the assistant music director of Archbishop Sigismund von Schrattenbach's chapel in Salzburg. In this role, he wrote music and directed the court orchestra for the archbishop. Archbishop Schrattenbach was a man who encouraged music and the arts—even keeping a permanent orchestra of twenty-one to thirty-three musicians.[10] He was very "well disposed towards the Mozart family," allowing Leopold leaves of absence for concert tours and training.[11] Leopold authored a well-known book on violin playing (actually published the same year as Wolfgang's birth), and he obviously fostered a love of music in his children, if by no other method than its constant presence in their house. He was an exceptional music teacher, who taught all other subjects in the Mozart household as well. Nannerl and Wolfgang never attended school outside their home. Leopold's influence helped Wolfgang excel as a musician, and it also helped him achieve the character and greatness he displayed throughout most of his life.[12] No wonder Wolfgang's motto was, "Next to God comes Papa."

1. Describe the Hagenauer House. _____

_____

2. Tell about the relationship between Marianne and Mozart. _____

_____

_____

3. Identify Father Mozart's position and role in Salzburg. _____

_____

_____

4. Discuss Mozart's view of his father. _____

_____

"Music Was Born in Him"

> *"Mozart did not choose to become a musician; music was born in him."*[13]
> ~Rachel Isadora

Dictionary definition of a genius: unusual mental ability, a natural talent; exceptional creative ability, someone who is dazzlingly skilled in any field; someone who has exceptional intellectual ability and originality[14]

Mozart definitely fit this description and is known as a genius worldwide. He seemed to be born to create music. Wolfgang Mozart rarely rested from composing, starting at age four until his death at thirty-five.[15] Mozart's ability to write music neatly improved with age. Most of the time, his music was already completed mentally before he would even put pen to paper.[16] He also could write pieces while visiting with friends, playing pool, or eating a meal.[17] "Composing is my one joy and passion," Wolfgang once wrote his wife.[18] It's interesting that he often used various colors of ink in writing his music. The most difficult passages were inked in bright blue.[19]

Attempt the following tasks.
1. Write a story about jungle animals **while talking** with someone about your favorite kind of music.
2. Play a game **AND** write new words to the tune of "Twinkle, Twinkle, Little Star" at the same time.
3. **While eating supper**, try to draw an accurate picture of the inside of your house.

Did you find yourself stopping one task to concentrate on the other? Can you imagine being able to write such complex musical pieces **WHILE** engaging in other everyday activities? Although we are not all geniuses by definition, **we each have special interests and abilities.**

Make a list of activities in which you enjoy participating.

At which of these activities do you excel?

> Mozart had to work hard and practice his skills even though he was brilliant at them (pp. 20, 32). We also need to put time and energy into what we love doing so that we can do our best and put those talents to good use.

German Words to Know

Match the following English words with their German translation.

One,
Two,
Three

Herr

Wonderful

Good
Evening

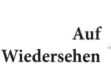

Auf
Wiedersehen

Mister

Eins,
Zwei,
Drei

Wundervoll

Wonder
Child

Guten
Abend

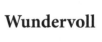

Good
Bye

Wunderkind

4ᵗʰ-6ᵗʰ grade:
Complete the following sentences as they are found in the book, *Mozart, The Wonder Boy.*

1. "_____ _____," he calls to his friend Peter, the candlestick maker,
     (Good)   (Night)

who stops a moment to chat over the news of the day. (p. 12)

2. "_____, _____, _____," he counts, keeping perfect
     (One)   (two)   (three)

time for such a small boy. (p. 16)

3. Wolfgang looks up with a merry smile—to him there is no one quite so _____ as
                                                                                              (wundervoll)

Father Mozart. (p. 24)

4. As the music goes on, _____ _____ plays more and more
                                    (Mister)   (Schachtner)
softly and then stops altogether. (p. 35)

5. "_____ _____," calls the cook as she waves them a last
          (Good)   (Bye)
farewell. (p. 39)

6. They nod their heads and say to each other, "Indeed he is rightly called a

_____ _____." (p. 57)
          (Wunderkind)

Mozart

Chapter Two Comprehension Questions

1. How did Father Mozart, Nannerl, and Wolfgang entertain each other in the coach on the way to Munich? _____

_____

_____

2. For which royal person were Nannerl and Wolfgang invited to play? _____

_____

3. When the Mozart children gave concerts for the people of Munich during their three-week visit, what was the response they received? _____

_____

_____

4. In this chapter, what new instrument did Wolfgang prove he could play—self-taught? (He demonstrated this ability when Herr Schachtner, Herr Wentzel, and his father began to rehearse new trios.) _____

_____

5. Why was Leopold crying at the end of this chapter? _____

_____

1. To what city were the Mozarts headed on a tour at the beginning of this chapter?

   _____

2. In addition to Father Mozart, which family member accompanied the children on this trip?

   _____

3. When the Mozarts stopped in towns and inns along the way to Vienna, what did the children

   give? _____

4. Do you remember how long it took the family to get to Vienna by coach on the rough, bumpy

   roads? _____

5. How did the Mozarts get through the customs house without having to pay duties on all the

   gifts they had received along the way? _____

   _____

   _____

6. Among the invitations they received from nobles in Vienna, the children were finally asked to

   play for whom at Schönbrunn castle? _____

   _____

7. Can you supply proof that Wolfgang was not intimidated by or scared of the king and queen?

   _____

   _____

   _____

8. Why did Wolfgang "propose" to the young princess, Marie Antoinette? _____

   _____

   _____

9. What gifts did the children receive from Queen Maria Theresa? _____

   _____

10. What illness did Wolfgang endure toward the end of this tour? _____

    _____

Wit and Sense of Humor

(p. 28) – The silly little song on this page hints at Wolfgang's love for laughter. Wolfgang had a lively disposition and fun-loving nature, which he is said to have received from his mother.[20] He had difficulty keeping still and was fond of jokes, games, dancing, masquerade balls, and singing.

"There was a crooked man
And he had a crooked pig,"
Hey,—dee—dle—deedle,
"They started off to town
In a two-penny gig,"
Hey,—dee—dle—deedle.

Industriousness *(p. 32, 83)* –

While the children were highly praised and had great successes on this concert tour, they were willing to practice harder so they could play even better in the future. Wolfgang never stopped composing, even in the midst of court music duties, concert tours, giving lessons, and so forth. He wrote three operas in a short span of time.

Humility *(p. 41, 44, 50)* –

The children were unspoiled by all the praise and gifts they received. Nannerl was not jealous of Wolfgang's success and the attention paid to him during concerts. And they loved their good little home better than any king's palace.

Playfulness *(p. 44, 45)* –

Don't you wish you could have seen Queen Maria Theresa's response to Wolfgang springing into her lap and kissing her at their first meeting? Wolfgang played with the royal children and even played some musical "tricks" for the king.

Kindness *(pp. 41, 46, 47)* –

Wolfgang was attracted to Marie Antoinette because of her kindness when he tripped and fell on the polished floor. The children were also kind in performing concerts for the townsfolk along the way to Vienna.

Tidbits of Interest

Chapter 2

Page 28: Munich is the capital of Bavaria, which is a state in southern Germany, right along the Austrian border.

Page 30: The Mozart children played for Prince Joseph, who was the court elector of Bavaria. His full title was Elector Maximilian Joseph III, and he was prince from 1745–1777. He was very influential in developing opera as a courtly entertainment in Bavaria.

Pages 34, 35: When the men were practicing the new trios, Herr Wentzel played first violin (the hardest music in a composition); Herr Schachtner played second violin (a supporting, usually harmonizing role in music); and Leopold accompanied with a bass violin. Once

again, we know about this event because Herr Schachtner wrote a detailed letter to Nannerl about that astonishing day and about the men's amazement at Wolfgang's natural talent with the violin.

Chapter 3

Page 41: Wolfgang and Nannerl remained remarkably unspoiled in the midst of all the attention they received.[21] In fact, Leopold once wrote Wolfgang, reminding him, "[A]s a boy you were so extraordinarily modest that you used to weep when people praised you overmuch."[22]

Page 46: Georg Christoph Wagenseil was the Hapsburg family's court composer and music teacher from 1739 until his death in 1777.

Wagenseil's compositions would have been very familiar to the Mozart children. An interesting sidelight is that one of Wagenseil's pupils went on to teach Ludwig van Beethoven.

Page 46 – One of the princesses Wolfgang met was Marie Antoinette, who was only two months older than Wolfgang.[23] Marie Antoinette married King Louis XVI of France. During the tumultuous months before and during the French Revolution, the people of France criticized her for her extravagance. It is alleged that she once replied, when told that the people had no bread to eat, "Let them eat cake!" In 1792, she secretly tried negotiating help from her imperial brother, Leopold II, in Austria, but the rioting revolutionaries overthrew the French monarchy. After a year in prison, this once kindly princess was tried and guillotined during the infamous "Reign of Terror."

Page 48 – A portrait was later painted of both of the Mozart children in those gift clothes from the queen, so the coloring and designs are carefully documented in art. Wolfgang was very concerned about his appearance—fussing over his clothes, choosing elegant fashions as he grew older, and being very particular about how his hair looked.[24] It was difficult to work on the young composer's hair, however, because he would suddenly flit from his grooming chair to the keyboard to note a musical idea—with his barber in hot pursuit.[25]

Pages 48, 49, 51 – Wolfgang had an exhausting childhood with a wearying schedule of concerts, fatiguing travel conditions, and exciting public appearances. Physical exhaustion would make anyone more susceptible to diseases such as scarlet fever, which is an acutely contagious disease that has symptoms of fever, a sore throat, and a red rash. It is caused by streptococci bacteria. Later, while they were in Holland, Nannerl came down with a severe illness in September—to the point that Leopold feared she would die. Wolfgang also came down with a fever and did not feel like composing again until January 1766.[26] A common thought in most biographies about Wolfgang's life is that he was an affectionate lad who was eager to please. In spite of his illness and the physical toll such concerts took on him, Wolfgang was eager to do more concerts. He was not yet six when they left for Munich and was on one musical tour or another for over half his life![27] One tour lasted for three years! In his short thirty-five-year lifespan, Wolfgang spent the equivalent of fourteen years on concert tours throughout Europe.

Musical Vocabulary Notes

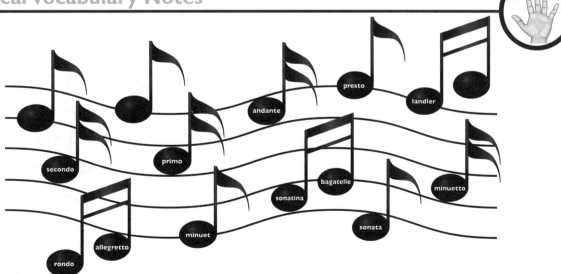

Using the *Musical Vocabulary Notes* lapbook pages, follow the directions to cut out and assemble the pieces. Glue the bottom piece to your Mozart lapbook on sections #7.

Mozart's Favorite Instrument

On pages 16 and 17 of *Mozart, The Wonder Boy,* you read about the clavier and Mozart's longing to learn how to play it.

A clavier is the keyboard of a musical instrument. In some cases, it refers to a particular early keyboard instrument, or it can be used to indicate other instruments with keyboards, including the clavichord, the harpsichord, or the piano.

The piano actually became Wolfgang's favorite instrument, and it was used for his most personal expressions in music.[28] At the time of Mozart's death, his most expensive possessions were a pool table and a walnut piano.[29]

Later, when Wolfgang was older, he was allowed to play the organ (pages 58-59). The organ is a keyboard instrument in which sound is produced by air passing through pipes of varying size and construction to give a wide variety of pitches and timbres. In Wolfgang's time, bellows attached to foot pedals were the means of forcing air through the pipes of the organ. It is incredible that a boy of seven could "man" the bellows and play lovely music after only the second attempt of playing this instrument in his short lifetime!

Instrument Word Search

Find the names of the instruments Mozart played in this word search. The words can go horizontally, vertically, diagonally, and in all eight directions.

R	C	P	M	R	V	R	M	D	Z	D
L	D	L	X	X	M	K	V	R	R	T
N	N	D	A	Z	W	I	C	O	K	N
L	P	P	K	V	O	N	H	H	Y	N
O	C	D	N	L	I	C	Y	C	T	X
R	T	Z	I	R	I	E	D	I	N	F
G	R	N	W	S	H	K	R	V	N	Q
A	W	Z	P	K	B	R	V	A	H	L
N	B	R	N	C	K	M	Y	L	P	L
N	A	W	P	I	A	N	O	C	Q	W
H	M	Z	M	K	L	N	Q	F	G	L

Clavichord
Harpsichord
Piano
Clavier
Organ
Violin

The rulers of England at this time were King George III and Queen Charlotte. King George was a king who appreciated the musical styles of George Frederic Handel (who had been the British court composer from 1714 to 1759) and Johann Sebastian Bach. The influence of Bach's music in the royal court was undoubtedly enhanced by the fact that the current music master for the imperial family was Bach's youngest son, Johann Christian Bach. J.C. Bach wrote some fifty symphonies, and his musical works became the prototypes of the Classical style that Mozart followed in his own works. The music master introduced Mozart to the spirit of Italian music, which Bach admired for its form and beauty.[30]

Music in the classical style has qualities associated with the art of ancient Greece and Rome, such as a focus on balance, symmetry, logic, and the natural expression of feeling—as opposed to technically complex or overwrought expressions.

**The Classical Period (1750 – 1820) was not so much a period of invention
as one of development and perfection.**

Using the *Music of the Classical Period* lapbook pages, follow the directions to cut out and assemble the pieces. Adhere the box book to section #6 in your Mozart lapbook.

Instruments of the World (Review)

Review: Match the instrument name to the correct picture <u>and</u> correct continent.

Europe   Didgeridoo

United Kingdom   Native American Drums

South America   Panpipes

North America   Gong

Australia   Bagpipes

Asia   Harpsichord

Below are pictures of some of the instruments you learned about in a previous chapter. Cut out the instruments and glue them to the appropriate area of origin on the map.

Harpsichord   Panpipes   Native   Gong   Bagpipes   Didgeridoo
from   from   American   from   from   from
Europe   South   Drum   Asia   United   Australia
               America   from   Kingdom
                           North
                           America

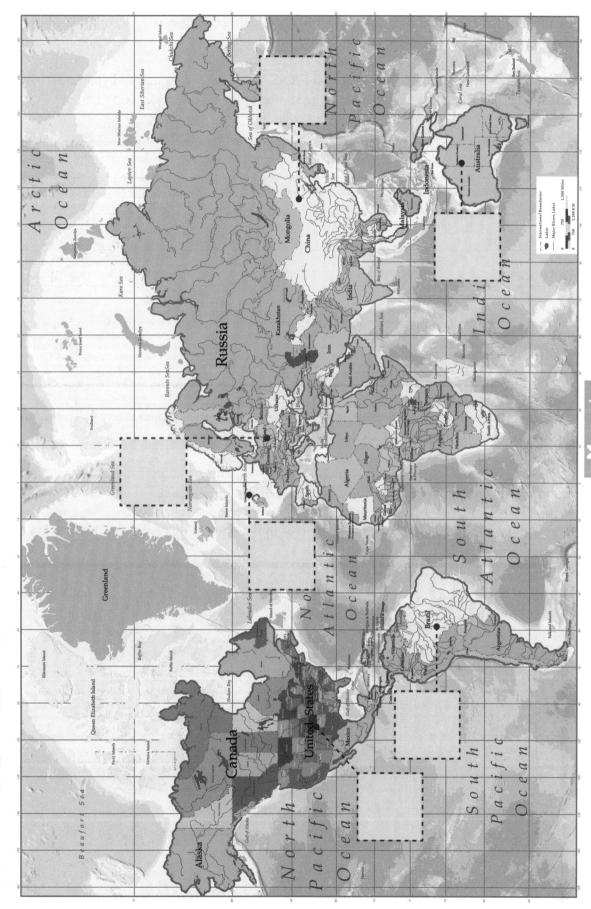

Spend some time listening to music from your own culture. This can be accomplished by listening to different local radio stations.

Write down your reaction to the music you heard. What styles of music did you find? Which ones did you enjoy? Were there more stations playing one style than another?

_____

_____

_____

_____

_____

Music In Your World

If you were to take a trip around the world, you would hear many different types of music. The style would change based on the region and purpose of the music.

Your family has a unique music style and preference all your own. This style is derived from the region where you live, your family heritage, and personal preferences.

Write a short paragraph describing what kind of music your family enjoys and how you engage in that music.

Now pretend that you are a news reporter for the local newspaper. The editor has assigned this week's culture and entertainment section to you. Now you must interview your friends and family in order to write this piece.

Ask the following questions of at least three different people. (Make sure each person is from a different family so that you have variety in your answers.)

WHO is your favorite music artist?
WHAT kind of music do you enjoy?
WHERE do you sing or listen to music?
WHEN do you like to listen to music the most?
HOW often is music a part of your life?

Compare all of the answers you received from the individuals. Then write a short article describing the different styles and usages of the music you researched.

Remember there are typically two kinds of newspaper articles…

NEWS ARTICLES
and
FEATURE ARTICLES

*News articles are very concise and answer the questions who, what, where, when, and how. This kind of article includes facts and lists.

*Feature articles usually cover one topic but do so from many different viewpoints. They are typically written with a more personal touch and are quite engaging to read. A feature article is also longer and more detailed than regular news articles.

You must decide what style of article you will chose to write. Don't forget to include an attention grabbing headline and perhaps even a related picture.

Week 3 Activity Pages

Mozart

Chapter Four Comprehension Questions

1. As the chapter began, the Mozart children were preparing to start a concert on a warm night in Frankfurt. Do you recall what costumes they were wearing? _____

_____

2. This concert tour had many stops along the way—so many that it took them five months to reach which joyous city along the River Seine in France? _____

_____

3. What were some of the unique features of the king's palace at Versailles, near Paris? _____

_____

_____

4. King Louis XV, ruler at this time, was so impressed by the children that he even allowed Wolfgang to play on which instrument in the royal chapel? _____

_____

5. Their next visit on the tour was to a city across the English Channel. What was the city, and what was their reception there? _____

_____

6. Queen Charlotte's music master in London was the son of a famous composer. Can you remember the master's name, or at least the last name of his family? _____

_____

7. Leopold became ill and the children had to stop doing something for several weeks. (Most of you wouldn't object to this "silencing" demand.) What did they temporarily stop doing?

_____

8. What did Wolfgang write during this sentence of musical silence? _____

_____

9. The Prince of Orange and Princess Caroline invited the Mozart children to visit them in what region? _____

10. How long did this entire concert tour last? _____

Character Qualities

Generous *(p. 57, 72)* – Wolfgang gave long concerts because he loved music and wanted to please the people. The children played generously for royalty and common townsfolk alike.

Gracious *(p. 72)* – Nannerl and Wolfgang delighted everyone with their gracious ways. The praise that they received from listeners all over Europe and England, particularly from nobility, did not change how they treated those around them.

Page 57: The people of Frankfurt hailed Wolfgang as a "wonder child." Both Wolfgang and Nannerl were dubbed *Wunderkinder*, the German word meaning "wonder children," because of their remarkable musical talents. Wolfgang also became known as the most kissed little boy in Europe during these musical tours.[31]

Page 62: King Louis XIV (the "Sun King") built the Palace of Versailles (pronounced \ver-sigh\) in the 17th century, and it was an enormous complex that housed some 5,000 aristocrats, ministers, servants, and royal family members. Thirty-six-thousand workers labored for almost thirty years on the palace. It was lavishly decorated and became the masterpiece of formal grandeur showing the glory of France. It also became the palatial ideal throughout Europe and the Americas for many decades after its construction. One hall, known as the Hall of Mirrors, had numerous mirrors to reflect candlelight and the "sparkle of the crystal chandeliers," which amazed visitors like the Mozart children.

Page 72: The Mozarts were in England for fifteen months, and it remained a country dear to Wolfgang's heart.[32] Before leaving for Holland, he underwent a "scientific examination" by a lawyer and musician named Daines Barrington. Some people were claiming that Wolfgang was a cheat (with his father writing the music but crediting Wolfgang with the works), or that he was a man pretending to be a boy. In order to prove or disprove these claims, Barrington tested Wolfgang by observing him for several hours and reporting his observations in the *Philosophical Transactions* publication. Mr. Barrington recorded that Wolfgang was like any other boy of nine in many ways—chasing cats, instead of playing the piano during practice hours, for instance.[33] Wolfgang also proved his musical genius by playing any difficult piece Barrington handed

him and by writing a complicated composition before Barrington's eyes. These scientific tests put an end to the horrible rumors regarding Wolfgang's abilities.

Page 74: Wolfgang declared that the canary still sang in the key of G. Wolfgang had perfect pitch, which is the ability to sing or name a note requested or heard. (It's also called absolute pitch.) People declared that Wolfgang's ears were "magically sensitive," and that he could tell the pitch of an instrument to the eighth of a tone before he could even read.[34] Advertisements for the Mozarts' concerts even highlighted his ability to name all notes played at a distance, "singly or in chords," and "on the harpsichord, bells, glass, or clock."[35]

Wunderkinder Concerts

The children's reputation had preceded them to England, and they were well received by the British. Advertisements for their concerts promised that "lovers of music, and all those who find some pleasure in extraordinary things" would be astounded "by the incredible dexterity of a girl of twelve and a boy of seven who astonished the Electoral Courts of Saxony, Bavaria, the Palatinate, and His Imperial and Royal Majesty during a four months' visit to Vienna."[36]

Design your own concert poster
Create your own *Wunderkinder* (wonder children) Concert Flyer using the template on the next page. Cut out and paste it to sections #11-14 of your Mozart lapbook.

Mozart and Money

Throughout Mozart's career, he often received gifts rather than money for his musical compositions and concerts. As a child, this trend may not have been much of a concern, but as he matured and married, imperial dignity, jeweled boxes, and special costumes did not help pay the rent.[37] Yet, until his death, Mozart composed for the love of music and not for financial reward or man's acclaim. Some of his last and greatest symphonies, for example, were written without any promise of commission, or even the promise of an upcoming performance of those works.[38] Wolfgang and his wife, Constance, moved twelve times in their nine years of marriage, and they always seemed to be scrabbling for the needed finances.[39] At one point, some friends came to visit the Mozarts only to find them dancing in one of the rooms during the middle of the day. Wolfgang explained that they had run out of firewood, and they were dancing to stay warm! In spite of these hardships, Wolfgang's last ten years of compositions—during his marriage—are among his most famous and artistically beautiful.

Using the *Mozart and Money* lapbook pages, follow the directions to cut out and assemble the pieces. Adhere the envelope to section #5 in your Mozart lapbook.

Mozart

The Music of Mozart

Mozart wrote music in many different styles (genres) during his career as a composer. Listed below are several different types of music that Mozart composed.

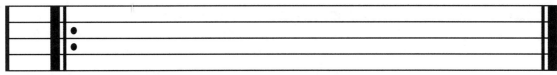

Symphony: elaborate music written for the instruments of a full orchestra, consisting of three or four movements
- allegro movement: a portion of music to be performed quickly in a brisk, lively manner
- presto movement: a portion of music to be performed at a quick tempo (faster than allegro)
- andante movement: a portion of music to be performed moderately slowly, yet distinctly and flowing

Concerto: music written so that one or more instruments stand out from the orchestra or accompaniment in order to display the instrument's qualities or the performer's skill

Sonata: a lengthy piece of music written for one or two instruments

Sacred Music: music written for religious services

March: a piece of music designed or fitted to accompany and guide the movement of troops

Organ Music: music specifically written to be played on an organ

Opera: a dramatic play set to music where the performers communicate mostly through song with appropriate costumes, scenery, and action

Vocal Arrangement: music specifically written to be sung by one or more voices

Dance music:
- Minuet: a stately court dance performed in a slow, graceful way
- Waltz: a ballroom dance performed by two people in circular, whirling motions
- Folk Dance (i.e. Landler, English Country Dance): a song that is traditionally played by the common people of a region and forms part of their culture

Rondo: lively, cheerful music in which the first section repeats itself after each of the other sections

Bagatelle: a light piece of music written for piano

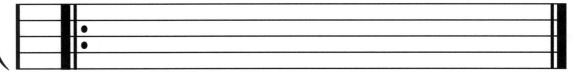

Using the *The Music of Mozart* lapbook pages, follow the directions to cut out and assemble the pieces. Glue the pocket to your Mozart lapbook on section #2.

Music and Culture

In many cultures and religions, music plays a key role in celebration, worship, and communication. It is important that we understand how and why music was created. Music has long been used for entertainment purposes. Even the ancient Greeks put poetry to music, and some Chinese instruments have been around for centuries. It is crucial to realize, however, that music is not just entertaining, but it is also very powerful.

There are several instances throughout history where music was used to communicate and stir up emotion.

- Negro Spirituals: These songs were a way for African American slaves to share the hard living conditions they endured. The spirituals "were used for expressing personal feeling and for cheering one another…[Some] negro spirituals like 'Wade in the Water,' 'The Gospel Train,' and 'Swing Low, Sweet Chariot' directly refer to the Underground Railroad." [40]
- Africans: Drums were often used for long distance messages or signals, and they were often referred to as "talking drums" [41]
- Native Americans: Drums were used to help tell stories and were also used during ritual and war dances. [42]
- Romanian Gypsy Music: The fiddle is the most widely used instrument in this genre of music. This music is "often played at a frantic pace by Rom musicians on fiddles… The sheer energy of performance overwhelms listeners and dancers." [43]

> Culture is defined as "the beliefs, customs, practices, and social behavior of a particular nation or people." [44] These beliefs and customs have a tremendous influence on how and why music is created.

Each people group and religion creates its own songs to meet the needs of the community. Songs are written for weddings, religious worship, tribal ceremonies, war, festivities, etc. These songs are then passed down from generation to generation and become part of the culture of that land.

Sing the following songs aloud. What event comes to your mind as you sing?

"Happy Birthday:"

"Star Spangled Banner:"

"Amazing Grace:"

Many songs were written with specific events in mind. They were written to help us celebrate or remember something important.

Think about some of your favorite things to do and places to go. Is music associated with any of those events? (church, sports games, parties, movies…) Make a list of how music is used during those times.

Week 4 Activity Pages

Mozart

Chapter Five Comprehension Questions

1. What new form of musical stories was Wolfgang beginning to compose in his pre-teen and teen years? _____

2. Explain what happened during Easter Week at the Sistine Chapel in Rome, according to this chapter. _____

   _____

   _____

   _____

3. When Wolfgang returned to Salzburg from his Italian tours, he became the court organist and concert master for whom? _____

4. There was one thing Mozart never stopped doing from age five to his death. What was it?

   _____

5. Why do you think Wolfgang could speak several different languages so well? _____

   _____

6. Do you recall the name of Wolfgang's wife? And who was one of his dearest friends who was a fellow composer of note (no pun intended)? _____

   _____

7. What was Wolfgang's comment or vision for the future when he heard the young Beethoven play the clavier? _____

   _____

8. Why was the first performance of Wolfgang's opera *Don Giovanni* a little late in starting? _____

   _____

   _____

9. Can you name one of the other two operas that are mentioned in this chapter as among Wolfgang's greatest compositions? _____

   _____

Character Qualities

Attentive *(pp. 78, 79-81, 86)* – He wrote Nannerl while they were apart. He memorized the whole papal music composition in Rome during one service. He recognized and attended to talent in others, such as in Beethoven.

Learned *(p. 78, 85)* – He spent hours studying and writing each day. He was educated by his father in other academic areas, as well. He could speak several languages fluently.

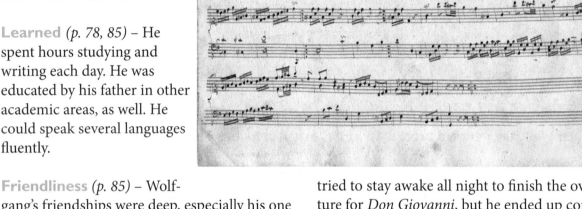

Friendliness *(p. 85)* – Wolfgang's friendships were deep, especially his one with Joseph Haydn, in whose honor he wrote six quartets.

Perseverance *(pp. 86, 87)* – Though Wolfgang's days were not always happy or struggle-free, he continued to work on his music. He tried to stay awake all night to finish the overture for *Don Giovanni*, but he ended up completing the work in a remarkable two hours of musical perseverance on the day of the opera's first performance.

Joyful *(p. 91)* – His music is pure, beautiful, and filled with joy—for an entire world.

Tidbits of Interest

Page 77 – Four years before this chapter's opening scene, Wolfgang fell ill with smallpox on a trip to Vienna. Smallpox is an acute, contagious disease that is now almost completely eradicated in the world. It causes skin blisters, or pustules, that are filled with pus. These blisters dry up, slough off, and leave pocked scars on the skin. It is believed that the fever accompanying this illness caused kidney damage in Wolfgang and precipitated his early death at the age of thirty-five. Wolfgang was scarred from the smallpox and had yellowish skin with bulging blue eyes (more hints at possible kidney failure). He became very ill again in 1784, when it is thought one kidney failed him entirely.

Pages 79–81: A papal decree protected Gregorio Allegri's *Miserere*, sung by the Papal Choir only during Holy Week. (*Miserere* is Latin for "have mercy.") A special guard was even established to keep the manuscript from being seen, copied, or used anywhere else, and those found in possession of a copy were immediately punished by excommunication from the Catholic church.[45] Nevertheless, Pope Clement XIV showed mercy, and perhaps a slight sense of humor, by ignoring the punishment of excommunication, and instead he bestowed on Wolfgang (at age fourteen) the honor of the Order of the Golden Spur. This Order was an honorary knighthood given by the pope, but requiring no specific obligations—particularly none of a martial or military nature. Wolfgang didn't even notice the ceiling art in the Sistine Chapel because he was so enthralled by the music. Michelangelo Buonarroti, the famous Italian artist and sculptor, spent four years (1508–1512) painting the ceiling and vault of the chapel with intricate decorations that include scenes from the book of Genesis, the prophets, and ancestors of Christ.

Page 85: Wolfgang learned fifteen languages in all his travels.[46] He married Constance Weber in 1782, a young lady eight years younger than himself, but who outlived him by fifty years.[47] They had a steadfast and loving marriage, in spite of many hardships they endured. Constance was a faithful helpmeet (living up to her name), who encouraged Wolfgang in his composing and shared six children with him—though only two lived to adulthood: Karl Thomas (1784–1858) and Franz Xaver (1791–1844).

Page 91: Sadly, Wolfgang died at only thirty-five years of age. He was in physical misery with complications most historians believe were related to kidney failure, malnutrition, and exhaustion.[48] He died on December 5, 1791, dictating another composition from his bed. Mozart composed over six hundred pieces of an amazing variety: quartets, concertos, sonatas, divertimentos, serenades, symphonies, church music, and operas.[49] If one were to listen to all Mozart's works in a row, it would take eight and a half days (202 hours)![50] No one is certain where Johannes Chrysostomus Wolfgangus Theophilus Mozart was buried in Vienna. At his death, Wolfgang only had 38 dollars' worth of worldly goods, not nearly enough for a funeral.[51] So a friend and musical admirer paid for his burial—but only in a pauper's grave. As the coffin was taken into the cemetery, a thunderstorm broke forth and caused the escorting mourners to run for shelter. Only the gravediggers were present when the body of this musical genius was lowered in an unmarked grave. (Even Constance was not present; she had just had a son a few months before, and she was so distraught by Wolfgang's death that she was under a doctor's care at the time of the funeral.) The graveyard caretaker had no recollection of where the renowned composer had been buried when Constance later questioned the caretaker about her husband's grave.

Fellow Composers Bookmark

Franz Joseph Haydn was born in Rohrau, Austria in March, 1732. He has been called the "Father of the Symphony." He was twenty-four years older than Wolfgang, but they still became close friends. They were fellow Austrian composers who first met each other in 1782, yet they never experienced any musical rivalry or jealousy between them. In fact, they inspired each other, and it is said that "the contemporary master from whom Mozart learned most, after Johann Christian Bach, was the elder of the brothers Haydn—Joseph Haydn."[52] Haydn's adventurous compositions influenced Mozart's creativity, and Wolfgang dedicated six string quartet pieces to his older friend.

When Haydn first heard these six quartets, he turned to Wolfgang's father and proclaimed,

"Before God and as an honest man, I tell you that your son is the greatest composer known to me either in person or by name."[53]

Ludwig van Beethoven was born in Bonn, Germany in December, 1770. He moved to Vienna in his twenties and requested that Mozart take him on as a student. Mozart recognized the incredible talent in this young German musician and knew he would succeed.

He is quoted as saying to his friends,

"Watch that young man. He will make a noise in the world someday."[54]

In 1826, years after Mozart's death, Beethoven stated,

"I have always reckoned myself among the greatest venerators [admirers] of Mozart, and I shall remain so until my last breath."[55]

Cut out the bookmark, by cutting along the solid line. Fold the bookmark accordion style, on the dotted lines. Using the information shared on the previous page, list several facts about each composer and their interaction with each other.

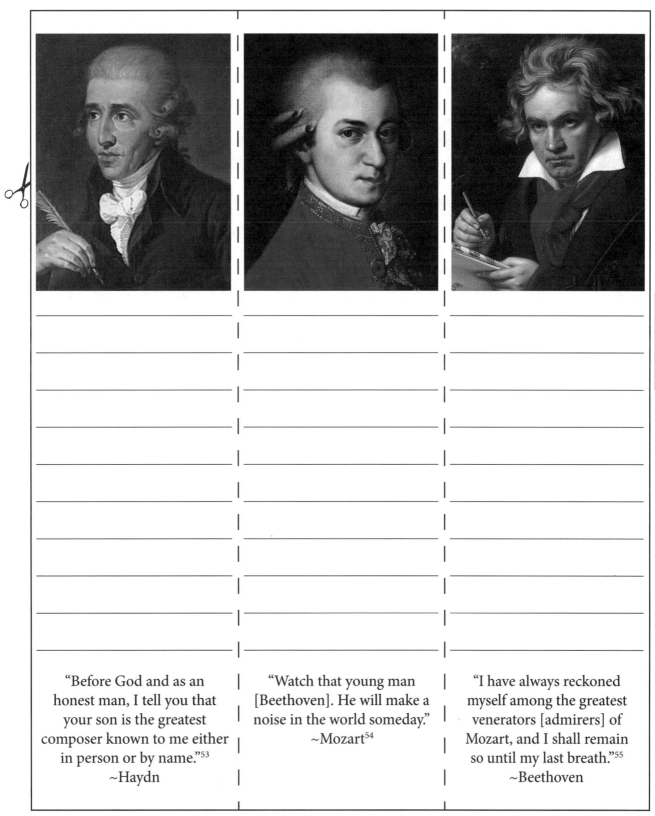

"Before God and as an honest man, I tell you that your son is the greatest composer known to me either in person or by name."[53]
~Haydn

"Watch that young man [Beethoven]. He will make a noise in the world someday."
~Mozart[54]

"I have always reckoned myself among the greatest venerators [admirers] of Mozart, and I shall remain so until my last breath."[55]
~Beethoven

Mozart—Week 4 Activity Pages

Learning About the Opera

Opera is a musical drama in which the performers sing most or all of their lines, and the music is just as important as the words. Opera was considered the premier style of music to write in the 18th century. "When a composer was asked to write an opera, he knew he had reached the top."[56]

Wolfgang wrote his first opera at age twelve, and it was performed in Milan when he was only fourteen. His favorite style of opera to write was comic opera. (That matches his playful, cheerful personality, does it not?) *The Marriage of Figaro*, written in 1786, caused a tremendous sensation in Prague, the capital city in what is now the Czech Republic. Prague was famous for its opera houses, theaters, and puppet theaters, and *Figaro* played to a packed house each performance. Wolfgang wrote of its overwhelming success in Prague: "[For] here nothing is talked about but 'Figaro,' nothing played but 'Figaro,' nothing whistled or sung but 'Figaro,' no opera so crowded as 'Figaro,' nothing but 'Figaro,'—very flattering to me, certainly."[57]

Wolfgang's next opera, *Don Giovanni*, was written just a few months after his father's death in 1787. Action appears to have been Wolfgang's remedy for discouragement.[58] Instead of succumbing to depression, or resting on his laurels as a child prodigy, Wolfgang constantly tried new and innovative compositions to ease his sense of loss or distress. Wolfgang could write music more quickly than almost any other composer in history, but he sometimes procrastinated, which often necessitated late-night composing sessions. Constance was known to stay awake with Wolfgang to tell him stories of Aladdin and Cinderella,[59] share jokes with him, and bring him his favorite punch while he composed.[60]

Using the *Learning about Opera Booklet* and the *Mozart's Operas Fact Matchbook* lapbook pages, follow the directions to cut out and assemble these pieces. Adhere the booklet to sections #15 & 16 in your Mozart lapbook. Then glue the matchbooks vertically on sections #9 & 10.

Mozart

In many ways, opera is similar to American musical theatre. These music styles have several things in common.

However, though they are similar, these music styles also have some distinct differences that make them stand apart as unique music forms.

Opera and American Musical Theatre:
- Usually both forms of music are long productions, with extensive scenery and special effects. (Scenery and stage effects can be elaborate or simple.)
- Opera uses a sizable orchestra during each performance. There is often an orchestra in musical theatre, but the size may vary.
- The stories presented in both styles often reflect society, history, and people's attitudes at the time the musical was written.
- Musicals are an outgrowth from opera.

American Musical Theatre:
- Most musicals have been written more recently, and the composers or librettists are still living.
- The length is similar to that of a movie.
- The actors usually use microphones.
- The songs are similar to a popular song style.
- There is spoken dialogue.
- Musicals are generally presented in English.
- The solos tend to be in a popular song style.
- The story can be funny or dramatic.

Opera:
- Operas were first written in about 1600.
- Many of the composers are no longer living.
- Singers do not generally use a microphone.
- Opera singers have trained a very long time to be able to perform.
- There is usually no spoken dialogue.
- Solos in operas are difficult and complex pieces.
- Operas are written in the native language of the composer or lyricist.
- The stories are often very tragic.

Information referenced from *Opera and American Musical Theatre, Grade Five.* Ohio Department of Education.[61]

Compare and contrast opera and American musical theatre by completing the Venn diagram. Use the information on the previous page to fill in each part of the circles.

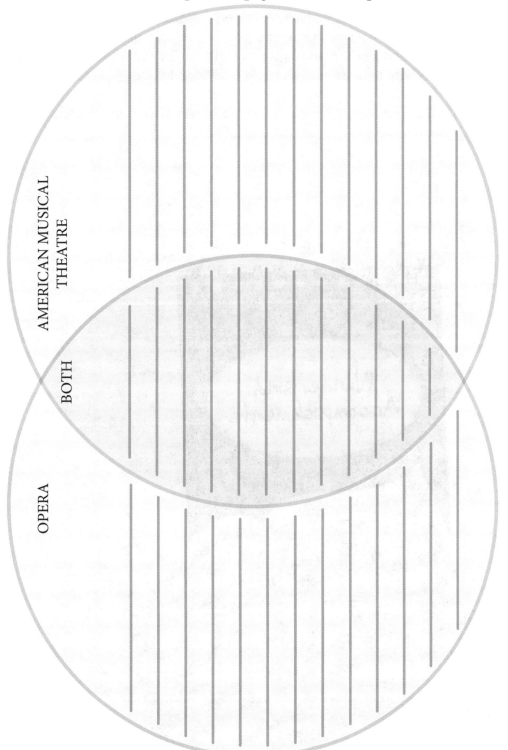

AMERICAN MUSICAL THEATRE

BOTH

OPERA

1. Opera: What characteristics are unique to opera?
2. Both: What characteristics do these musical forms share?
3. American Musical Theatre: What characteristics are unique to American musical theatre?

NOTE: It may be enjoyable for your students to watch an opera and a musical theatre production. This can be accomplished by attending a performance and/or by watching a movie. Ask your students to identify the various elements they have studied concerning each production.

Wunderkind Accomplishments

Wolfgang Mozart was a composer of indefatigable enthusiasm, action, and spirit. When an emperor once told Wolfgang that his music had too many notes, Mozart retorted, "Just as many notes as are necessary, Your Majesty."[62] Perhaps that is what could be said about Mozart's life: "Just as many notes as are necessary..." and just as many days as were necessary to compose music that has brought delight to listeners around the world for decades.

Using the *Wunderkind Accomplishments* lapbook pages, follow the directions to cut out and assemble the pieces. Adhere the book to section #8 in your Mozart lapbook.

Wolfgang Mozart's greatest accomplishment was the way he lived his life with honor and dignity. He demonstrated many admirable qualities throughout this life.

Review the character qualities presented in chapters 1-4 by writing an example of how you could demonstrate that trait in your life.

1. Family-oriented: _____

2. Enthusiastic: _____

3. An eager learner: _____

4. Sweet-tempered: _____

5. Creative: _____

6. Reverent to parents: _____

7. Sense of humor: _____

8. Industrious: _____

9. Humble: _____

10. Playful: _____

11. Kind: _____

12. Generous: _____

13. Gracious: _____

14. Attentive: _____

15. Learned: _____

16. Friendly: _____

17. Perseverant: _____

18. Joyful: _____

Do not hesitate to look up the definitions of these traits in a dictionary if you are not sure of their meaning!

Mozart

Using the *Mozart's Life at a Glance* lapbook pages, follow the directions to cut out and assemble the pieces. Adhere the book to sections #3-4 in your Mozart lapbook.

The Life and Times of Mozart

- 1756
- 1757
- 1758
- 1759
- 1760
- 1761
- 1762
- 1763
- 1764
- 1765
- 1766
- 1767
- 1768
- 1769

Mozart, The Wonder Boy Quiz

Name: _____   Date: _____

Short Answer:

1. Whom did Mozart love the most, next to God? _____

2. What could Mozart do while composing? _____

3. Which instrument did Mozart teach himself to play? _____

4. Name one other famous composer who knew Mozart personally. _____

Matching:

Match the instrument name to the correct picture <u>and</u> correct continent.

Europe	Didgeridoo
United Kingdom	Native American Drums
South America	Panpipes
North America	Gong
Australia	Bagpipes
Asia	Harpsichord

Match the following with their definition.

_____rondo   a.   a short, light-hearted piece

_____sonata   b.   instrumental music, often in several movements.

_____minuet   c.   this music carries a theme over a series of episodes

_____bagatelle   d.   a triple meter French dance

Week One: Chapter One Comprehension Questions

1. To see his new son, p. 13
2. Wolfgang, or Wolferl, p. 14
3. A cat, a yellow canary, a puppy named Bimperl, p. 15
4. Court composer and conductor of the court orchestra, p. 16
5. Play the clavier, p. 17
6. By figuring out or doing sums (math problems), p. 20
7. Playing music, or composing, pp. 17, 20
8. Papa Leopold, p. 24

Week One: The Mozart Family
(Answers may vary.)

1. Their home consisted of at least three floors, a kitchen, small chamber, living room, bedroom, and a study.
2. Marianne and Wolfgang were very close and remained dear siblings their whole lives. They enjoyed touring together and often wrote letters to each other.
3. Leopold Mozart was the assistant music director of Archbishop Sigismund von Schrat-tenbach's chapel in Salzburg. In this role, he wrote music and directed the court orchestra for the archbishop.
4. Mozart respected his father very much and was very thankful for his influence. He recognized that his father helped him achieve the character and greatness he displayed throughout most of his life. Wolfgang's motto was, "Next to God comes Papa."

Week One: German Words to Know

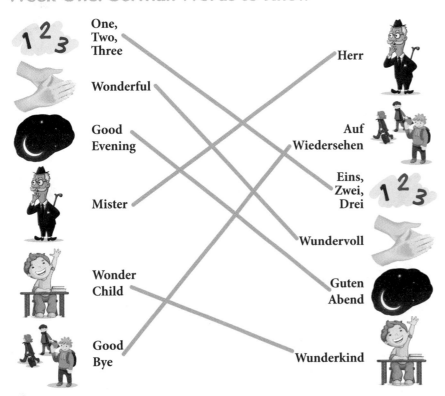

1. Guten Abend
2. Einz, zwei, drei
3. Wonderful
4. Herr Schachtner
5. Auf wiedersehen
6. Wonder child

Week Two: Chapter Two Comprehension Questions

1. They told funny stories and sang silly tunes, p. 28.
2. They played for Prince Joseph, p. 30.
3. They received praise, gifts, cheers, and amazement, pp. 30, 31.
4. He played the violin, p. 34.
5. He was astounded by Wolfgang's musical ability, p. 36.

Week Two: Chapter Three Comprehension Questions

1. They were headed to Vienna, p. 39.
2. Mother Mozart, p. 39.
3. They gave concerts — which were warmly received and praised, p. 41.
4. It was almost four weeks…nearly an entire month, p. 42.
5. Wolfgang entertained the customs officials who were so awed by the music of this small boy that they forgot all about the duties and let the Mozarts pass through, p. 42.
6. They played for King Francis and Queen Maria Theresa, p. 43.
7. Wolfgang sat on the queen's lap and kissed her; he played with their children; he allowed the king to sit right next to his clavier while he played; and he performed one-finger and "blind" fingering tricks at the clavier for the king, pp. 44–46.
8. She helped him up when he fell on the polished court floors, p. 46. Her kindness moved him deeply, p. 47.
9. The received very elegant hand-me-downs… court clothes her own children had worn, p. 48.
10. He caught scarlet fever, p. 49.

Week Two: Mozart's Favorite Instrument
Answer key for word search

Week Two: Instruments of the World (Review)

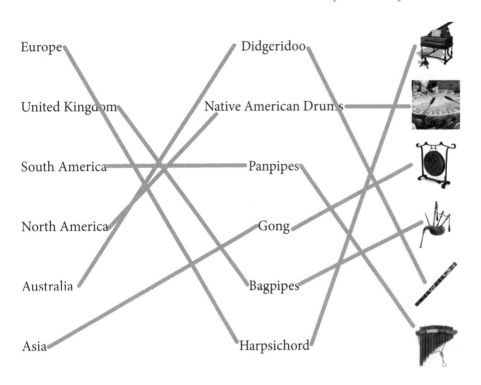

Europe

United Kingdom

South America

North America

Australia

Asia

Didgeridoo

Native American Drums

Panpipes

Gong

Bagpipes

Harpsichord

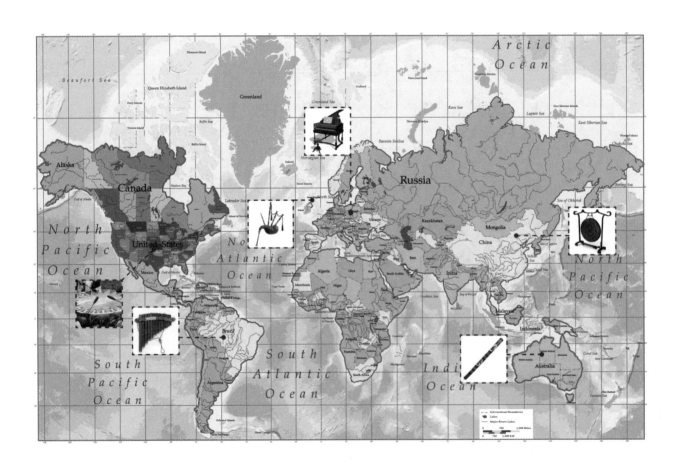

Week Three: Chapter Four Comprehension Questions

1. They wore the royal costumes from Queen Maria Theresa, p. 55.
2. The finally reached Paris, p. 61.
3. Versailles had Glittering lights, crystal chandeliers, rare tapestries, and bright ceiling paintings, p. 62.
4. He played the gilded organ (which means it was covered with a thin layer of gold), p. 62.
5. They visited London, where they were greeted even more cordially and successfully than in Paris, p. 63.
6. His name was Johann Christian Bach, p. 65.
7. Practicing their music so that the house would be quiet for Leopold's recovery process, p. 67.
8. He wrote his first symphony, at age eight, p. 67.
9. They visited in Holland, p. 72.
10. It lasted three years, p. 73.

Week Three: Music and Culture
(Answers may vary.)

Happy Birthday—a birthday party
Star Spangled Banner—a 4th of July celebration, a sporting event
Amazing Grace— church

Week Four: Chapter Five Comprehension Questions

1. He composed Opera, p. 79.
2. Mozart memorized a special choral piece that was only to be seen by those taking part in the Easter service. Wolfgang wrote out his memorized copy, but it was against the pope's rules to possess a copy. However, instead of punishing Wolfgang, the pope presented him with the honor of the Order of the Golden Spur to recognize his rare talent. pp. 79–82.
3. He served the Archbishop of Salzburg, p. 83.
4. Yes, breathing is a correct answer, but for this chapter the answer we were hoping to receive was *composing*, p. 83.
5. He had visited so many different countries in his travels and tours, p. 85.
6. Constance was his wife, and his notable friend was the composer Haydn, p. 85.
7. Paraphrased it is: "Keep an eye on this man; he'll make a noise in the world some day," p. 86.
8. Copies of his overture, written in two hours on the day of the performance itself, were still being made for the orchestra, pp. 87, 88.
9. *The Marriage of Figaro*, p. 86, and *The Magic Flute*, p. 90, are among his greatest composisitions.

Week Four: Fellow Composers Threefold Bookmark

Franz Joseph Haydn
- born in Rohrau, Austria
- born in March, 1732
- called the "Father of the Symphony"
- twenty-four years older than Wolfgang

He and Mozart were close friends. They met in 1782, yet did not feel any musical rivalry or jealousy between them. Instead they inspired each other. Haydn influenced Mozart's creativity, and Wolfgang dedicated six string quartet pieces to Haydn.

Wolfgang Mozart
- born in Austria
- twenty-four years younger than Haydn
- learned the most from Johann Christian Bach

• lived in Vienna, Austria

Mozart and Haydn were close friends. They met in 1782, yet did not feel any musical rivalry or jealousy between them. Instead they inspired each other. Haydn influenced Mozart's creativity, and Wolfgang dedicated six string quartet pieces to Haydn. Beethoven requested that Mozart take him on as a student. Mozart recognized the incredible talent in Beethoven and knew he would succeed. Beethoven greatly admired Mozart.

Ludwig van Beethoven
• born in Bonn, Germany
• born in December, 1770
• moved to Vienna in his twenties

Beethoven requested that Mozart take him on as a student. Mozart recognized the incredible talent in Beethoven and knew he would succeed. Beethoven greatly admired Mozart.

Week Four: Opera and American Theatre Venn Diagram

Opera:
• Operas were first written in about 1600.
• Many of the composers are no longer living.
• Singers do not generally use a microphone.
• Opera singers have trained a very long time to be able to perform in operas.
• There is usually no spoken dialogue.
• Solos in operas are difficult and complex pieces.
• Operas are written in the native language of the composer or lyricist.
• The stories are often very tragic.

Both:
• They are both usually a long productions, have scenery and special effects. Scenery and stage effects can be elaborate or simple.

• Often, there is an orchestra but the size may vary. Opera uses a sizable orchestra.
• The stories often reflect society, history, and people's attitudes at the time the musical was written.
• Musicals are an outgrowth from opera.

American Music Theatre:
• Most musicals have been written more recently and the composers or librettists are still living.
• The length is similar to that of a movie.
• The actors usually use microphones.
• The songs are similar to a popular song style.
• There is spoken dialogue.
• Musicals are generally presented in English.
• The solos tend to be in a popular song style.
• The story can be funny or dramatic.

Mozart, The Wonder Boy Quiz

Short Answer:

1. His father
2. He could visit with friends, play pool, or eat a meal.
3. The violin
4. Franz Haydn and Ludwig Beethoven

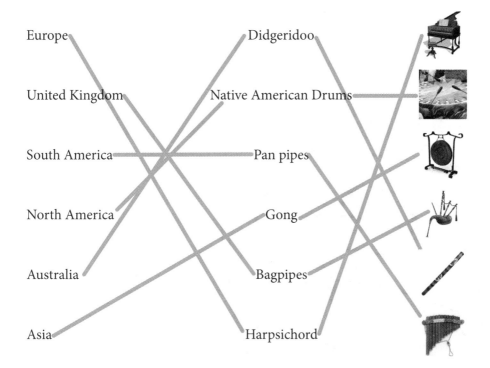

Europe   Didgeridoo

United Kingdom   Native American Drums

South America   Pan pipes

North America   Gong

Australia   Bagpipes

Asia   Harpsichord

Match:
   c.
   b.
   d.
   a.

Mozart

Weekly Lesson Outline

(Activities marked with an * are required in order to meet national music appreciation standards.)

Week One:

- Read Chapter 1*
- Answer Comprehension Questions
- Character Qualities
- Tidbits of Interest
- Assemble Lapbook Folder
- Geography Oral Report
- Life With the Beethovens
- The Family Business (LB)
- Boy Beethoven's Favorite Things (LB)
- How Music is Created, Part 1*

Week Two:

- Read Chapter 2*
- Answer Comprehension Questions
- Listen to Music Disc 5, tracks 2-5*
- Character Qualities
- Tidbits of Interest
- The Rhine River (LB)
- Beethoven's Variations (LB)*
- Composers Three*
- How Music is Created, Part 2*

Week Three:

- Read Chapters 3*
- Answer Comprehension Questions
- Listen to Music Disc 5, tracks 6-10*
- Character Qualities
- Tidbits of Interest
- Slow Cooker Porridge
- Keyboard Cousins (LB)*
- "Living in Exile"
- How Music is Created, Part 3*

Week Four:

- Read Chapter 4*
- Answer Comprehension Questions
- Listen to Music Disc 5, tracks 12-35*
- Character Qualities
- Tidbits of Interest
- The World of Nature
- The Vocabulary of Ludwig's Music (LB)*
- Beethoven's Favorite Foods (LB)
- Beethoven's *Fidelio* Opus (LB)*
- Revolutionary Times (LB)
- The Chiming Tower Bells (LB)
- How to Judge Greatness (LB)
- How Music is Created, Part 4*
- A Timeline of Beethoven's Life*

Beethoven

Chapter One Comprehension Questions

1. What neighbor and family member lived across the street from Ludwig's house in Bonn?

   _____

2. What was Ludwig's father's job? _____

   _____

3. Can you recall the two instruments Ludwig learned to play at an early age? _____

   _____

4. Name or list some ways that Ludwig "escaped" from the exhausting hours of music practice his

   father required of him. _____

   _____

   _____

   _____

5. Why would neighbors of the Beethovens often meet at their home in the evening?

   _____

6. One night the carillon began ringing in the late night hours. What happened? _____

   _____

   _____

7. When did Ludwig sometimes have his music lessons—particularly under Herr Pfeiffer and his

   father? _____

   _____

8. Why did Father Johann remove Ludwig from school at age eleven? _____

   _____

1685	Johann Sebastian Bach	1750
1685	George Frederic Handel	1759
1732	Franz Joseph Haydn	1809
1756	Wolfgang A. Mozart	1791
1770	**Ludwig van Beethoven**	1827
1782	Nicolò Paganini	1840
1797	Franz Schubert	1828

Character Qualities

Hard-working *(pp. 16, 18, 24, 27)* – Ludwig spent many wearying hours practicing the piano and the violin so he could be "another Mozart some day." He devoted hours daily to practicing scales and difficult exercises. He also wanted to help his family financially so that his mother wouldn't have to work so hard; this meant even longer hours of practice. Sometimes the hard work was forced on him during the late night hours under his father and Herr Pfeiffer's demanding eyes.

Helpful *(pp. 18, 24, 31)* – Whether he was drawing water for his mother, practicing diligently for a concert at the palace, or leaving school to go on a concert tour, Ludwig devoted himself to helping his family.

Attentive *(pp. 14, 19, 21, 28)* – Ludwig was particularly attentive to his loved ones and to music. Ludwig relished time with his grandfather, listening to the older Kapellmeister's stories. He was always attuned to hearing the carillon ringing, and he enjoyed the music of the impromptu concerts at the Beethoven home. He was attentive to the details needed to *write* music, as well.

Imaginative *(pp. 19, 29)* – Ludwig enjoyed sitting alone at the window seat where he could dream of faraway lands and let wonderful melodies creep into his mind. Later, Ludwig was imaginative in that he played music that didn't follow the rules of music. He dreamed of and dared to play music "just as it sang itself in his mind."

Tidbits of Interest

Page 11: Ludwig was baptized in St. Remigius Church, the same Roman Catholic church in which his parents were married. Though Beethoven did not attend church regularly,[1] he is recognized as an intensely religious man.[2]

Page 20: The old red ferry called the flying bridge was a ferry that moved across the river without man or animal power. A strong rope (nearly 1,000 feet long) was anchored in the middle of the river and then was tied to the mast of a ferry at the height of about twenty feet. This rope was held out of the water by several small hulls (or boat-like floats) that helped keep the rope from wearing out. The ferry would start from one bank of the river by taking a diagonal yaw position. The rudder maintained an angle so that the current would push the ferry sideways. This pendulum motion allowed the ferry to swing from bank to bank. There is still such

a ferry, named the *Flying Bridge*, in fact, in operation at the crossing of the Rhine near Bonn.

Page 23: Benjamin Franklin's famous kite experiment occurred in 1752 and ignited, or sparked, an interest in kite-flying around the world.

Page 24: When Ludwig gave his first concert in Bonn, the false age of six was listed as his age. It was probably an age given by his father so Ludwig would seem to be more of a musical prodigy like Mozart. The elector at this point was Maximilian Friedrich, who had employed Beethoven's grandfather as Kapellmeister.[3] This description of Ludwig's special costume for his first concert in Bonn was apparently the gala dress of all court musicians that year.[4] Electors often established orchestras for their own pleasure and to entertain guests.

Geography Oral Report

Beethoven visited several different places during his lifetime.

- Rotterdam, Holland (northern part of the Netherlands)
- Berlin, Germany
- Bonn, Germany
- Heiligenstadt, Germany
- Leipzig, Germany
- Dresden, Germany
- Vienna, Austria
- Baden, Austria
- Prague, Czech Republic (modern day name for this area)

Using print or internet sources, research ten facts about one of these countries. Pay close attention to **location**, **historical events**, **culture**, and **political leaders**.

Write a short essay (1-3 paragraphs) describing the country you chose and present it as an oral report.

- Prepare for your oral report by reading through the written report several times.

- When it is time for your presentation, stand up straight and speak clearly.

- Be sure that you add voice inflection and do not read your report too quickly.

Life with the Beethovens

Life with Grandfather: Grandfather Louis (or Ludwig) Beethoven had moved from Antwerp, Holland, first working as a bass singer for the Elector of Cologne, and then rising to Kapellmeister, or senior musician, for the Court. Grandfather was Ludwig's dear companion. He was always very kind to the boy and cared for him. Young Ludwig was only three years old when his grandfather died (December 24, 1773). (pp. 12-14)

Life with Father: Johann, Ludwig's father, was appointed to the post of Court Tenor and gave violin and piano lessons. Though Johann wanted Ludwig to play concerts like Mozart and bring their family wealth, Ludwig was not the natural prodigy that Mozart or Handel had been. Nevertheless, Beethoven's father made him study music for hours every day. Once Johann had taught the boy all he could, he hired Tobias Pfeiffer, a twenty-nine-year old actor and musician (and tavern buddy of Johann Beethoven's) to teach his son. Herr Pfeiffer would awaken Ludwig in the middle of the night to make him practice the piano.[5] No wonder neighbors recall the boy weeping before the piano.[6] When Beethoven was only eleven, his formal education ended. He had attended primary schools—Neugasse, Münster-schule, and Tirocinium—but his father pulled him from school in 1781 to focus on his musical career. (pp. 16, 27, 31)

Life with Mother: Ludwig's mother was named Anna Maria Magdelena Keferig (or Keverich) and was described as tall, with earnest eyes and polite manners. She was well respected and a good domestic woman who would sew, knit, and pay the rent and baker's bills promptly.[7] Anyone who knew Ludwig remembered him as always referring to his mother with "love and feeling, calling her often an honest good-hearted woman."[8] As a teenager, Ludwig used much of his earnings to help supply for his family's needs. Before Ludwig's trip to Vienna, his mother suffered from tuberculosis (sometimes called consumption). She needed rest and proper food to recover from this bacterial disease of the lungs. In addition, she had an infant daughter named Margaret for whom to care.[9] Unfortunately, Maria Beethoven died July 17, 1787, shortly after Ludwig's return to Bonn. When she died, Ludwig wrote, "She was such a kind, loving mother to me, and my best friend."[10] Ludwig was only seventeen, and a year that started with hope and joy was ending in despair, sorrow, and bitterness. (pp. 19, 41–44, 73–76, 82)

Beethoven

Life with Brothers: The Beethoven's had seven children, only three of whom survived infancy. Four months after his mother died, Ludwig's seven-month-old sister (Margaret) also died. Ludwig's two surviving siblings were his younger brothers Caspar Anton Karl Beethoven (1774–1815) and Nikolaus Johann Beethoven (1776–1848). Karl eventually became a Viennese bank clerk, and Johann became an apothecary and small landowner. Ludwig's younger brother Karl developed tuberculosis (just as his mother had) and left guardianship or care of his son with Beethoven. Nephew Karl was nine years old and Ludwig was forty-seven when they began dwelling in the same house. While their relationship was often rather stormy, Beethoven never failed to do whatever he needed to do to provide for his nephew's needs.[11] (pp. 41,133)

Using the information on the previous page and above, complete the crossword puzzle below.

ACROSS

5. Ludwig's age when he was pulled out of school
6. The reason Ludwig left school
7. Ludwig's father's occupation
8. How Beethoven described his mother
9. Whom Ludwig supported with his earnings
10. Ludwig's age when his mother died

DOWN

1. The name of Beethoven's nephew that came to live with him
2. The disease that killed Beethoven's mother and brother
3. Beethoven's teacher that held late night practices
4. Ludwig's age when his grandfather died
6. What Ludwig's grandfather was to him
7. Whom Ludwig's father wanted him to be like

The Family Business

Using the *Family Business* lapbook pages, follow the directions to cut out and assemble the pieces. Adhere this activity to section #16 in your Beethoven lapbook.

Boy Beethoven's Favorite Things

The book, *Ludwig Beethoven, and the Chiming Tower Bells* shares some of Beethoven's favorite things. When given the opportunity, Ludwig would play with neighborhood children in the Fischers' courtyard, in the palace garden and in the sand along the Rhine River.[12] He also enjoyed daydreaming while sitting on the window seat in his house and listening to the carillon, or bells, at the palace tower. Sometimes he would stop to play marbles with the boys on his way home from school. But more than anything else, he loved to fly his homemade kite. (pp. 17, 19, 20, 23)

Using the *Boy Beethoven's Favorite Things* lapbook pages, follow the directions to cut out and assemble the pieces. Write your favorites things on the opposite flap. How much different are Beethoven's favorite things than yours?

Adhere this activity to section #13 in your Beethoven lapbook.

Beethoven

How Music is Created Part I

Contextual elements shape the development of music. The progression of music is dependent on several basic things. (Definitions are from Encarta® World English Dictionary.[13])

1. **Time**: a moment or period at which something takes place
2. **Location**: the site or position of something
3. **Culture**: the beliefs, customs, practices, and social behavior of a particular nation or people
4. **Current Events**: important political and social events or issues of the present time
5. **Social Climate**: the current attitude of human society concerning social issues
6. **Political Climate**: the current attitude of human society relating to civil administration or government

Match the following descriptions with the correct songs.

1. _____ **Location**: This song was written aboard an English ship during the War of 1812. Frances Scott Key was watching the bombing of Fort McHenry and saw that the American flag was still flying "through the rocket's red glare."

2. _____ **Time**: This song was written about the death of an Old West outlaw. It provides the specific events surrounding his demise such as day and time.

3. _____ **Culture**: This is a traditional cowboy song that describes the heart of those who worked the range and their desire to live in that country.

4. _____ **Current Events**: This song was written by Woody Guthrie about the Great Depression. It portrays the life of a farmer who has to move away from the prairie and find new work out west. This song describes the daily events that affected so many during that time.

5. _____ **Social Climate**: This song was written in 1863 to convey the deep longing friends and family members had for their loved ones to return home from the American Civil War.

6. _____ **Political Climate**: This song was written as an anthem for the woman's suffrage movement. This cry for "woman's freedom" would dramatically change the face of politics in America.

a. "Star Spangled Banner"

b. "When Johnny Comes Marching Home Again"

c. "Chant of the Wanderer"

d. "Song For Equal Suffrage"

e. "Ballad of Jesse James"

f. "Dust Bowl Refugee"

Historical and cultural contexts have also greatly influenced music. Changing times, momentous events, and various people and places have all inspired musicians to write new songs and develop new styles of music.

An example of how cultural events during a specific period in history have had a direct effect on the music of that era is protest songs.

During the 1800's many songs were written in response to social events. During the American Civil War, some hot social issues were slavery, political differences between the states, and the casualties of war. This social climate stirred many to write music expressing their points of view, lamenting the tragedies of war, or rallying others to fight for a cause.

In the 20th century, other issues provoked the writing of protest songs. Women's suffrage, development of labor unions, the Great Depression, Civil Rights, and the Vietnam War were all cultural issues that greatly divided society.

Example of a Civil War Protest Song:

One song that was popular on both sides of the Mason Dixon Line was the "Battle Cry of Freedom." This song was written during the War Between the States by an American composer named George F. Root. It was composed in 1862, in response to President Abraham Lincoln's plea for more troops to join the dwindling Union Army. The song became so popular that new lyrics were later written as a rallying cry for the Confederacy. It is said that this ballad gained such popularity during the war that the song's publisher could not keep up with the demand. At one point, the company had fourteen print- ing presses printing this song alone, and that still was not enough. It is estimated that over 700,000 copies of this song were put into circulation.[14] Matthew Sabatella describes the influence of the "Battle Cry of Freedom" this way "…[it] was soon sung by millions of Americans from New York to California. There are many anecdotes in diaries, reminiscences, and newspapers concerning the inspirational effects of the song. One such claim from a Union soldier states that the song 'put as much spirit and cheer into the camp as a splendid victory.'"[15]

The lyrics for the "Battle Cry of Freedom" (Union version) and "Rally Round the Flag" (Confederate version) are on the following page. As you read these two protest songs, compare the different people and places to which they refer.

• Listen to "Battle Cry of Freedom" on Disc 5, track 1.

Note: It is interesting to note that although these people were fighting on different sides in the war, they were essentially singing the same song.

Union Lyrics:

Yes we'll rally round the flag, boys, we'll rally once again,
Shouting the battle cry of freedom,
We will rally from the hillside, we'll gather from the plain,
Shouting the battle cry of freedom!

Chorus:
The Union forever! Hurrah, boys, hurrah!
Down with the traitor, up with the star;
While we rally round the flag, boys, rally once again,
Shouting the battle cry of freedom!
We are springing to the call of our brothers gone before,
Shouting the battle cry of freedom!
And we'll fill our vacant ranks with a million freemen more,
Shouting the battle cry of freedom!

(Chorus)
We will welcome to our numbers the loyal, true and brave,
Shouting the battle cry of freedom!
And although he may be poor, he shall never be a slave,
Shouting the battle cry of freedom!

(Chorus)
So we're springing to the call from the East and from the West,
Shouting the battle cry of freedom!
And we'll hurl the rebel crew from the land we love best,
Shouting the battle cry of freedom!

(Chorus for the 1864 election campaign)
For Lincoln and Johnson, hurrah, boys, hurrah!
Down with the rebellion and on with the war,
While we rally round the cause, boys, we'll rally in our might,
Singing the holy cause of freemen.

Confederate Lyrics:

Our flag is proudly floating on the land and on the main,
Shout, shout the battle cry of freedom!
Beneath it oft we've conquered, and we'll conquer oft again!
Shout, shout the battle cry of freedom!

Chorus:
Our Dixie forever! She's never at a loss!
Down with the eagle and up with the cross!(albatross)
We'll rally 'round the bonny flag, we'll rally once again,
Shout, shout the battle cry of freedom!
Our gallant boys have marched to the rolling of the drums.
Shout, shout the battle cry of freedom!
And the leaders in charge cry out, "Come, boys, come!"
Shout, shout the battle cry of freedom!--

(Chorus)
They have laid down their lives on the bloody battle field.
Shout, shout the battle cry of freedom!
Their motto is resistance -- "To tyrants we'll not yield!"
Shout, shout the battle cry of freedom!--

(Chorus)
While our boys have responded and to the fields have gone.
Shout, shout the battle cry of freedom!
Our noble women also have aided them at home.
Shout, shout the battle cry of freedom!--

(Chorus)

Chapter Two Comprehension Questions

1. Mother Beethoven and Ludwig sailed down the Rhine River to what country and why? _____

   _____

2. When he returned to Bonn, what new musical instrument did Ludwig learn to play? And do you remember his first teacher's name on that instrument? _____

   _____

   _____

3. When he later took organ lessons from Zenser at the Münsterkirche, Ludwig wrote his own compositions. What did Zenser see as a "problem" with those works, and what was Ludwig's response to the difficulty Zenser pointed out? _____

   _____

   _____

4. Do you remember the names of Ludwig's younger brothers? _____

   _____

5. How did Ludwig and his family celebrate his mother's birthday? _____

   _____

   _____

6. What major musician from the court did Ludwig next study under, practicing Bach's difficult works, in particular? And how did this musician describe Ludwig's future? _____

   _____

7. As a youth, what conducting position did Ludwig undertake, and was he successful? _____

   _____

8. Can you provide an anecdote (or a story) from this chapter that shows Ludwig was a bit of a tease? _____

   _____

   _____

Diligent *(pp. 37, 39, 47, 63)* – Playing an organ as a young man was not an easy task, but Ludwig never shrank from the job and even learned how to play the bass notes with the foot pedals. Ludwig practiced diligently for the chapel services, memorizing the music, playing for the early morning services, and playing for special services at another nearby church. He learned difficult pieces, composition rules, and writing variations to improve his musical abilities. Furthermore, he proved that even as a young lad, he understood the necessity of patient, diligent practice of difficult passages when he conducted the theater orchestra.

Respect for Others *(pp. 41, 44, 47, 65)* – His treatment of his mother, particularly honoring her on her birthday, demonstrated his deep respect for his mother. And he was glad for a yearly income so that his mother would not have to work so hard. Ludwig's appreciation for the skill of other musicians, such as the court organist Herr Neefe, showed respect for others. He even agreed to Neefe's rules and composition requirements, although it saddened him not to be able to write variations as he heard them in his mind. Ludwig also recognized that the elector deserved respect and bowed low to him.

Leadership *(pp. 38, 49, 62)* – Even as a young man, Ludwig was given important responsibilities: playing for church services and for the court chapel when the senior organist was absent and taking on the role of conductor for the theater orchestra. He took on that role in spite of the fact that many musicians expected the

task to be too difficult for a child. By the end of the first rehearsal, however, they applauded the young conductor and appreciated his leadership.

Visionary *(pp. 39, 40, 47)* – Ludwig composed music that he couldn't even play because his hands were not large enough, but it didn't deter his enthusiasm for composing, and he even expressed an attitude of, "I'll play it when I'm bigger." He had a view of the future even as a youngster. He practiced and experimented with the organ, and he risked writing music that didn't "follow the rules" for composing variations. His visionary quality transformed music forever!

Tidbits of Interest

Page 34: Rotterdam is a port city in the Netherlands province of South Holland. Currently, Rotterdam has the second largest port in the world (after Shanghai). Much of the Netherlands is flat, about half of its surface area being less than four feet above sea level, and large areas are below sea level. An extensive system of dykes and canals is used to protect these low areas from flooding. Windmills are used to pump water out of low areas in which a water level must be maintained, which explains why Holland (a province in the Netherlands) is commonly associated with windmills.

Page 35: Beethoven studied organ with Brother Willibald Koch from the Franciscan monastery in Bonn. Brother Willibald eventually accepted Beethoven as his assistant. Playing organs in Ludwig's time required lots of physical activity and strength. The organ is a keyboard instrument in which sound is produced by air passing through pipes of various size and construction to give a wide variety of pitches and timbres. In Beethoven's time, bellows attached to foot pedals were the means of forcing air through the pipes of the organ. But even as a child, Ludwig was known as a boy of musical ambition and physical strength.[16]

Page 40: Ludwig loved experimenting with the organ and writing new compositions. In fact, even as a youth he began keeping notebooks of

various musical ideas that were crowded in with other ideas in all stages of development — similar to Leonardo da Vinci's notebooks of science and art ideas.[17] These notebooks were masses of corrections and enthusiastic writings, sometimes difficult for anyone but the composer to decipher.[18]

Pages 44-49: The elector's court organist and theater director was Christian Gottlob Neefe (1748–1798), who is described as a Protestant believer who mentored Ludwig.[19] Neefe was a master organist who taught Ludwig classical rules of composition and helped him develop his technique as a keyboard player. Neefe taught Ludwig the *Well-Tempered Clavier* by Bach, which Ludwig still practiced during his years in Vienna. Ludwig always had a deep respect for the music of earlier masters — particularly the music of Bach, Mozart, and Handel. Beethoven excelled under Neefe's teaching, and he essentially was apprenticed, or deputized, for the position of Kapellmeister at age twelve![20] Neefe once wrote in a letter that he thought Ludwig was a genius worthy of and "deserving of help to enable him to travel. He would surely become a second Wolfgang Amadeus Mozart were he to continue as he was begun."[21]

Music Appreciation for the Elementary Grades—Beethoven

223

Beethoven

Map Activity

The Rhine River

The Rhine River is one of the longest rivers in Europe. It begins in Switzerland, flowing north and east approximately 820 miles, but it can also be navigated from the North Sea to Basel, Switzerland. Almost eighty percent of its ship-carrying waters pass through Germany, although not all oceangoing vessels can go the entire distance on the Rhine. Many ships must end their journey in Cologne, Germany (near Bonn). From Cologne, cargo must then go by barges pushed by smaller ships until the Rhine reaches the intersection of the three countries of France, Germany, and Switzerland. During the Middle Ages and beyond, feudal lords and landowners built castles along the Rhine to protect their lands from marauders and land-grabbing neighbors. There are more castles on the short stretch of river from the city of Mainz to Bonn, a length of only thirty-five miles, than there are in any other river valley in the world.

The Rhine River

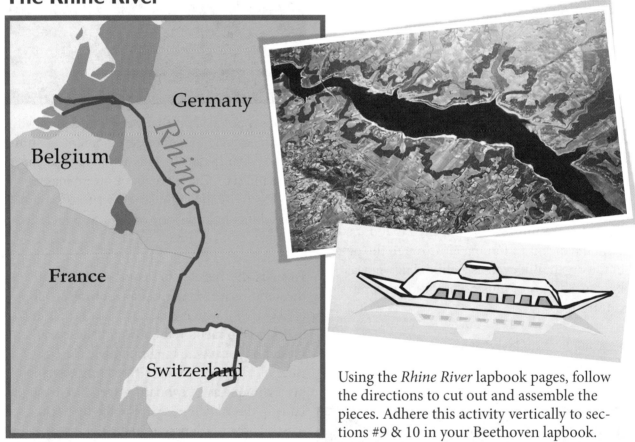

Using the *Rhine River* lapbook pages, follow the directions to cut out and assemble the pieces. Adhere this activity vertically to sections #9 & 10 in your Beethoven lapbook.

Hands-on

Beethoven's Variations

Ludwig's first published composition, *Nine Variations on a March*, came out when he was only twelve years old. Variations are changes to a given theme of music through changes in the melody, harmony, rhythm, or addition to the theme.

Using *Beethoven's Variations* lapbook pages, follow the directions to cut out and assemble the pieces. Adhere this activity vertically to section #15 in your Beethoven lapbook.

Composers Three

Beethoven Meets Mozart

Ludwig is described as having unkempt hair when he first approached Mozart. The style of the day was careful pigtails, but Ludwig let his thick hair grow long and wild — his entire life.[22] Mozart initially recognized Ludwig as a good pianist, but at that time Vienna had hundreds of good pianists. Amazingly enough, during Beethoven's time, Vienna had some 200,000 residents, of whom at least 6,000 were pianists![23] Nevertheless, Vienna was a better location for musical success than any other city in the Hapsburg empire, because Vienna's imperial family and several other wealthy families supported musicians there. It was Ludwig's improvisation (composing on the spur of the moment, or making and arranging offhand) that led to Mozart's prophetic comment about Ludwig making a noise in the world someday. Beethoven later said that Mozart had "a fine but choppy way of playing" because the manner of playing a clavier or a harpsichord was different than that used for piano, and Beethoven's interest was in the piano.[24] In the years that Ludwig lived in Vienna, composers were becoming more appreciated in their own right as gifted artists, rather than servants who had to write under a patron's demands or restrictions. Ludwig did receive help from many friends, including Prince Karl Lichnowsky, a musical aristocrat who had once studied with Mozart.[25] The prince offered Beethoven numerous opportunities to perform, gave him rooms to live in, and understood Ludwig's eccentricities. (pp. 78, 79)

Beethoven Meets Haydn

Count Ferdinand Ernst Gabriel Waldstein helped introduce Ludwig to the famed composer Joseph Haydn (1732–1802) who passed through Bonn in 1790 on his way to London, and again on his return from London in 1792. Franz Joseph Haydn was Austria's premier composer of the time. He was particularly known for his symphonies (over 100 of them), and he was a primary shaper of Classical style music. Ludwig wrote a new composition, a cantata, to commemorate the recent death of Emperor Joseph II in 1790, which he then gave to Haydn to critique. His work so impressed the older composer (sometimes called Papa Haydn) that he offered to teach the young musician. Ludwig began studying with Haydn in late 1792 and continued through October of 1793. They shared cups of chocolate and coffee[26], and Haydn even loaned him money at one point.[27] However, Ludwig considered Haydn a poor teacher because Haydn was preoccupied with his own compositions for his second London journey.[28] Even so, Haydn wisely predicted, "…Beethoven will in time fill the position of one of Europe's greatest composers, and I shall be proud to be able to speak of myself as his teacher."[29] (pp. 87, 88, 94)

Haydn • Mozart • Beethoven

Beethoven

Using all of the facts you have learned about Haydn, Mozart, and Beethoven, complete this compare/contrast graphic organizer.

Compare and Contast Diagram

| Franz Joseph Haydn | Wolfgang A. Mozart | Ludwig van Beethoven |

How were these composers alike?

_____

_____

_____

_____

_____

_____

_____

How were these composers different?

Franz Joseph Haydn	Wolfgang A. Mozart	Ludwig van Beethoven
_____	_____	_____
_____	_____	_____
_____	_____	_____
_____	_____	_____
_____	_____	_____
_____	_____	_____

How Music Is Created Part 2 (4th-6th grade activity)

Music is a fluid picture of the values and moral direction of our society. It is constantly changing in its style and message, based on current developments in our world. Political policies, personal ethics, and the current worldview are often communicated throughout the lyrics of a song.

List your five favorite songs.

1. _____   4. _____

2. _____   5. _____

3. _____

What do your musical choices reveal about your personal moral convictions and world view?

_____

_____

_____

Now research the current top five hits of today and write the titles here.

1. _____   4. _____

2. _____   5. _____

3. _____

What can you tell about the current direction of our society based on these <u>song titles</u>?

_____

_____

Write a short paragraph discussing what the current direction of modern music reveals about the world in which we live.

Chapter Three Comprehension Questions

1. To whom does Herr Neefe encourage Ludwig to go for more musical instruction?_____
   _____

2. Why did it take Ludwig a long time to save enough money for a trip to Vienna? _____
   _____
   _____
   _____

3. When Ludwig first played for Mozart in Vienna, was Mozart highly impressed by the lad? What
   finally captured Mozart's attention in Ludwig's playing, and what did he predict about Ludwig?
   _____
   _____
   _____

4. Why did Ludwig hurriedly return to Bonn from Vienna? _____
   _____

5. Can you give the names of at least two dear friends from this chapter who helped Ludwig out in
   times of need or exhaustion? _____
   _____

6. Ludwig was again allowed to move to Vienna to continue his music studies. From what famous
   composer did Ludwig begin taking lessons when he returned to Vienna? _____
   _____

7. Ludwig was soon called upon to give concerts for many of the prince's friends, but this was a
   struggle for Ludwig. Why did he feel he needed to leave the palace? _____
   _____
   _____

8. By the end of this chapter, what physical struggle was Ludwig fighting, and how did he respond
   to it as it worsened? _____
   _____
   _____
   _____

Character Qualities

Frugality *(pp. 73, 88, 96)* – Ludwig carefully saved any extra pennies he earned from playing special music, with the hopes of using the money for a trip to Vienna to study under Mozart. He was very frustrated at losing even one coin from his savings box. He even rode in an open coach to Vienna to save money. When he moved to Vienna permanently (somewhat permanently, at least), Ludwig was willing to live in an attic room offered by a generous prince so that his expenses were diminished a bit more.

Passionate Determination *(pp. 77–79, 82, 95)* – Ludwig's eyes burned with his passion for music, and he was determined to show Mozart that he was more than just a decent pianist. Mozart was impressed by Ludwig's spirit and musical power. After returning home from Vienna, Ludwig was determined to provide for his family's needs after his mother's death — to the point that he overworked himself and became ill from a lack of food and rest. Furthermore, Ludwig's *music* displayed his passion. He wrote with emotion and ignored "rules" in order to share the thoughts that burned in his mind. He was equally determined to cope with his deafness on his own.

Creativity *(pp. 79, 95)* – Mozart recognized Ludwig's creative genius at their first meeting when Ludwig improvised richly on a Mozart melody. Mozart told his friends to keep an eye on Ludwig: "He will make a noise in the world some day." When Ludwig began studying under Albrechtsberger and Salieri, they scolded him for not following the rules of composition in his works, but Ludwig argued that he needed to write the music as he felt it, as it sang itself in his head.

Tidbits of Interest

Pages 71–72: Many considered Ludwig a piano virtuoso by age eleven.[30] But when Ludwig was about fifteen or sixteen, Master Neefe encouraged him to go on for more training under a new master. Beethoven later wrote Master Neefe a letter of gratitude, stating, "I thank you for the counsel which you gave me so often in my progress in my divine art. If I ever become a great man yours shall be a share of the credit."[31]

Page 95: Ludwig's burning emotions were played out in his music — even if that music went against the rules that Salieri and Albrechtsberger were teaching him. His compositions bridged the Classical achievements of the 18th century to the Romanticism of the 19th century. He moved music from its focus on form and rules (restraints from the Classical era) to the wildly emotional and personalized expression of the Romantic era.

Page 96: Most contemporaries of Beethoven and biographers admit that Ludwig was very disorganized and even sloppy in his personal life and appearance. When his clothes became too dirty or tattered, his friends would snatch them in the night and replace them with new ones.[32] Once when he was at the height of his musical career in Vienna, he took a walk in such a disheveled state that he was arrested by a police officer who thought he was a tramp![33]

Page 99: Ludwig often directed from his piano, but sometimes he became so involved in the music that he would forget he was a soloist, and jumping up from his piano, he would begin conducting in his own peculiar fashion.[34] His conducting style included leaping in the air in the loud parts, waving his arms to the skies, crouching in quiet parts (almost under the music stand), and later (during his deafness) even shouting out loud without being aware.[35] One time, another composer witnessed Ludwig conducting with such fury that "when he struck the first chord of the solo he broke six strings" on the piano.[36]

Beethoven

Slow Cooker Porridge

Beethoven ate a bowl of porridge before leaving for the Easter services. Perhaps you would enjoy a bowl of warm porridge while you read Chapter Three.

Slow-Cooker Porridge Recipe

¼ c. cracked wheat
½ c. raisins
¾ c. rolled oats (not instant oatmeal)
¼ c. wheat germ
3 c. water

½ c. apple, grated
¼ tsp. cinnamon
Milk and honey

Combine all ingredients except the milk and honey in a slow-cooker. Turn to lowest setting. Cook overnight. Spoon into bowls, and serve with milk and honey.

Keyboard Cousins: The Piano and the Harpsichord

Ludwig quickly "made his reputation as the most exciting keyboard player in Vienna just at the time when the piano was beginning to replace the harpsichord."[37] Pianos were cheaper to make than harpsichords, and they allowed for greater dynamics, which suited Beethoven's style and music perfectly. Beethoven even introduced bent finger playing to get more dynamics and character from the piano.

Pianos in Beethoven's day were made with wooden frames, rather than metal ones like today, which meant they were more fragile. The wooden frames also meant they could support less tension on the strings, so they made less sound than modern pianos. At least four of Beethoven's pianos were gifts from piano manufacturers.[38]

Moonlight Sonata is perhaps the most recognized piano sonata in history. The piano was central to Beethoven's art. He composed thirty-two piano sonatas.

Although the piano and harpsichord are similar, they have several distinguishing characteristics.

Harpsichord	Piano

Harpsichord	**Piano**
The strings of a harpsichord are plucked.	Hammers strike the strings of a piano.
This instrument was popular long before the piano was invented.	The piano was introduced in the 18th century.
It has five octaves.	It has seven octaves.
The keys are slimmer and have to be hit hard for any sound to be produced.	The notes on a piano can be sustained and the keys have little resistance.
The volume of a harpsichord is constant.	Varying dynamics can be produced simultaneously on a piano.

(Information above is from www.differencebetween.net[39])

Using the chart above, mark an H beside each fact that describes a harpsichord, and a P beside each fact that describes a piano.

1. _____ The notes can be sustained and the keys have little resistance.
2. _____ It has five octaves.
3. _____ The volume is constant (either loud or soft).
4. _____ This instrument was introduced in the 18th century.
5. _____ The keys are slimmer and have to be hit hard for any sound to be produced.
6. _____ Varying dynamics can be produced simultaneously.
7. _____ The strings are plucked.
8. _____ Hammers strike the strings.
9. _____ This instrument was popular first.
10. _____ It has seven octaves.

• Listen to the harpsichord in No. 2 Allegro on Disc 4, Track 19.
• Listen to the piano in *Moonlight* Sonata on Disc 5, Track 11.

Using the *Keyboard Cousins* lapbook pages, follow the directions to cut out and assemble the pieces. Adhere this activity vertically to sections #12 & 14 in your Beethoven lapbook.

"Living in Exile"

Weariness, exhaustion, and a raging fever caused by typhus weakened Beethoven's body in 1797.[40] By 1801, sickness had settled in his ears, causing buzzing and ringing day and night. Ludwig later claimed that the shelling of Vienna by Napoleon Bonaparte's troops caused his deafness. His rooms were in line of the shelling, and he covered his head with pillows to shut out the noise.[41] Ludwig also claimed that exposure to cold caused his deafness, but it is more likely that his deafness was due to nerve damage from a combination of factors.

Melancholy, loneliness, and pride or fear seems to have caused Ludwig to move from Vienna. He wrote his brothers that he felt his deafness meant he "must live as an exile."[42] Yet in the midst of his struggles, he sought God to make sense of life's unfairness: "Therefore, calmly will I submit myself to all inconsistency and will place all my confidence in your eternal goodness, O God! My soul shall rejoice in Thee, immutable Being. Be my rock, my light, forever my trust."[43]

Doctor Johann Adam Schmidt, a professor of general pathology and therapy at Josephine Academy, treated Ludwig and became his personal physician.[44] On the advice of Dr. Schmidt, Beethoven went to Heiligenstadt, a village north of Vienna that was famous for its sulfur springs and its views of the Danube River and Carpathian Mountains. This visit to Heiligenstadt started as a low point in Beethoven's life. However, he would not remain silent in his world of silence. In fact, it was in Heiligenstadt that Beethoven wrote his dear friend Wegeler in 1801 insisting, "I will seize Fate by the throat; it shall certainly not bend and crush me completely."[45]

Beethoven used a number of different ear trumpets, also called acoustic cornets, in an effort to hear more clearly. Ludwig's Fifth Symphony is a musical depiction of his struggle with deafness.[46]

His pianos were without legs because he moved so often. It has also been suggested that by placing the piano on the floor, lying on the floor, and holding a stick with his teeth to the frame of the piano Ludwig could feel the sound vibrations.[47]

Beethoven's Conversation Notebooks

As Beethoven's hearing declined, he began using notebooks to communicate with others. They would write down questions, and Beethoven would respond verbally. It is thought that there were somewhere around 400 of these books when he died, but the actual number is not known. However, 137 of these books, along with some loose pages, were sold to the Berlin Royal Library in 1846.

Beethoven invited Stephen von Breuning to Baden, a place of cures and relaxation. Stephen nursed Beethoven through illnesses, came alongside him during his anger and humiliation in his deafness, and even helped the composer pull *Fidelio* into shape from its original 1805 production.[48] While the spas in Baden did not lessen his deafness, Beethoven began composing harder than ever. His musical excellence and creativity seemed to burst forth even more in his world of increasing silence (1802–1816). It is believed he was completely deaf by 1817, but in those fourteen years of deepening deafness, Beethoven wrote six symphonies, an overture, an opera, two piano concertos, piano sonatas, and quartets.

At the close of Beethoven's final concert in Vienna, he cried when someone turned him to see the audience applauding—applause he could no longer hear.[49]

According to the Gallaudet Research Institute, close to a million people in the United States are "functionally deaf."[50] It is important to understand that deafness is a physical difference, not the defining characteristic of a person. Although there have been many advancements in treatment since Beethoven's time, deafness can still cause someone to feel isolated.

In order to gain a slight understanding of how someone who is deaf might feel, complete the two activities described below.

1. Turn on your favorite TV show, but turn the volume down all the way. (Do not use closed captioning for this activity.) How long does it take for you to feel frustrated and confused because you cannot follow the story line or understand what is happening?
2. For the next several minutes, try to communicate by only using hand signals. Ask a person in the room for something or where something is. Do not use any written words or sounds to communicate. Can they understand your signals? Do you feel irritated that you cannot get the information you need?

Write down five adjectives to describe how these activities made you feel.

» _____

» _____

» _____

» _____

» _____

Imagine how someone who is deaf might feel when those around him/her cannot understand what is being expressed or cannot communicate back effectively.

Beethoven used an ear trumpet when trying to hear others speak. Modern science technology has produced hearing aids, cochlear implants, closed captioning, and text telephones to help those that are deaf communicate with others in the hearing world. Other developments include sign language, lip reading, and hearing assistance dogs. You may enjoy learning some sign language on your own. Michigan State University Communication Technology Laboratory has an American Sign Language website with videos of the ASL alphabet and many word signs.

Recommended Reading: *Moses Goes To a Concert* by Isaac Millman is a delightful book about a class of young students who attend an orchestra concert with their teacher, Mr. Samuels. Many other children are also attending the performance, but the students in Mr. Samuels's class are deaf. He devises a clever way for them to "hear" the music, and they have the opportunity to meet the orchestra's percussionist, who is also deaf.

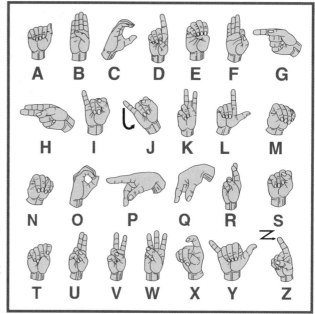

How Music Is Created Part 3

The sounds of music alone can communicate great meaning. The choice of instruments, note arrangement, and tempo can alter the effect that music has on the listener. The style of music can suggest many different things by influencing our emotions and moods. Different types of music generate different images in our minds, and the lyrics are often secondary in communicating feeling.

Think about how the <u>sound</u> of a musical piece influences the kind of music you like. **Circle the words that describe the kind of music you enjoy the most.**

Fast	Depressing	Harmonious
Slow	Powerful	Discordant
Loud	Calming	Elegant
Quiet	Uplifting	Spirited

No matter what kind of music you enjoy, there is an emotional connection to the musical experience.

Look at the faces below these songs. Cut out the squares and glue the face under the song that makes you feel that way.

"Happy Birthday"	"Twinkle, Twinkle Little Star"	"Pop, Goes the Weasel"

"Three Blind Mice"	"Oh, Where Oh, Where Has my Little Dog Gone?"	"America, The Beautiful"

Happy   Disgusted   Proud   Sad   Surprised   Calm

Chapter Four Comprehension Questions

1. What did Beethoven do in Heiligenstadt to help him forget about his deafness?

   _____

   _____

   _____

   _____

2. What did Beethoven keep around his neck to help him communicate with others?

   _____

   _____

   _____

3. How did the world of nature seem to help Beethoven with his music?_____

   _____

   _____

   _____

4. Can you provide a story or anecdote from this chapter that shows Beethoven was not always careful with things or mindful of things, especially when he was composing? _____

   _____

   _____

   _____

   _____

5. When Beethoven returned to Vienna, what young boy greeted him near his front door?

   _____

6. What beverage did Beethoven enjoy, especially before sunrise? _____

   _____

7. How do we know that Vienna never forgot Beethoven even in the midst of his struggle with deafness? _____

   _____

   _____

Character Qualities

Appreciated Nature (*pp. 103, 104, 107, 116*) – Ludwig reveled in going for walks in the mountains and meadows where he could feel the wind and see the trees. Neither thunderstorms nor darkness deterred him from these walks. (He might have been an excellent postman if he had not continued with music, eh?) He found peace in the stars, clouds, and trees, and they all helped him to remember sounds for his melodies. At one point he felt that even the trees were crying out, "Holy! Holy!" (By the way, Isaiah 55:12 indicates that this is not a far-fetched notion at all.)

Generous (*pp. 117, 134, 140, 144*) – Beethoven welcomed friends to his home (though he was in a nightcap and offered watery soup for supper). He welcomed his needy nephew Karl into his home and provided for his needs, setting aside a large gift he had received specifically for Karl's education. Ludwig gave a first-performance concert of his Ninth Symphony and Mass to the people of Vienna, a rare appearance at this stage in his deafness. And he gave music for generation upon generation to enjoy and cherish.

Attribute Acronyms (Review)

Ludwig Beethoven was a man that demonstrated many attributes in his day to day life. Some of them should not be emulated, but there is much we can learn from his life.

Follow the acronym of Beethoven's name to review some of the character traits he demonstrated.

L—Leader
U—Unconventional
D—Diligent
W—Willing
I—Imaginative
G—Generous

B—Brusque
E—Enthusiastic
E—Economical
T—Tireless
H—Helpful
O—Observant
V—Visionary
E—Earnest
N—Nature-loving

What attributes do you demonstrate each day? Would other people want to be like you? Make an acronym with your name and assign a character trait to each letter that best describes yourself. (A thesaurus may be helpful.)

Tidbits of Interest

Page 104: Beethoven used small notebooks that could fit in his pocket or hang from his neck so that he could document musical ideas when he was away from home. He would stitch together these notebooks himself since ready-made musical manuscript notebooks were too expensive.[51] He would sometimes mull over the musical ideas or "sketches" noted in the booklets for years before developing them into composition building blocks. As his deafness increased, the small notebooks also became "conversation notebooks" in which visitors could write what they wanted to ask Beethoven or what they wanted him to know.

Page 105: Beethoven claimed he was too clumsy to sharpen a quill, and his broad fingers weren't suited for sharpening and using a regular pencil because the point broke too quickly.[52] He chose to use a carpenter's pencil with its broad, thick lead.

Page 135: Ludwig loved strong coffee. (Sixty beans per cup seems like a caffeine-fix for a full day!) He also enjoyed afternoons at a coffeehouse where he could read the newspaper and share in local gossip.[53]

Page 140: Beethoven's Ninth Symphony, called *Choral*, is set to a poem entitled "Ode to Joy" by Johann Christoph Friedrich von Schiller. Schiller was a German poet and playwright whose works championed the cause of political freedom.[54] The poem speaks of the brotherhood of man and the arrival of joy through suffering.[55] It is little wonder, then, that the Ninth Symphony was played during the Chinese student protest in Communist China in 1989 and during the fall of Germany's Berlin Wall, also in 1989.

The World of Nature

Ludwig loved walks in the out-of-doors, regardless of the weather. This is demonstrated in the book, *Ludwig Beethoven and the Chiming Tower Bells* on page 107.

> "Through the long summer months, in every kind of weather, Beethoven roamed through the woods and fields. And even at night, long after the sun had set behind the purple mountains, he could not go to bed, for he must walk in the restful moonlight and lie in the meadows to gaze up at the stars and the clouds, for in them he found peace."

Max Ring, a doctor who once visited Ludwig at one of his summer residences, described him as "not quite right in his mind; he would often run, bareheaded, without a hat, around in the great park . . . hours on end, even if it were raining with lightning and thunder."[56]

Being outside in nature brought Beethoven great joy and inspiration. Do you enjoy being out in nature? Do you have a favorite place in the out-of-doors that you like to visit?

Write a cinquain ('siŋ-ˌkān) poem describing how you feel about the outdoors. (It can be positive or negative.)

A cinquain poem is a five line poem that follows one of three patterns.

Style #1:	**Examples**
Line 1: One word	Nature
Line 2: Two words	Big, beautiful
Line 3: Three words	No matter what
Line 4: Four words	I love it here
Line 5: One word	Wilderness
Style #2:	
Line 1: A noun	Outside
Line 2: Two adjectives	Colorful, bright
Line 3: Three -ing words	Blowing, shining, raining
Line 4: A phrase	It's my favorite place
Line 5: Another word for the noun	Nature
Style #3:	
Line 1: Two syllables	Nature
Line 2: Four syllables	In the country,
Line 3: Six syllables	I find calm and beauty
Line 4: Eight syllables	How my heart aches to travel there
Line 5: Two syllables	Peaceful

The Vocabulary of Ludwig's Music

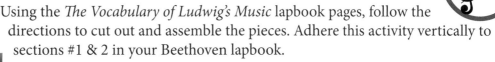

Using the *The Vocabulary of Ludwig's Music* lapbook pages, follow the directions to cut out and assemble the pieces. Adhere this activity vertically to sections #1 & 2 in your Beethoven lapbook.

overture   quartet   mass

symphony

concerto   sonata

Beethoven's Favorite Foods

Ludwig was notorious for his poor cooking skills. He liked macaroni and cheese, red herrings, and a mushy soup of bread and eggs.[57] (He was also a notoriously poor housekeeper. He moved nearly eighty times in his thirty-five years in Vienna!)

Using *Beethoven's Favorite Foods* lapbook pages, follow the directions to cut out and assemble the pieces. Write your favorite things on the opposite flap. How much different were Beethoven's favorites than yours? Adhere this activity to section #11 in your Beethoven lapbook.

Beethoven's Opera: *Fidelio* Opus 72

Fidelio was Ludwig's only opera. Napoleon's troops marched into Vienna and shelled the city one week before the opera's opening.[58] Some people consider it among the greatest operas, but Ludwig rarely wrote well for voices because he treated them as just another musical instrument, causing him to ignore the limitations of the human voice.[59]

Fidelio was written in honor of the Congress of Vienna (1814–1815) in which Europe's leaders met with the aim of stamping out current revolutionary ideas, putting an end to Napoleon's political influence, and restoring old political orders.

Using the *Beethoven's Opera: Fidelio Opus 72* lapbook pages, follow the directions to cut out and assemble the pieces. Adhere this activity to section #6 in your Beethoven lapbook.

Beethoven

Revolutionary Times

The 1700's were a time of "sudden, radical, or complete change"—of revolution. [60]

1750	1775	1789
The Industrial Revolution (1750-1850)	The American Revolution (1775-1783)	The French Revolution (1789-1799)

In 1792, Ludwig made his second trip to Vienna, but travel to that city was not safe because of the growing conflict that started in France three years before (the French Revolution). Commoners in Paris had revolted against the rulers, and they deposed King Louis XVI in 1792. Austria (and other European countries) sided with the imprisoned king, declaring war against the French people. Two years after Ludwig left Bonn, in fact, the French invaded the city, causing Elector Maximilian Franz to flee the city and never return. [61]

Ludwig nearly took the post of senior musician or Kapellmeister for the King of Westphalia, Jerome Bonaparte, Napoleon's brother, who ruled in Westphalia from 1807–1813. Three Viennese aristocrats combined their resources to offer Ludwig a salary for life if he remained in Vienna. [62] The Napoleonic Wars made this arrangement difficult to fulfill, but Beethoven was never penniless, though he rarely had much money after the Congress of Vienna in 1815. [63]

Beethoven's Third Symphony, incidentally, was originally to be dedicated to Napoleon, because Beethoven had idealized him as a hero of humanity, leading mankind into an age of liberty, equality, and fraternity (the ideals of the French Revolution). When Beethoven learned that Napoleon had crowned himself emperor, Beethoven ripped up the dedication page and renamed it *Eroica* (*Heroic*) in honor of the heroic "common man."

Make a circle book to help you record major world events that were going on during Beethoven's time. Using the *Revolutionary Times* lapbook pages, follow the directions to cut out and assemble the pieces. Adhere this activity to section #4 in your Beethoven lapbook.

The Chiming Tower Bells

It is intriguing to note how Wheeler uses bells chiming in each chapter to tie the story of Beethoven's life together — from the carillon in Bonn to the tower bells in Vienna.

Trace this strand of chiming bells on pages 19, 35, 69, 131, and 141 of the biography, and recognize that a well-crafted story will have threads and ideas carefully woven throughout it. This concept also gives the book's title even more meaning.

In chapter one, we see Beethoven's love for the bells expressed for the first time. A carillon is a set of at least twenty-three cast bronze bells that are fixed and tuned chromatically. While the bells are sounded by hammers, they are controlled from a keyboard. They are usually located in a tower. In this biography, the carillon was in the elector's palace tower.

In chapter two, the bells call Ludwig to the morning church service, where he enjoys hearing the organ played. The bells ring again in chapter three, rousing Beethoven from his bed early on Easter morning. Chapter four describes the "sweet sound of bells [that] broke the stillness of the valley." Near the end of this same chapter, we see the bells once more. Beethoven is returning home, when he comes to a little church. He looks above and "the old bells [are] turning and swinging over his head . . ." However, he cannot hear the chiming tower bells any longer, ". . . the sounds rang only in his mind."

Using the *Chiming Bells* threaded book lapbook pages, follow the directions to cut out and assemble the pieces. Adhere this activity to section #8 in your Beethoven lapbook.

How to Judge Greatness

On March 26, 1827, Beethoven died of complications from pneumonia and liver failure. His final words were appropriately, "I shall hear in heaven."[64] Twenty thousand Viennese came to watch Beethoven's funeral procession[65] — that's one out of ten people in Vienna at the time.[66]

Patrick Kavanaugh's statement perhaps best summarizes Beethoven's life: "The judgment of a man's greatness is not only to be measured in the mission he accomplishes but in the obstacles he has overcome in the process."[67] Beethoven overcame innumerable difficulties to give mankind music of passion, joy, and emotion that has been cherished by every subsequent musical age.

Using the *How to Judge Greatness* lapbook pages, follow the directions to cut out and assemble the pieces. Adhere this activity to section #3 & 5 in your Beethoven lapbook. Take some time to ponder Patrick Kavanaugh's statement and write what you think it means in the space provided in the lapbook.

> *"The judgement of a man's greatness is not only to be measured in the mission he accomplishes but in the obstacles he has overcome in the process."*[67]
> **~Patrick Kavanaugh**

How Music is Created Part 4

In Week Three, you learned that the sound of a musical piece has great influence on personal preferences. We discussed several words that could describe songs.

Fast	Depressing	Harmonious	Slow	Powerful
Discordant	Loud	Calming	Elegant	Quiet
Uplifting	Spirited			

People respond to different kinds of music in a variety of ways. If you were to listen to music from each category above, you would feel something different with each song. Here are some ways that people may respond to music:

 Dance

 Cry

 Fall asleep

 March

 Shout

 Cover their ears

 Stop and listen

 Run

 Get Angry

 Smile

 Sing

Stand at Attention

Everyone has different emotional connections and responses to music. These differences are based on personality, upbringing, personal interests, and cultural heritage.

Music is constantly developing. It is often a reflection of society and its current views, as well as a way for people to express themselves in a creative way. Music transcends age, national boundaries, and economic status. It can be a powerful vehicle to promote change and brings great pleasure to many all around the world.

Choose five of the responses above and list a song that would make you want to react that way. Give the list to someone else and have them list five songs for the same responses. (Do not let them see your answers beforehand.) Were your song choices similar?

A Timeline of Beethoven's Life

1770

On December 16, Ludwig van Beethoven is born in Bonn, Germany. The "Boston Massacre" occurs between civilians and British troops in the American colonies. In Paris, the first public restaurant opens.

1773

On December 24, Beethoven's grandfather (also named Ludwig van Beethoven) dies. The Boston Tea Party, protesting the tea duty, occurs. The waltz becomes fashionable in Vienna.

1778

On March 26, Beethoven gives a public concert in Cologne, Germany. American colonies sign treaties with France and Holland, and reject the British peace offer. James Cook discovers Hawaii.

1781

Beethoven is taken out of school, at age 11, by his father.

1782

Beethoven's first pieces are published, the 9 Variations on a March by Dressler for piano. He becomes deputy court organist to Neefe, and his friendship with Wegeler and the von Breuning family begins. Thomas Greenville is sent from London to Paris to open peace talks with B. Franklin. Spain completes its conquest of Florida. The Montgolfier brothers construct a hot air balloon.

1783

Beethoven travels with his mother to Rotterdam. The Peace of Versailles is signed, and Britain recognizes the independence of the United States. Famine breaks out in Japan. Simon Bolivar, a Latin-American soldier/statesman, is born.

Using a separate sheet of 11x17 paper, create your own timeline of Beethoven's life. Draw a horizontal line in the middle of the paper. Cut out the date boxes and those on the following page. Adhere the dates in chronological order along the line. Match the correct event to each date. (Refer to the notes above.)

1787

Beethoven makes his first visit to Vienna and meets with Mozart. Beethoven's mother dies of consumption, and Beethoven returns to Bonn to provide for his family.

1790

Beethoven composes a cantata to honor Emperor Joseph II. Joseph Haydn visits Bonn and shares dinner with court musicians, including Beethoven.

1792

Beethoven leaves Bonn forever, traveling to Vienna to study under Haydn. Beethoven's father dies in Bonn in December. French forces invade Cologne and Bonn, and the court orchestra is abandoned.

1795

Beethoven gives his first public performance in Vienna (March 29).

1796

Beethoven takes a concert tour to Prague, Dresden, and Berlin with Prince Lichnowsky.

1797

Signs of Beethoven's deafness are apparent.

1805

Beethoven works on his opera *Fidelio*. The French invade Vienna.

1815

Brother Karl Beethoven dies and **Beethoven becomes guardian of his nephew Karl.** The Congress of Vienna closes.

1822

Beethoven begins work on the *Choral* **(Ninth) Symphony, which he completes in 1824.**

1827

Beethoven dies on March 26. He is buried March 29 in Vienna.

1770	1773	1778	1781
1782	1783	1787	1790
1792	1795	1796	1797
1805	1815	1822	1827

Beethoven

Beethoven's first pieces are published, the Nine Variations on a March by Dressler for piano. He becomes deputy court organist.

On December 24, Beethoven's grandfather dies.

Beethoven makes his first visit to Vienna and meets with Mozart. Beethoven's mother dies of consumption, and Beethoven returns to Bonn to provide for his family.

On December 16, Ludwig van Beethoven is born in Bonn, Germany.

Beethoven composes a cantata to honor Emperor Joseph II.

Beethoven gives his first public performance in Vienna (March 29).

On March 26, Beethoven gives a public concert in Cologne, Germany.

Beethoven travels to Vienna to study under Haydn. Beethoven's father dies in December.

Beethoven travels with his mother to Rotterdam.

Beethoven takes a concert tour to Prague, Dresden, and Berlin.

Signs of Beethoven's deafness are apparent.

Beethoven becomes guardian of his nephew Karl.

Beethoven begins work on the *Choral* (Ninth) Symphony.

Beethoven dies on March 26.

Beethoven is taken out of school, at age 11, by his father.

Beethoven works on his opera *Fidelio*.

Beethoven

Beethoven—Quiz

Ludwig Beethoven and the Chiming Tower Bells Quiz

Name: _____ Date: _____

Multiple Choice:
Circle the correct answer.

1. As a child, when would Ludwig often be given music lessons that would make him cry?
    a. lunchtime
    b. the middle of the night
    c. during church
    d. after school

2. What is the definition of a variation?
    a. making changes to a song, but the melody stays the same
    b. a slow dance
    c. playing a song from memory
    d. none of the above

3. What physical struggle did Beethoven develop as he grew older?
    a. numbness in his legs
    b. allergies
    c. blindness
    d. deafness

4. Who came to live with Beethoven in 1815?
    a. His friend, Jean Baptiste Cramer
    b. Antonio Salieri
    c. His nephew, Karl
    d. Dr. Schmidt

Fill in the Blank:
Mark an H beside each fact that describes a harpsichord, and a P beside each fact that describes a piano.

1. _____ The notes can be sustained and the keys have little resistance.
2. _____ It has five octaves.
3. _____ The volume is constant (either loud or soft).
4. _____ This instrument was introduced in the 18th century.
5. _____ The keys are slimmer and have to be hit hard for any sound to be produced.
6. _____ Varying dynamics can be produced simultaneously.
7. _____ The strings are plucked.
8. _____ Hammers strike the strings.
9. _____ This instrument was popular first.
10. _____ It has seven octaves.

Week One: Chapter One Comprehension Questions

1. His grandfather, Grandfather Beethoven, his dear companion, lived across the street, pp. 11, 14.
2. Father Johann sang in the elector's royal choir at the palace, and he gave violin and piano lessons, p. 11.
3. Ludwig learned to play piano and violin, p. 16.
4. He played in the garden with neighbor children, p. 17; he sat on the window seat in his house and dreamed, p. 19; he listened to the carillon, or bells, at the palace tower, pp. 19–20; he flew kites, p. 23.
5. Impromptu concerts were held in their home, pp. 11, 21.
6. The bell tower caught fire and the carillon crashed to the ground, p. 22.
7. In the middle of the night, after being awakened from his sleep Ludwig had music lessons, p. 27.
8. He wanted Ludwig to focus on his music, p. 31.

9. ### Week One: Life With the Beethovens Crossword Puzzle

```
K       T
A       U
R       B           P   T
E L E V E N         F   H
        R       C A R E E R
M U S I C I A N     O   I   E
O       U       C   M   F   E
Z       U       O   P   F
A       L       G O O D H E A R T E D
R       S       S   N       R
T       I   F A M I L Y
        S       O
        S E V E N T E E N
```

Week One: How Music is Created Part I

1. a.
2. e.
3. c.
4. f.
5. b.
6. d.

Week Two: Chapter Two Comprehension Questions

1. They sailed to Holland, to give musical concerts for the royal families, pp. 33–34.
2. He learned to play the organ, and his teacher's name was Brother Willibald, pp. 35, 37.
3. The music was too hard for Ludwig's small hands; however, Ludwig determined that he would simply play it when he was bigger, pp. 39–40.
4. Karl and Johann were his younger brothers, p. 41.
5. They made a special bower of birthday flowers for her, gave her a concert with the neighbors, and danced and enjoyed music all night, pp. 41–43.
6. He studied with organist Herr Neefe, pp. 46–47. Neefe predicted that Ludwig would be another Mozart someday, p. 49.
7. He became court conductor for the theater orchestra, p. 62. His own orchestra applauded him for his leadership, p. 63.
8. He challenged the soloist, Herr Heller, in chapel to stay on his part while Ludwig attempted to throw him off with his accompaniment, p. 65.

Week Two: Composers Three
(Answers derived from Haydn, Mozart, and Beethoven chapters.)

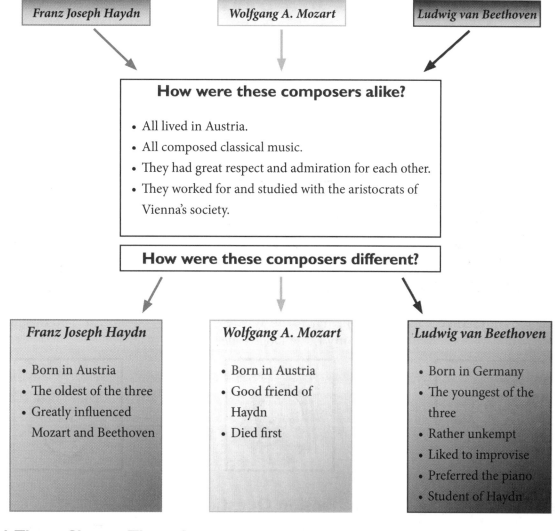

| Franz Joseph Haydn | Wolfgang A. Mozart | Ludwig van Beethoven |

How were these composers alike?

- All lived in Austria.
- All composed classical music.
- They had great respect and admiration for each other.
- They worked for and studied with the aristocrats of Vienna's society.

How were these composers different?

Franz Joseph Haydn

- Born in Austria
- The oldest of the three
- Greatly influenced Mozart and Beethoven

Wolfgang A. Mozart

- Born in Austria
- Good friend of Haydn
- Died first

Ludwig van Beethoven

- Born in Germany
- The youngest of the three
- Rather unkempt
- Liked to improvise
- Preferred the piano
- Student of Haydn

Week Three: Chapter Three Comprehension Questions

1. He went to the great Mozart in Vienna, p. 72.
2. He had to play special music at the palace to earn the extra money, p. 73; he dropped a coin while putting it in his savings box and lost it through a crack in the floor, p. 73; he used the money to help his family buy clothes and food, p. 76.
3. Mozart was not overly impressed at first. Vienna was filled with many other young men who played the keyboard as well as Ludwig, p. 78. When Ludwig began improvising a theme of Mozart's, however, Mozart's opinion changed, p. 79. He predicted that Beethoven would make a noise in the world someday.
4. Mother Beethoven died and he had to earn a living for his father and brothers, p. 82.
5. Stephen Breuning, a pupil, p. 82; Count Waldstein, p. 86; Prince Lichnowsky in Vienna, p. 88; and Wegeler, a friend, p. 95, all helped Ludwig.
6. Joseph Haydn, p. 88.
7. He was overwhelmed and couldn't find the time to compose as he wished, p. 95. He also did not like having to dress carefully, care for his beard, attend dinner at four, and so forth, p. 95.
8. Sickness had settled in his ears so that they buzzed continually, and he couldn't hear clearly, p. 100. He determined to leave Vienna before his friends knew he was going deaf, p. 101.

Beethoven

Week Three: Keyboard Cousins

1. P
2. H
3. H
4. P
5. H

6. P
7. H
8. P
9. H
10. P

Week Three: How Music is Created Part 3

Possible Answers:

"Happy Birthday to You"

Happy

"Twinkle, Twinkle Little Star"

Calm

"Pop, Goes the Weasel"

Surprised

"Three Blind Mice"

Disgusted

"Oh, Where Oh Where, Has my Little Dog Gone?"

Sad

"America, The Beautiful"

Proud

Week Four: Reading Comprehension Questions

1. He wore his favorite old coat, went for walks in the meadows and mountains, ran through the rains, sat beneath trees to compose, and let the music in his mind carry him away, pp. 103, 105.
2. He carried a little pad of paper, or a notebook, on which to write, p. 104.
3. Nature offered him peace and helped him to remember sounds so that he could write out melodies in his notebook, pp. 107, 116.
4. He stomped and pounded around the room, upsetting ink on the piano, p.106; he danced away from a festival, waving his arms to the music in his head, p. 110; he greeted dinner guests in a nightcap and apron, pp. 117–118; his rooms were in disarray, with boots wrapped in music, p. 118; his pianos had no legs because he moved so often, p. 119; he poured cold water on his head while he composed, but he didn't consider that it would leak through to apartments below his, p. 120–121.
5. His nephew Karl, who had been left in Beethoven's care when Karl's father died greeted him, p. 133.
6. He enjoyed coffee — sixty beans per cup, p. 135.
7. They asked him to give the premier performances of his Ninth Symphony and Mass, Missa Solemnis, for them, p.140. Moreover, they applauded and waved their handkerchiefs to him to show their appreciation at the close of the concert, p. 143.

Week Four: A Timeline of Beethoven's Life

1770
On December 16, Ludwig van Beethoven is born in Bonn, Germany.

1773
On December 24, Beethoven's grandfather dies.

1778
On March 26, Beethoven gives a public concert in Cologne, Germany.

1781
Beethoven is taken out of school, at age 11, by his father.

1782
Beethoven's first pieces are published, aVarations on a March by Dressler for piano. He becomes deputy court organist.

1783
Beethoven travels with his mother to Rotterdam.

1787
Beethoven makes his first visit to Vienna and meets with Mozart. Beethoven's mother dies of consumption, and Beethoven returns to Bonn to provide for his family.

1790
Beethoven composes a cantata to honor Emperor Joseph II.

1792
Beethoven travels to Vienna to study under Haydn. Beethoven's father dies in December.

1795
Beethoven gives his first public performance in Vienna (March 29).

1796
Beethoven takes a concert tour to Prague, Dresden, and Berlin.

1797
Signs of Beethoven's deafness are apparent.

1805
Beethoven works on his opera *Fidelio*.

1815
Beethoven becomes guardian of his nephew Karl.

1822
Beethoven begins work on the *Choral* (Ninth) Symphony.

1827
Beethoven dies on March 26.

Beethoven

Ludwig Beethoven and the Chiming Tower Bells Quiz

Multiple Choice:

1. b.
2. a.

3. d.
4. c.

Fill in the Blank:

1. P
2. H
3. H
4. P
5. H
6. P

7. H
8. P
9. H
10. P

Weekly Lesson Outline

Paganini

(Activities marked with an * are required in order to meet national music appreciation standards.)

Week One:

- Read Chapter 1*
- Answer Comprehension Questions
- Character Qualities
- Tidbits of Interest
- Assemble Lapbook Folder
- Italy, Color by Number

- "Many Hands Make Light Work"
- Spaghetti Soup
- Variations on a Theme Booklet (LB)
- Learn A Little Italian Flashcards (LB)
- Instruments Paganini Played (LB)
- Develop Personal Music Criteria*

Week Two:

- Read Chapter 2 & 3*
- Answer Comprehension Question
- Character Qualities
- Tidbits of Interest
- Quoteworthy

- The Music Paganini Played (LB)
- What Is So Special About a Violin? (LB)
- Concert Advertisements (LB)
- Is Money a Good Motivator?
- Personal Music Preferences*

Week Three:

- Read Chapters 4 & 5*
- Answer Comprehension Questions
- Character Qualities
- Tidbits of Interest
- The Little Corporal (Napoleon Bonaparte) (LB)

- Knight of the Golden Spur
- Paganini Reviews*
- The Jokester
- The Language of Music
- Using the Music That You Enjoy*

Week Four:

- Read Chapter 6*
- Answer Comprehension Questions
- Listen to Music Disc 5, tracks 40-41*
- Character Qualities

- Tidbits of Interest
- Crossing the English Channel (LB)
- A Timeline of Paganini's Life (LB)*
- Music, the Language of the Heart

Chapter One Comprehension Questions

1. What major body of water was Nicolò running to in this chapter? What industry was apparently key in the city? _____

_____

2. What instruments are mentioned in this chapter?

_____

3. For what purpose did Antonio teach Nico to play the violin? _____

_____

_____

4. Provide two evidences that Nico's violin sessions under director Servetto's leading were not easy rehearsals. _____

_____

_____

_____

5. Who promised Nico's mother, Teresa, that Nico would be the world's greatest violinist? _____

_____

6. What were some of the opportunities Signor Costa, music director of the Cathedral, gave Nico that he may not have otherwise enjoyed? _____

_____

_____

7. Based on this chapter, what would you say "variations" means in music? _____

_____

1685	Johann Sebastian Bach	1750
1685	George Frederic Handel	1759
1732	Franz Joseph Haydn	1809
1756	Wolfgang A. Mozart	1791
1770	Ludwig van Beethoven	1827
1782	**Nicolò Paganini**	1840
1797	Franz Schubert	1828

Character Qualities

Fun-Loving (*pp. 8, 10, 34, 66*) – Nico asked Romano to join him in the fisherman's sing-song sales pitch. He enjoyed his father's fu-ni-cu-li song and composed a cheerful French military song. Nico also liked to eat cake. He could not remember a time before the festival in Lucca when he had played his violin for sheer fun and joy.

Diligent (*pp. 14, 19, 24, 30*) – Paganini learned violin at five years old. He started playing in the streets to earn coins. He also practiced for six hours in a locked room. Nicolò became the Cathedral's soloist and he studied with as many masters as possible.

Tidbits of Interest

Page 7: Genoa was a seaport city in northern Italy. It was the birthplace of Christopher Columbus in 1451.

Pages 8–12, 14, 23: Nicolò had a rare musical ability. He had "perfect pitch," which means he could naturally recognize notes that were played off key and tune his own instruments without the aid of a tuning device.

Pages 10, 11: Paganini had the measles at age four and scarlet fever at the age of seven.

Page 24: Nico's father taught him to play the mandolin at the age of five, then violin when he was seven years old. He began to compose music before his eighth birthday. His father imposed very strict demands upon his young son and expected him to play with perfection. When Paganini did not play to his father's satisfaction, he would punish Nico with a cane until he improved. He also made Nico practice for his supper, pushing his son to play better and better. Nico was always skinny and sickly because of the poor treatment he endured during his childhood.

Paganini

Italy Color by Number

Paganini was born in Genoa, Italy and visited each of the other towns shown on the map below.

Here are five interesting facts about Italy that you may not have known before:
1. Soccer (football) is the most popular sport in Italy.
2. There are many volcanoes in Italy (Etna, Stromboli, and Vesuvius are all currently active).
3. Italians call their country Italia.
4. Over 75% of Italy is covered with hills and mountains.
5. Italy has the second lowest birth rate in Europe. Most families only have one child.

After you finish coloring your map, you may want to cut out and adhere the smaller map, included with the lapbook pages, to section #8 in your Paganini lapbook.

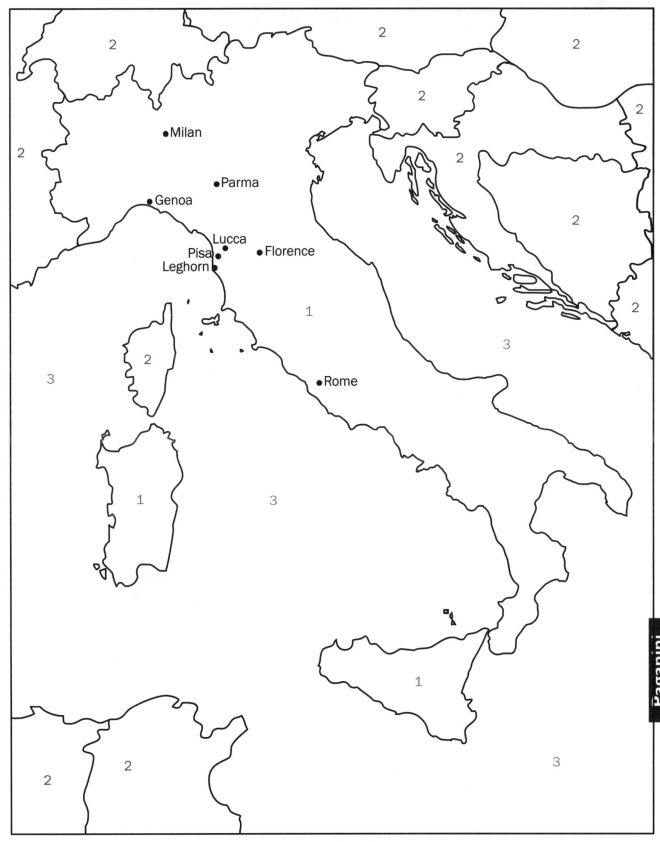

Color the map following this color code.

1 - Green
2 - Brown
3 - Blue

Paganini

"Many Hands Make Light Work"

Nicolò's family was very poor. They often did not have enough food to eat and were cold and hungry. Even at a very early age, Nico went to work so he could earn money to help his family. When he was just six years old, he began to play in the streets of Genoa. Later, he played at weddings and festivals to help pay for his lessons.

It takes a lot of work to care for a family. Each person must help out as much as they can. When everyone shares the responsibility, much good is accomplished. A famous quote says, "Many hands make light work."

What can you do to help your family? Even if you have daily chores or assigned responsibilities, there is always more that can be done. Look around your house or ask an adult if there is a job you could do to be extra helpful.

Disclaimer: Make sure that you ask an adult to help you or get permission before you tackle a new responsibility.

Take time today to do this extra job around the house. (Remember, it is even better when you do it with a happy spirit!)

Spaghetti Soup

On page 25 of *Paganini, Master of Strings*, Mrs. Paganini brings Nicolò some spaghetti soup. This hearty soup[1] would have helped to nourish the boy after his long day of practicing.

Spaghetti Soup

2 tablespoons vegetable oil
½ pound skinless, boneless chicken breast halves, cut into cubes
1 medium onion, chopped
1 large carrot, chopped
1 stalk celery, finely chopped
2 cloves garlic, minced

4 cups chicken broth
1 (10.75 ounce) can condensed tomato soup
1 cup water
3 ounces uncooked spaghetti, broken into 1 inch pieces
2 tablespoons chopped fresh parsley (optional)

Heat 1 tablespoon oil in a saucepot over medium-high heat. Add the chicken and cook until it is browned, stirring often. Remove the chicken. Stir in the remaining oil and heat over medium heat. Add the onion and cook for 1 minute. Add the carrots and cook for 1 minute. Add the celery and garlic and cook for 1 minute. Stir in the broth, soup and water. Heat to a boil. Stir in the pasta. Cook for 10 minutes or until pasta is tender. Add the chicken and parsley, if desired, and heat through.

Maybe you would enjoy eating this soup for supper tonight.

Variations on a Theme Booklet

Nicolò Paganini had a brilliant mind when it came to composing, even as a young boy. He once said, "Why- it just ran into my head, and out again on the strings."[2] He also liked to create variations of a specific musical theme. This simply meant that he would start with a recognizable tune and alter it many times throughout a song. In *Paganini, Master of Strings*, the author provides a beautiful description of one such occasion. "Simply [the song] started, then grew more difficult as the same melody was played in many different ways,- now sad, now merry, and ending in a spirited march." (pp. 33, 34)

Using the *Variations on a Theme* lapbook pages, follow the directions to cut out and assemble the pieces. Adhere this activity to sections #13 & 14 in your Paganini lapbook.

Learn a Little Italian Flashcards

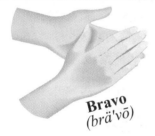

Bravo
(brä'vō)

Pesce
(pā'shā)

piu
(p'yoo)

Mrs. Wheeler introduces her readers to some Italian words throughout the story of Paganini.

Using the *Learn a Little Italian Flashcards* lapbook pages, follow the directions to cut out and assemble the pieces. Adhere this activity vertically to section #15 in your Paganini lapbook.

Each flashcard shows the page number where the English or Italian word is used in the story. Have fun leaning and using these words with your family and friends.

Signor
(sēn'yôr)

Arrivederci
(ar'rē-ve-der-chē)

bambino
(bam'bē-nō)

Lire
(lē'rĕ)

Signora
(sin-yôr'a)

Instruments Paganini Played

Using the *Instruments Paganini Played* lapbook pages, follow the directions to cut out and assemble the pieces. Adhere this activity to the top of section #1 in your Paganini lapbook.

Viola   Mandolin   Violin   Guitar

Develop Personal Music Criteria (4th-6th grade activity)

As you learn how music is made, its role in society, and the influence it can have, it is important for you to develop personal standards concerning your musical choices.

Throughout this activity you will be developing criteria ("a standard on which a judgment or decision may be based"[3]) for specific musical works. You will also learn how to apply these standards to the music you hear.

One way to make a clear decision about a particular song is to think about positives (+) and negatives (-).

Ask yourself these questions:
1. Do I like this style of music?
2. Is the sound of the instruments and voices of high quality?
3. What is the message being communicated by this song?

Using the positive (+) and negative (-) signs, evaluate songs that you hear. You can use a chart like this to help you make your decision. Write down a song's name, and then give it a positive or negative mark in each category.

Name of Song:	Style of Music	Sound Quality	Song's Message
Beethoven's 5th Symphony	+	+	+
Dying Cowboy	+	-	-
Meet me in St. Louis, Louis	-	+	+

This method can help you make better musical choices concerning a song's musical quality and message.

Throughout the week, pay attention to the music around you. (TV, radio, in stores and restaurants, etc...) Use the following chart to record the songs you hear and rate each one based on the questions above. Pay close attention to the message (lyrics and music) of each song and the sound quality. The results may surprise you!

Name of Song:	Style of Music	Sound Quality	Song's Message

After you have spent some time evaluating the music you hear, think about your personal preferences. Music is a direct reflection of your beliefs and standards. It can reveal your inner attitude and thoughts. Developing criteria can help you make better music choices and become a more discerning listener.

Look at your chart again. Talk to your parents or another trusted adult and ask them to help you develop specific standards for your musical choices. Create a chart, similar to the one already used, but insert your personal criteria. List all of your favorite songs and see if they match the standards you made. Continue to use these standards to help you develop your own personal music preferences.

Chapter Two Comprehension Questions

1. When Nico's abilities exceeded any further training in Genoa, to whom did Nico go in Parma for more teaching? Provide one of this teacher's three musical jobs. _____

_____

_____

2. Signor Rolla was so sick, he was not planning on taking any new students. How did Nico convince Rolla otherwise? _____

_____

3. What did Master Ghiretti instruct Nico to do? _____

_____

4. Provide at least one proof from this chapter that Nico was very dedicated to playing his violin well. _____

_____

_____

5. What title was given to Nico after his first concert as a teenager? _____

_____

6. What were two of the ways Nico bartered for things he needed for a personal concert tour?

_____

_____

_____

7. What rare violin does Nico get to play at a violin shop? _____

_____

_____

Chapter Three Comprehension Questions

1. How did Nicolò earn his keep at homes and inns along his way to Lucca's festival? _____

   _____

2. How did Nico show that he still cared for his family at home when he gave concerts in Lucca?

   _____

   _____

3. What contest had the Parma painter, Pasini, devised that so intrigued Nicolò he walked 100 miles to Pasini's home? _____

   _____

   _____

4. Name two responsibilities that Nico's young lawyer companion, Germi, undertook when he became Nicolò's manager. (There are several options.) _____

   _____

   _____

   _____

5. What did Nico do to have money for his new clothes that made giving his next concert very difficult? _____

   _____

   _____

6. How did Nicolò become the owner of a Guarenius violin? _____

   _____

Character Qualities

Perfectionism *(pp. 46, 47)* – Paganini kept practicing and playing works or portions of compositions until they were perfect.

Clever *(pp. 54, 55, 60)* – Nicolò planned bartering options for getting shoes and clothes he needed for a personal concert tour. He also timed the talk with his father to let him tour alone.

Daring *(pp. 75, 81)* – Nico dared to try sight-reading Pasini's composition, even walking 100 miles to get to his home in order to try to win the Stradivarius violin. He dared (or perhaps risked is a better word) to pawn his violin in ordered to pay some debts he owed, not knowing how he would get his beloved violin back.

Tidbits of Interest

Chapter 2:

Page 39: "La Carmagnole" was the name of a short jacket worn by working class militants in the French controlled portion of Italy. The title was from a French song made popular during the French Revolution involving a tune and a wild dance. Apparently it is a revolutionary song, in general, and came to convey the idea that "everything will be okay."

Page 46: Alessandro Rolla was a true virtuoso and composer. He was particularly skilled in the viola and taught Paganini many of the musical "tricks" that later propelled Nico to great fame.

Page 48: It wasn't long before Nicolò outpaced all of his tutors. He then began to train himself, finding new ways of bouncing the bow and plucking the strings. He worked and practiced for two years before his first concert tour.

Page 51: Nicolò was a young teenager when he went on his first concert tour. He was one of the first musicians to tour as a solo act. One source describes it this way. "He became one of the first 'superstars' of public concertizing. He made a fortune as a touring musician, and was uncanny in his ability to charm an audience."[4] During one year alone, he gave more than one hundred concerts in forty different towns.

Chapter 3:

Page 68: Paganini struggled with poor health all throughout his life. His emaciated condition and recurring fevers may be traced to neurasthenia, stemming from his childhood attacks of measles, scarlet fever, and hypersensitive skin. He also received treatments for another illness (syphilis) that involved mercury and opium, which resulted in stomach ulcers and rotting gums. In the early 1830's, when Paganini first consulted with Dr. Francesco Bennati, he already had all his bottom teeth removed and part of his lower jaw removed because of infected bone.

Page 72: "Germi" was Luigi Germi, an amateur musician and professional lawyer. Germi acted on Nicolò's behalf in Genoa for many years while he was on tour. Much of Paganini's biographies are based on correspondence between himself and Germi.

Page 77: Paganini won the Stradivarius from the famous painter. Then he worked and played so heartily for three years that his health broke. A noblewoman took pity on him, inviting him to her castle where she cared for him for several years. He did not touch his violin in all that time.

Page 84: A wealthy businessman lent Nico a Guarneri violin for a concert in Leghorn. The man was so impressed by Nicolò's playing that he told Paganini to keep the violin. "Keep the instrument, dear Paganini, and look upon it as a souvenir."[5] It is said that the Guarnerius violin was Nico's favorite and most prized possession. It was the last thing he touched before he died.

Quoteworthy

When Nico met the great teacher, in Parma, Signor Rolla said "Work, boy, work is what does it, eh?… think carefully as you practice." (p. 46)

This principle has been taught throughout the centuries, and is still a valuable truth for us today.

"No one has ever drowned in sweat."
~Lou Holtz

"There is no substitute for hard work."
~Thomas A. Edison

"Go to the ant, thou sluggard; consider her ways, and be wise: which having no guide, overseer, or ruler, provideth her meat in the summer, and gathereth her food in the harvest. How long wilt thou sleep, O sluggard? When wilt thou arise out of thy sleep? Yet a little sleep, a little slumber, a little folding of the hands to sleep: So shall thy poverty come as one that travelleth, and thy want as an armed man."
~Proverbs 6

"The daily grind of hard work gets a person polished."
~Unknown

"Opportunity is missed by most people because it is dressed in overalls and looks like work."
~Thomas A. Edison

The Music Paganini Played

Nicolò Paganini was truly the "Master of Strings!" His compositions were elegant in form, rich in harmony, and clever in their instrumentation.[6] A bit of a showman, Nico liked to impress his audiences with his unusual skill. He could play twelve notes a second and cover three octaves in a single hand span, because of his unusual flexibility.[7]

Paganini's twenty-four capriccios for the violin were believed to be unplayable until he proved otherwise.[8] His most difficult piece, Caprice No. 24 in A Minor, and his other caprices are still a measuring stick in identifying virtuosos.[9]

Using *The Music Paganini Played* lapbook pages, follow the directions to cut out and assemble the pieces. Adhere this activity vertically to section #2 in your Paganini lapbook.

Caprice   Lullaby   Concerto   Sonata   Quartet   Fugue

What Is So Special About a Violin?

Using the *What Is So Special About a Violin?* lapbook pages, follow the directions to cut out and assemble the pieces. Adhere this activity vertically to section #10 in your Paganini lapbook.

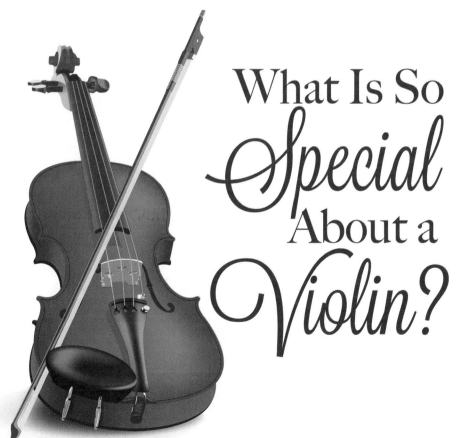

Concert Advertisements

During Nico's younger years, his father created posters promoting upcoming concerts. One of the concerts was to fund a trip to visit the great teacher, Signor Rolla.

Grand Paganini Concert
Funds Needed for Study
Come One, Come All
Help the Wonder Violinist to Greater Fame

Fundraisers are still popular today. It is a good way to raise money and is often used to support a specific cause.

Is there a special organization for which you would like to raise money? Design a poster promoting your fundraiser. Include details like time, date, cause, event, and cost.

Perhaps you and your family could do this fundraiser for real. It would be exciting to see how much money you could raise for your organization!

Is Money a Good Motivator?

Several times throughout this story, Nico and his father proclaim their excitement over the great riches his talent would bring them.

> As they started homeward, Antonio laughed happily.
> "Soon you may play as well as the boy Mozart!" he cried. "And then
> we can live in better quarters. Why, we might even have a fine car-
> riage, like the one coming towards us." (p. 26)

> "But Romano, could we catch enough fish so that we could live in
> beautiful houses and ride around in fine carriages?" (p. 29)

> His father went on jubilantly, "Then houses and lands and carriages
> will be ours for the asking, when we return home again." (p. 48)

> "And now we are rich, Father!" cried the children. "Houses and
> lands and carriages and beds we will have!" (p. 52)

Although Nico did use his earnings to help his family (pp. 68, 113, 114), and his father warned that it was best to gain wealth slowly (p. 52), money was definitely a driving factor for both of these men.

The question must then be asked - **Did money make Nico truly happy?**

The answer is a resounding, **"No!"** Mrs. Wheeler demonstrates this throughout her book. His relationship with his father was strained, he made himself sick on food and parties, and he struggled to find peace and quiet away from his admiring fans.

History reveals that as a young man, Paganini did not respond well to his instant success. At nineteen- after some lost fortunes to gambling—he vanished into the villa of a mysterious countess, supposedly for several years.[10]

Probably the best description of this emptiness that money could not fill is found on pages 131, 132 of *Paganini, Master of Strings*.

> "Happy times there were for Nicolò, but lonely times, as well. Often his thoughts wandered to Italy… and [his] young son, Achille… How he longed to see him. Nicolò sighed over his simple breakfast. Ah, yes, it would be good to have the child with him. But it would mean giving up his concerts. Concerts! Always they had kept him from home… Any sum that he asked was given without a murmur, and Nicolò grew very rich, indeed, as the months rolled by. But many days there were when he was far from well… Letters from France or Italy gave him the greatest joy…"

What did Nicolò finally realize was his greatest treasure? *His son, Achillino and his dear friends from home!* (pp. 138, 150) This was the treasure that money could not buy. These people brought him joy and satisfaction that could not be found in lands, houses, or fine carriages. No amount of money in the world could equal the pleasure he found from being with those he loved.

Do you ever think,

"If only I had _____, then I would be happy!"

or

"I wish I could just have _____, then I wouldn't need anything else."

Stop for a moment and think about the things you already have right now.

List ten people or things that bring you joy.

1. _____
2. _____
3. _____
4. _____
5. _____
6. _____
7. _____
8. _____
9. _____
10. _____

The next time you start to feel ungrateful, remember this list and focus on the good things you do have. Remember Nicolò Paganini, and the lesson he learned about <u>true</u> wealth and happiness!

Personal Music Preferences

Using the music vocabulary below, explain your personal music preferences. Circle the words that best describe the kind of music you enjoy. You may circle more than one in each category. (Music vocabulary definitions are from Cal Poly College of Liberal Arts, San Luis Obispo, CA.[11])

1. <u>Type of Song</u>

   Instrumental (music performed by instruments; no lyrics)

   Vocal (music with lyrics; with or without instruments)

2. <u>Style of Music</u>

   A cappella Music (singing without instrumental accompaniment)

   Classical Music (music written from approximately 1750 to 1815)

   Twentieth-Century Music (music written from approximately 1900 to the present)

   Religious Music (music performed or written for religious use)

3. <u>Dynamic Level</u> (the relative volume level in music)

   piano (p - soft / quiet)

   forte (f - loud / strong)

4. <u>Number of Performers</u>

   Solo (one performer)

   Ensemble (the possible groupings of singers or instrumentalists) (duet - two performers, trio – three, quartet – four, quintet – five, sextet – six, septet – seven, octet – eight)

5. <u>Musical Tempo</u>

   Adagio (slow)

   Moderato (moderate)

   Allegro (fast)

Paganini

5ᵗʰ-6ᵗʰ Grade Activity:
Write a brief paragraph describing why other people may have different musical preferences than you do.

Think about the terms above and what you have already studied about music's ability to communicate values and ideals before you begin to write.

(Remember to include a topic sentence, several supporting sentences, and a concluding sentence in your paragraph.)

_____

_____

_____

_____

_____

_____

_____

_____

Paganini

Chapter Four Comprehension Questions

1. What royal person was impressed by Nicolò's concert in Lucca, and what position was Nico commanded to take afterwards? _____

_____

_____

2. What were two of Nicolò's responsibilities as the orchestra director? (There are several options.)

_____

_____

_____

3. After being released from his duties at the princess's court, how did Nico make a living?

_____

_____

4. How did Nico help Gioacchino Rossini in Rome? _____

_____

_____

5. Under what circumstances did Nico meet the cellist Ciandelli? _____

_____

_____

_____

Chapter Five Comprehension Questions

1. What were some of the things accomplished in Genoa when Nicolò was healthy enough to visit? _____

_____

_____

2. Provide three proofs that Vienna was excited about and pleased by Paganini's visit. _____

_____

_____

3. What other cities or countries did Nico visit during this concert tour, besides Vienna, Austria. _

_____

_____

4. Why were concerts in London unique? (There are two options here.) _____

_____

_____

5. Why did audience members want to touch Paganini?_____

_____

_____

Character Qualities

Submissive *(pp. 91–93)* – Nicolò submitted to Princess Elise's command to join her court as the orchestra director. He stayed under poor conditions and low pay. He even humbly submitted to get permission to play concerts in other cities to supplement his income.

Talented *(pp. 91, 105)* – Paganini composed an entire sonata on one string in less than a week. He developed works with double tone, like "Prayer from Moses," and he wrote orchestra music for Rossini's opera. He could also play on the cello as well as the violin.

Compassionate *(pp. 96, 118, 109)* – Nicolò provided a comfortable home for his family. He played a lullaby for his driver's wife, and he agreed to help out Jehu, a cab driver, by letting him paint Paganini's name on the side of the cab, which increased Jehu's cab traffic. Nicolò also played in the streets to raise money for a poor Italian boy.

True to His Word *(p. 122)* – Even when he had to walk thirty miles and arrived late for a concert because he missed his carriage, Nicolò stayed and performed the concert a day later.

Adventurous *(pp. 122, 123)* – Nicolò risked leaving the safety of Italy to give concerts in other cities around Europe; he was especially challenged to play in Paris, the music center of the world, where he felt his true abilities as a musician would be tested.

Tidbits of Interest

Chapter 4:

Page 91: As director of Princess Elise's court orchestra, Nicolò only earned a pittance of a salary, just over 1,000 francs a year. In Paganini's own words it was "a piffling little salary."[12]

Page 91: After being challenged by the Princess, Paganini composed a piece for the G string alone. He called it *Napoleon's Sonata* and presented it in time for the emperor's birthday.

Page 97: Paganini gave the impression of being filled with some special kind of power or "electricity" that left him drained of energy, perspiring heavily, and shaking all over when he was finished playing.

Page 103: Gioacchino Rossini was a composer who was famous in Italy for his operas from 1810-1823. He then experienced success in Paris until 1829. The Revolution of 1830 limited any further presentations. Rossini wrote three dozen or so operas, the most recognized being *The Barber of Seville.*

Chapter 5:

Page 112: A person who makes and repairs violins is called a luthier.

Page 115: Nico's gaunt appearance, white skin, black clothing, eerie walk, and rolling white eyes all added to the bizarre nature of his concerts. Plus all his teeth dropped out, leaving a toothless grin.

Page 116, 117: Paganini's reception in Vienna was a huge success. His portraits were sold by the hundreds, his face was reproduced in sugar on cakes and in jewels on snuffboxes. Bread was shaped like a violin, and "a la Paganini" gloves were made with a "bow embroidered on the right hand and a violin on the left."

Page 122: While touring in Germany during 1829 and 1830, Paganini gave more than one hundred concerts in forty different towns.

The Little Corporal (Napoleon Bonaparte)

During much of Paganini's life, Napoleon Bonaparte and his family ruled Italy. Chapter four opens with Paganini being hired to direct Princess Elise's royal court and compose music for her enjoyment.

Using *The Little Corporal* newspaper lapbook pages, follow the directions to cut out and assemble the pieces. Adhere this activity to sections #3-6 in your Paganini lapbook.

NOTE:
In 1808, Napoleon promoted his sister to grand Duchess of Tuscany, which expanded her domain greatly. She spent most of her time in Florence, Pisa, and Poggio.

When Napoleon's empire fell, Elisa began a life of exile and homelessness. She was eventually allowed to live at Trieste, under a false name, the Countess of Campignano. The Princess died at this place in 1820. After receiving news of her death, Napoleon responded by saying, "I used to think that death had forgotten our family; but now he has begun to strike. He is taking Elisa, and I shall soon follow her." Ironically, he died less than six months from that time.[13]

Napoleon Bonaparte

Napoleon's Empire

The EMPIRE of NAPOLEON about 1810

The Knight of the Golden Spur

While in Rome, Nico Paganini was made a Knight of the Golden Spur. The **Order of the Golden Spur** was an honorary knighthood bestowed by the pope, which required no military obligations. Paganini received this honor in 1827 from Pope Leo XII. (This honor was also bestowed on Wolfgang Mozart when he was fourteen years old.)

Each order of chivalry had its own badge, which was easily recognizable when worn. This is a picture of the badge awarded to Nico Paganini in 1827.[14]

Design and draw a badge decoration. Determine what you want the badge to look like and what trait you want to honor. (Remember to keep it uniform and simple so that it can be quickly recognized.)

The Order of

Paganini

MUSIC REVIEWS

"Whenever anything wonderful was spoken of [we] named [it] Paganini."[15]
–MENDELSSOHN, LISZT, AND CHOPIN, classical composers

"I shall not be able to sleep, for thinking of these songs of the strings."[16]
–LUIGI CHERUBINI, Italian composer

"It was the Paganini-inspired Liszt, stirred by the emotional appeals of a Paganini-inspired Chopin who set Wagner on his triumphant way in operas."[17]
–ROBERT FLOOD, author

"For the first time, the violin sings in all its glory. Never have I heard such sadness, such joy from four slender strings."[18]
–FRANZ LIST, classical composer

"Paganini [is a] Shakespeare among violinists because he [can] blend humor, coquetry, teasing, deep sorrow and the most agonizing heartache, with no disturbing transitions as a whole."[19]
–A REVIEWER FROM DRESDEN

"The greatest violinist that ever lived [with] brilliant and radical innovations in violin technique."[20]
–JASON EARLS, author

Write a review of Paganini's music, expressing your reaction to his musical style, ability, and compositions.

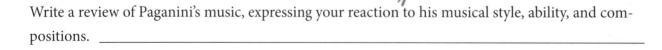

The Jokester

It is important to have fun with music and enjoy the instrument you play. Although Paganini was not always kind with his jokes, he did enjoy having fun with his violin and loved playing it. He found great pleasure in music.

Here is an example of Paganini's playful spirit:

Nico Paganini became famous for the ability to make animal sounds with his musical instruments. While he was in Italy, giving several well received concerts, "he was criticized for having played jokes in his performance, such as imitating cries of animals and other strange sounds."[21]

To help you remember how much fun music can be, here are some musical jokes[22] for you to read. Enjoy!

Q: Why couldn't the athlete listen to her music?
A: Because she broke the record!

Q: What makes music on your head?
A: A head band!

Q: What part of the turkey is musical?
A: The drumstick!

Q: What is the difference between a fish and a piano?
A: You can't tuna fish!

Q: What has forty feet and sings?
A: The school choir!

Q: Why did the girl sit on the ladder to sing?
A: She wanted to reach the high notes!

Paganini

The Language of Music

Paganini accepted the invitation of Prince Metternich to play for the people of Vienna, Austria. However, Nico could only speak Italian. How would he be able to communicate in this new land?

"A sudden thought made [Paganini] pause. How would he get along in a country whose language was so different from his own? Ah, well, **surely everyone could understand the language of music**."

~ *Paganini, Master of Strings*, **p. 115**

What is the "language of music"? Can everyone understand it?

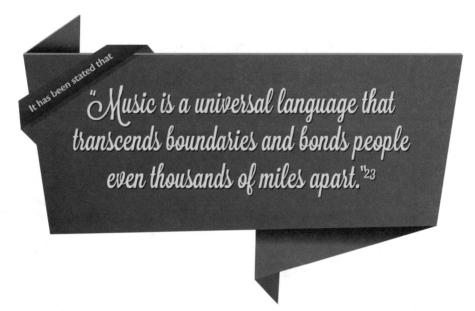

It has been stated that "Music is a universal language that transcends boundaries and bonds people even thousands of miles apart."[23]

Music can be appreciated and enjoyed by anyone, from any culture. Language barriers, social status, and education cannot hinder the ear from hearing and "understanding" the sounds of music. Even though you may not be able to understand the words of a song written in another language, you are still able to appreciate the music that the instruments are playing. Music is truly a universal language.

Use the following songs to test this truth for yourself. As you listen to music from different cultures, think about the instruments that are playing and the musical notes you are hearing.

Enjoy the sounds of music from other lands.

Listen to Music Disc 5, track 36 – Japanese instrumental music
Listen to Music Disc 5, track 37 – Mexican music and song
Listen to Music Disc 5, track 38 – Polish polka
Listen to Music Disc 5, track 39 – Jewish music and song

Using the Music That You Enjoy (5th-6th grade activity)

Read the following questions thoughtfully. Discuss the questions with an adult that you respect, and then answer them honestly.

How does the music that you enjoy **affect** you? How does it **affect** those around you?

Webster's Dictionary Definition: affect-"to produce an effect on someone or something: to cause a change"[24]

_____

_____

_____

_____

_____

_____

What are some of the ways that you use music in your daily **experiences**?
What are some specific ways that your musical choices could be used for good in your daily **experiences**?

Webster's Dictionary Definition: experiences-"the process of doing and seeing things and of having things happen to you"[25]

_____

_____

_____

_____

_____

_____

Paganini

Chapter Six Comprehension Questions

1. How long does Paganini claim it has been since he has practiced? _____
_____

2. What were two of the ways Paganini impressed the audience at the Paris Opera House?
_____
_____
_____
_____

3. What did Paganini do to encourage the master Berlioz? (There are several options here.)
_____
_____
_____
_____

4. Provide two ways that Nicolò showed his utter devotion to his son Achillino. _____
_____
_____
_____
_____
_____

5. What was one of Paganini's favorite drinks for breakfast? _____
_____
_____

6. What did the Duchess of Parma plan to do for Nicolò Paganini? _____
_____
_____
_____

Character Qualities

Dedicated (*p. 126*) – The years of dedication in practicing the violin early in his life now allowed Paganini to play with the orchestra in record time. Nicolò was dedicated to making life as pleasant and memorable as possible for his son Achille. He played the violin for others for fifty years!

Simple (*p. 141*) – Nicolò liked certain aspects of his life to be simple and plain – especially his food: hot cocoa, soup, chamomile tea, chicken pie, and such. His main goal towards the end of his life was simply to make his son content and poverty free.

Paganini's Character Trait Wheel (Review)
Paganini was a masterful musician, and even though he was not always careful in his actions and choices, he did demonstrate many valuable traits.

Using the *Nicolò Paganini's Character Trait Wheel* lapbook pages, follow the directions to cut out and assemble the pieces. Adhere this activity to sections #11 & 12 in your Paganini lapbook.

Tidbits of Interest

Page 126: Paganini rarely rehearsed after his 30th birthday, but in his formative years he often practiced up to fifteen hours a day behind closed doors.

Pages 132, 136, 137: Nico and Antonia Bianchi had a son whom they named, Achille Cyrus Alessandro Paganini. They nicknamed him Achillino. Their relationship was stormy and full of quarrels, but Nicolò loved Achillino. When Antonia left Paganini, she took as much money and wealth as she could carry, but she left him Achillino, Nico's pride and joy.

Page 133: Paganini was a virtuoso, unrivaled even by modern musicians. He could play his "Perpetual Motion" piece–"with the fullest expressiveness"–in three minutes flat, which means 126 beats each minute, eighth notes to the beat.[26]

Pages 129, 130: Throughout his musical career, Paganini used over one thousand violin strings. Most of those strings were broken on purpose, just for show.

Nicolò Paganini, 1782-1840

Ill health returned when Paganini was in his fifties, which even began to affect his playing. Nicolò Paganini died in Nice, France at the age of 57.

Nico had declined the Catholic Church's final rites, so it was another five years before he was allowed to be buried in sacred ground at the church. Paganini was reburied no fewer than three times in his adopted hometown of Parma between 1876 and 1896.

When finally buried in a grave at Parma, Paganini's monument epitaph reads—
"Here lie the remains of Nicolò Paganini,
A violinist who inspired the whole of Europe.
By his divine music and supreme talent,
Conferring great and unprecedented renown upon Italy."

Crossing the English Channel

Nico decided to "try his luck in the great French capital." (p. 123) In order to reach Paris, he had to cross the English Channel. The trip did not go well for Paganini, and he vowed to never again set foot in a boat!

Using the *Crossing the English Channel* lapbook pages, follow the directions to cut out and assemble the pieces. Adhere this activity vertically to section #9 in your Paganini lapbook.

A Timeline of Paganini's Life

Remove *A Timeline of Paganini's Life* pages. Follow the directions to cut out and assemble the pieces. Adhere this activity to section #7 in your Paganini lapbook.

Music, the Language of the Heart

While in Paris, Paganini was often asked to tell a story. Page 133 shares one such moment.

"With a smile, the master would begin. Waving his long arms, he spoke in such a mixture of English, Italian, German, and French that howls of laughter drowned out his words."

"Always those words—they are too difficult for me.
But in music, I can say what is in my mind and heart."

Paganini used his music to communicate. He couldn't always express himself clearly with spoken words, but through music he could say what was on his heart.

Paganini's playing had a deeply moving effect on all listeners, even the ones with little musical knowledge. He didn't play merely for the learned, but for all to love and feel it.[27]

In his later years, the Duchess of Parma wanted to honor Paganini. She surprised him with a special celebration to recognize his talent and accomplishments. When it came time for Paganini to speak he took up his beloved violin and responded this way—

"Happy tears filled his dark eyes, and his voice trembled as he began to speak to the notable gathering around him."

"My countrymen," said he, "I will try to thank you for this great
honor with which you have crowned my life. But what I feel is too
deep for words.

And so I must speak to you through music."
~ *Paganini, Master of Strings*, p. 150

Music was the true language of Nicolò Paganini's heart!

Paganini

Activity:

- Listen to Music Disc 5, tracks 40 & 41.
- As you listen to each song, draw what you hear.

Do you hear boldness? Use bold colors.
Do you hear speed and energy? Draw quickly.
Do you hear softness? Color with light color stokes.

As you listen to Paganini's music, think about what he was communicating. Around each drawing write <u>adjectives</u> to describe an emotion that Paganini may have been expressing through his compositions.

Paganini, Master of Strings Quiz

Name: _____ Date: _____

Multiple Choice:
Circle the correct answer.

1. What instruments did Paganini play?
   a. Violin and viola
   b. Guitar
   c. Mandolin
   d. All of the above

2. What two types of rare violins did Nico play?
   a. A Glasel
   b. A Stradivarius
   c. A Guarnerius
   d. B and C

3. What honor was awarded to Nicolò Paganini while he was in Rome?
   a. The Cross of St. Gregory the Great
   b. A Knight of the Golden Spur
   c. Grand Master of the Knights Templar
   d. A Knight of St. Sylvester

Sequencing:
Number the events of Paganini's life in chronological order.

_____ Paganini begins a six and a half year tour, starting in Vienna and ending in Paris.
_____ Nicolò Paganini dies in Nice, France at the age of fifty-seven.
_____ He becomes Director of the court orchestra for Napoleon's sister, Elisa.
_____ Paganini is born on October 27 in Genoa, Italy.
_____ Nico goes to Parma, Italy to study music.

Matching:
Match the music vocabulary word with the correct definition.

1. _____ Instrumental music
2. _____ Vocal
3. _____ A cappella Music
4. _____ Classical Music
5. _____ Twentieth-Century Music
6. _____ Religious Music
7. _____ Solo
8. _____ Ensemble

a. one performer
b. groups of singers or instrumentalists
c. music written from 1900 to 1999
d. music with lyrics; with or without instruments
e. performed by instruments; no lyrics
f. music performed or written for religious use
g. singing without instrumental accompaniment
h. music written from 1750 to 1815

Week One: Chapter One Comprehension Questions

1. The Mediterranean Sea, p. 1, fishing, pp. 1, 2
2. Bells, p. 1, mandolin, p. 10, violin, p. 15
3. So Nico could play enough in the streets of Genoa to earn some extra coins, p. 15.
4. He would not allow Nico to use his music to earn money in the streets, p. 19. His father locked Nico in his room to practice, p. 24. Practicing took six hours straight at times, p. 24.
5. An angel, p. 25
6. He gave Nico solos for the services, p. 30. He arranged for Nico to play for festivals and weddings, p. 32. He got composition lessons for Nico to take with master teacher Gnecco, p. 33.
7. Variations are different versions of a repeated theme by varying the melody, in its rhythm or harmony, or varying by addition of new parts. In this case, Paganini wrote eight variations on the same melody, pp. 33, 34.

Week Two: Chapter Two Comprehension Questions

1. He went to Signor Rolla, who was a violinist, composer, and conductor, pp. 41, 45, 46.
2. He played Rolla's new composition flawlessly, p. 44
3. Write music for all the instruments in the orchestra, p. 47
4. He wrote music (24 fugues in six months) that only he could play, p. 47. He would practice up to ten hours on one page, p. 48. He rehearsed for two years, p. 48.
5. "Boy Wonder of the Strings" or "Boy Wonder of the Violin," p. 51.
6. He bartered with Paolo (the cobbler) for new shoes in exchange for teaching Paolo's children to play violin, p. 53. He got the tailor to make a new coat for him in exchange for a private concert or festival with the tailor's friends and family, p. 54.
7. A Stradivarius, p. 58.

Week Two: Chapter Three Comprehension Questions

1. Nicolò played music for the guests and families, p. 65, 66.
2. He divided the banknotes into two piles—half for himself, and half for his father, p. 67.
3. Pasini wrote a musical piece so difficult that he promised whoever could play it flawlessly at first sight would receive a Stradivarius, p. 71.
4. He would make and post notices of Nico's upcoming concerts, print tickets for those concerts, find accompanists, rent halls, and keep Nico in contact with his violin, p. 74, 82.
5. He sold his violin to a pawnbroker, and he didn't have enough money to buy it back before his next concert, p. 81.
6. A friend or acquaintance of Germi's loaned it to Nico for a concert, and when he heard Nicolò play it, he offered it to the violinist as a gift, p. 84.

Week Two: Personal Music Preferences
5th-6th Grade Activity:

Example: (Answers may vary.)

Musical preference varies greatly from person to person. This difference in musical taste is a result of cultural differences, age, and moral values. Musical preference is also a result of personal likes and dislikes. While I may enjoy soft, instrumental music the most, someone else may enjoy loud, fast music. Musical style is vast and can bring pleasure to many different types of people. Although musical preference may vary greatly, the delight we derive from music can be to a similar degree.

Week Three: Chapter Four Comprehension Questions

1. Napoleon's sister, Princess Elisa, was so impressed by Nicolò's playing that she commanded him to become her court's orchestra director, pp. 89, 90.
2. He directed the orchestra (of course), composed special music for specific occasions, played solos, and gave lessons to the royal prince, p. 91.
3. He gave concerts throughout Italy, p. 96.
4. Nico wrote some of the opening orchestral parts for Rossini's newest opera, and he directed or led the orchestra, p. 105.
5. Nicolò had been turned out from his room at the inn because he was ill. A cellist from the orchestra, Ciandelli, recognized him as Paganini, and beat the innkeeper for his lack of hospitality. Ciandelli cared for Nico while he was ill, and Nico taught him to play better so eventually Ciandelli was able to give concerts of his own, pp. 107, 108.

Week Three: Chapter Five Comprehension Questions

1. Ricci repaired Nico's Stradivarius violin, pp. 112, 113. Nicolò moved his family to a larger home on the hill with lots of beds and blankets in the house, pp. 113, 114. He received an invitation from Vienna, Austria's Prince Metternich, to give a concert there, pp. 114, 115.
2. A band greeted him with a merry waltz, p. 116; numerous novelties were for sale with Paganini's portrait on them (perfumes, gloves, walking sticks, shoes, hats, and more)-"al- Paganini," p. 117; The Waltz King, Strauss, wrote a waltz for him; other composers (Brahms, Schumann, and Medelssohn) imitated and praised his works, p. 117; one cabbie gave him free cab rides anywhere in the country, p. 118.
3. He visited Germany, London, England, and prepared for Paris, France, pp. 122, 123
4. Prices were double his typical concert tickets fees. He had to have body guards to get through the throngs, p. 122.
5. They wanted to see if he was real. They believed only a person given powers by creatures of another world could play with his musical prowess, p. 123.

Week Four: Chapter Six Comprehension Questions

1. Seventeen years (p. 126)
2. They wondered if he was even strong enough to play. He played his own musical compositions. Nicolò plucked the strings of the violin, not just using the bow, to create new sounds. He continued playing a composition even after three of his four strings broke. (p. 128-130)
3. Paganini attended a concert of Berlioz's newest works and publicly praised him for his music. Nicolò kissed Berlioz's hand in gratitude for his music. He hired Berlioz to write him a solo, which turned into one of Berlioz's best known symphonies, *Harold in Italy*, but Nico paid him nonetheless. (pp. 138, 139)
4. He called Achillino his greatest treasure. (p. 138) He told his son stories all the way home to Genoa. (p. 140) Nicolò promised Achillino would never know poverty or hunger. (p. 141) He held Achille for eight days and eight nights so the boy would rest and his broken bone would mend properly. (p. 144) He spoiled Achille with lots of toys. (p. 145)
5. Hot chocolate (p. 146)
6. She plans to honor him as other countries had done. There was a day of feasting, dancing, speeches, music, and a presentation of a golden jewel- laden pendant. (pp. 149, 150)

Paganini, Master of Strings Quiz

Multiple Choice:
1. d.
2. d.
3. b.

Matching:
1. e.
2. d.
3. g.
4. h.
5. c.
6. f.
7. a.
8. b.

Sequencing:

4 — Paganini begins a six and a half year tour, starting in Vienna and ending in Paris.

5 — Nicolò Paganini dies in Nice, France at the age of fifty- seven.

3 — He becomes director of the court orchestra for Napoleon's sister, Elisa.

1 — Paganini is born on October 27 in Genoa, Italy.

2 — Nico goes to Parma, Italy to study music.

Weekly Lesson Outline

(Activities marked with an * are required in order to meet national music appreciation standards.)

Week One:

- Read Chapter 1*
- Answer Comprehension Questions
- Character Qualities
- Tidbits of Interest
- Assemble Lapbook Folder
- Web Diagram Map Activity
- Family Concert Night (LB)
- Playing the Hackbrett (LB)*
- The Stadtkonvikt (LB)
- An Introduction to Music Theory, Part I*

Week Two:

- Read Chapter 2*
- Answer Comprehension Questions
- Listen to Music Disc 5, tracks 43-47*
- Character Qualities
- Tidbits of Interest
- The Music of Schubert (LB)*
- Word Search
- Music Throughout the Ages (LB)*
- An Introduction to Music Theory, Part II* (Vocabulary and Symbols)

Week Three:

- Read Chapters #3*
- Answer Comprehension Questions
- Listen to Music Disc 5, tracks 48-56*
- Character Qualities
- Tidbits of Interest
- Apple Fun (LB)
- Musical Chairs (LB)*
- "Places, Everyone!" (Orchestra Review) (LB)*
- Franz Schubert, Teacher (LB)
- An Introduction to Music Theory, Part III* (Notes and Rests)

Week Four:

- Read Chapter 4*
- Answer Comprehension Questions
- Listen to Music Disc 5, tracks 57-63*
- Character Qualities
- Tidbits of Interest
- Schubert and Beethoven (LB)*
- Composers Scramble*
- Writing Poetry
- Did You Know?
- "Here Is My End" (LB)
- Timeline Fan*
- An Introduction to Music Theory, Part IV*

Week 1 Activity Pages

Schubert

Chapter One Comprehension Questions

1. What occupation did Franz Schubert's father have? _____
_____

2. What type of factory did the Schuberts live near that Franz would visit as often as possible?
_____

3. Can you provide one "proof" that the Schuberts were a rather poor family? _____
_____
_____

4. In order to be considered for a place in the Vienna court choir, what two things did Franz have
to do during tryouts? _____
_____
_____
_____

5. Can you name at least one person who helped Franz learn music in this chapter? _____
_____
_____
_____
_____

1685	Johann Sebastian Bach	1750
1685	George Frederic Handel	1759
1732	Franz Joseph Haydn	1809
1756	Wolfgang A. Mozart	1791
1770	Ludwig van Beethoven	1827
1782	Nicolò Paganini	1840
1797	**Franz Schubert**	1828

Character Qualities

Keen *(pp. 15, 19)* – Franz was a quick learner and had a keen ability for music. He rapidly learned violin from his father, piano from his brother Ignaz, and singing from choir director Michael Holzer.

Purposeful *(pp. 11–14, 23)* – Schubert appeared to be motivated by music even as an infant. He developed his own piano exercises, watched how pianos were put together at a nearby factory, played songs on the factory pianos until it was dark, and was unfazed by mocking comments of other musicians when he tried out for the royal choir.

Proud *(pp. 9, 21, 23)* – We know the Schuberts struggled to earn enough money for their family, yet they never gave up their work ethic. Mother Schubert carefully cleaned and patched Franz's ragged coat for his music exam at the Convict. Moreover, Franz ignored the remarks of the other singers about his poor clothes, and simply proved himself through his musical abilities.

Tidbits of Interest

Page 9: The Schubert family lived in a lodging house in Lichtental (spelled Lichtenthal in Wheeler's book), Austria, a suburb of Vienna. The house was named Zum Roten Krebsen, meaning The Red Crab. It had sixteen apartments, two of which were the residence for the Schubert family, and in two larger rooms Franz Theodore Schubert (the father) ran a school for one hundred eighty pupils.[1]

Pages 10, 11: Franz Peter Schubert was born January 31, 1797. Elizabeth and Theodore Schubert were Catholics who had fourteen children; sadly, only five survived beyond infancy. At the time of Franz's birth he had three living older brothers: Ignaz (1785), Ferdinand (1794), and Carl (1795). His sister Maria was born in 1801.

Pages 12, 15: Franz was six years old when his father began giving him violin lessons, and his brother Ignaz (then a seventeen-year-old assistant in his father's school) gave him piano lessons.

Page 15: The Schuberts attended church at Liechtental parish, where Michael Holzer was the choirmaster. Holzer started teaching Franz at age ten in organ, singing, and harmony. At one point the choirmaster marveled at Franz's musical abilities, exclaiming, "The lad has harmony in his little finger."[2] Holzer later said, "If I wanted to instruct him in anything new, he already knew it… Therefore I gave him no actual tuition but merely talked to him and watched him with silent astonishment."[3]

Schubert

Franz Schubert was born in Lichtental, Austria in 1797. He spent most of his life in Austria, rarely traveling outside of the country.

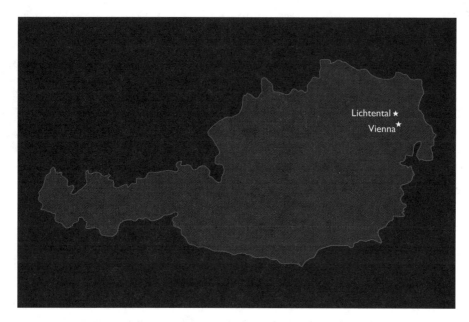

Using print or internet sources, research geographic information about Austria. (Geographic information includes physical features, climate, plant and animal life, cultures and religions, population, etc.) Arrange your research into a web diagram. (An example is provided below, but feel free to create as many informational circles as you want.)

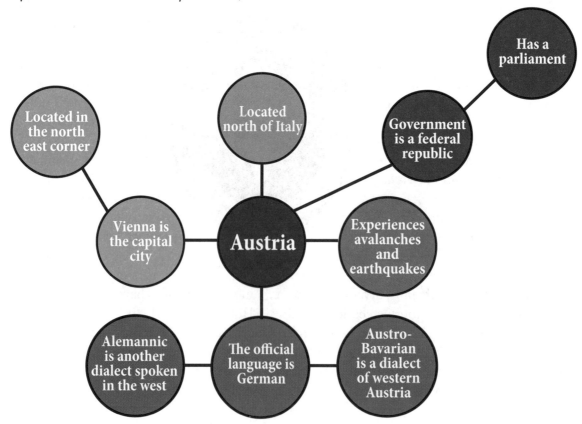

Family Concert Night

The Schubert family enjoyed playing music together, and would often spend evenings at home putting on concerts. Even as a baby, Franz Peter looked forward to this special time. When he was old enough, Franz was able to join his father and brothers. This family quartet is referenced several times throughout the book, *Franz Schubert and His Merry Friends*. It describes how Franz enjoyed being able to come home from the Convict on Sunday afternoons because of the little family concerts. (p.41)

Using the *Family Concert Night* lapbook pages, follow the directions to cut out and assemble the pieces. Adhere this activity to section #1 in your Schubert lapbook.

(Refer to p. 26 of *Franz Schubert and His Merry Friends* to complete this activity.)

Playing the Hackbrett

In Chapter 1 (p.12), Ms. Wheeler mentions Franz playing on a hackbrett, which is supposedly similar to a piano.

Actually, a hackbrett is a traditional musical instrument of the Alpine regions of Austria and Germany that is similar to a zither or a hammered dulcimer. It usually has a trapezoidal-shaped sound box with three or four strings for each musical note. The strings are played by striking them with a small wooden mallet or hammer.

Using the *Playing the Hackbrett* lapbook pages, follow the directions to cut out and assemble the pieces. Adhere this activity to section #8 in your Schubert lapbook.

Schubert

The Stradtkonvikt

In 1808, the Imperial and Royal City College (called the Convict) announced that a soprano was needed for the choir. The choir is now known as the Vienna Boys' Choir!

Students were usually eleven to sixteen years old and received a classical education in the daytime and musical lessons in the afternoon and evening. The Convict had recently been founded in 1803 by Emperor Franz to replace an earlier Jesuit seminary that had been dissolved.[4] It was also a university preparatory school, preparing choir members for life after their voices changed. It is remarkable that even without formal music training, Franz's natural musicality caused him to be accepted as a chorister in the court chapel.[5]

As a side note, the German name for the Imperial and Royal City College is Kaiserlich-königliches Stadtkonvikt, and it is from those final seven letters that the "Convict" arose.[6]

Using *The Stradtkonvikt* lapbook pages, follow the directions to cut out and assemble the pieces. Adhere this activity to section #2 in your Schubert lapbook.

An Introduction to Music Theory

Music theory is defined as "a study of the principles of music." In order to fully appreciate music, it is good to understand music theory. To create or participate in music, it is vital that you understand the basics of music theory.

"Theory is to music what grammar is to language."

Creative writing has certain rules and guidelines. If you want to be a good writer, you must understand punctuation, correct sentence structure, and the parts of speech. You will need to use grammatical rules and follow certain patterns.

Music also has specific principles that need to be understood in order to actively engage in written music.

Use this activity to help you remember the importance of music theory.

Using the *Theory is…* lapbook pages, follow the directions to cut out and assemble the pieces. Adhere this activity to section #9 in your Schubert lapbook.

Let us begin our study of music theory by reviewing four of its basic elements.

> **Dynamics:** the different levels of loudness and softness in a piece of music
> **Rhythm:** the regular pattern of beats and emphasis in a piece of music
> **Melody:** a series of musical notes that form a recognizable phrase, and usually have a distinctive rhythm
> **Syllables and Solfege:** sounds assigned to individual notes in order to aid in sight-reading (Definitions are from Encarta® World English Dictionary.[7])

Dynamics:

piano: an Italian word meaning "soft" (*p*). Whenever you see this dynamic written by the musical notes, play softly. [*mezzo piano* - means "moderately soft"(*mp*), *pianissimo* means "very soft" (*pp*)]

forte: an Italian word meaning "loud" (*f*). Whenever you see this dynamic written by the musical notes, play loudly. [mezzo forte means "moderately loud" (*mf*), fortissimo means "very loud" (*ff*)]

Sometimes there will be several different dynamic markings within one song. This change in volume generates excitement and climax in the music, and allows the composer to communicate a variety of emotions in a song.

$$p \quad mp \quad mf \quad f$$

Schubert

Using the written music in *Franz Schubert and his Merry Friends*, practice recognizing dynamic markings in music. Write each of the dynamic markings that you see throughout the song on the line.

Example: Page 40 <u>pp</u>

1. Page 52_____
2. Pages 102-103 _____ ➔ _____ ➔ _____
3. Pages 110-113 _____ ➔ _____ ➔ _____
4. Pages 122-123 _____ ➔ _____ ➔ _____ ➔ _____ ➔ _____

Dynamics of a song can also be indicated with a *crescendo* sign (<). This mark means gradually get louder. *Decrescendo* (>) means the exact opposite, gradually getting softer.

Rhythm:

Each song has a distinct rhythm. It is important that you learn to *hear* the rhythm of a song and be able to follow the pattern of the notes.

Sing and clap to the song "Twinkle Twinkle Little Star." You should give a clap for each syllable. Can you feel the rhythm?

Now touch the notes while you sing "Twinkle Twinkle Little Star." Each syllable of this song has its own note. As you follow the notes, you are beginning to read music!

The notes help you see and hear the rhythm of the song.

Note: We will introduce note values and time signatures in future lessons.

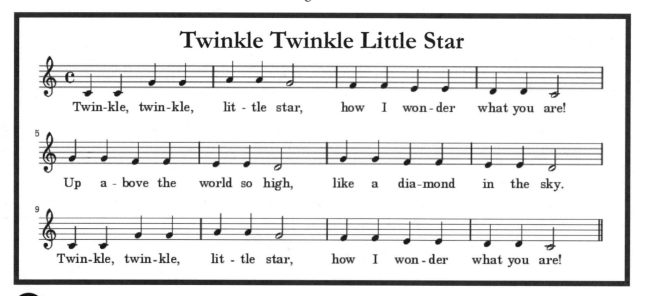

Melody:

The melody of a song is what allows us to recognize a tune and be able to sing it the same way over and over again.

Ask an adult to hum a song you know. Listen for a moment. Can you recognize the song that you are hearing? Write the name of the song on the line. Try a few more!

1. _____

2. _____

3. _____

4. _____

5. _____

You were able to recognize these songs because you knew their <u>melodies</u>!

Syllables and Solfege:

Lyrics are often written and then "put to music." This means that the syllables of the words are assigned to specific notes. To sing a song correctly, you must sing the right syllable with the right note.

Solfege (sol-fej) is a method that helps you learn how to sing the correct notes in music. Each note is assigned a sound—do-re-mi-fa-so-la-ti-do. These are the same sounds as the notes of a scale on the piano.

One of the best descriptions of solfege is from a classic musical called the *Sound of Music*. In this story the governess teaches the children how to sing. Read the following lyrics and think about how solfege helps us understand music better.

Continued...

Schubert

Do-Re-Mi [8]

Let's start at the very beginning
A very good place to start
When you read you begin with ABC
When you sing you begin with
Do-Re-Mi, Do-Re-Mi, Do-Re-Mi
The first three notes just happen to be
Do-Re-Mi, Do-Re-Mi,
Do-Re-Mi-Fa-So-La-Ti...
Let's see if I can make it easier.

Chorus:
Doe - a deer a female deer
Ray - a drop of golden sun
Me - a name I call myself
Far - a long, long way to run
Sew - a needle pulling thread
La - a note to follow so
Tea - a drink with jam and bread
That will bring us back to Do
Oh Oh Oh (repeat Chorus 3x)
Do-Re-Mi-Fa-So-La-Ti-Do-So-Do!

So-Do-La-Fa-Mi-Do-Re (echo)
Can you do that?
So-Do-La-Ti-Do-Re-Do (echo)
Now let's put it all together
So-Do-La-Fa-Mi-Do-Re
So-Do-La-Ti-Do-Re-Do
But it doesn't mean anything...
So we put in words,
One word for every note, like this:

When you know the notes to sing
You can sing most anything.
Together! (repeat)
Chorus

Do-Re-Mi-Fa-So-La-Ti
Do-Do-Ti-La-So-Fa-Mi-Re
Do-Mi-Mi-Mi-So-So
Re-Fa-Fa-La-Ti-Ti
Do-Mi-Mi-Mi-So-So
Re-Fa-Fa-La-Ti-Ti
Chorus

Listen to part of this song on Music Disc 5, track 42.

Week 2 Activity Pages

Schubert

Chapter Two & Three Comprehension Questions

Comprehension

1. Can you provide two ways that Franz helped out with the school orchestra? _____

_____

_____

_____

2. Explain who Spaun was in this chapter. _____

_____

_____

_____

3. When Franz once ran out of paper for writing a composition, what did he use instead? _____

_____

_____

4. What did Franz prefer to do over playing games or doing his studies? _____

_____

_____

5. What extreme response did Father Schubert have when Franz's grades at the Convict began to

fail? _____

Schubert

Character Qualities

Hungry *(pp. 31, 32, 34, 48)* – Franz was physically *and* musically hungry. His literal hunger seemed to be constant throughout his days at the Convict, as evidenced in a letter to his brother in chapter three. Franz's hunger musically was illustrated in his happiness when music lessons resumed during the daily classes, in his time spent writing music, and in his admission that he liked music above all else.

Goodwill *(pp. 44, 46)* – Franz's jolly nature and kindliness made him a young person of whom his masters and his friends were very fond. The long list of friends' names from his youthful days at the Convict also demonstrates Franz's goodwill toward men.

Tidbits of Interest

Page 31: Franz was always on the short side of life (only growing to an inch over five feet tall), rather stocky in nature, and nicknamed "Tubby" by his friends.[9]

Pages 32, 33, 49: Herr Wenzel Ruziczka was the court organist, conductor of the royal orchestra, and music teacher at the Convict.[10] He once explained that Schubert learned music so swiftly he believed Franz "has learned it from God."[11] Franz's role as the orchestral assistant involved looking after instruments, setting up the room for rehearsals, keeping the supply of music in good condition, and lighting candles for the next practice.[12] Franz met Joseph Spaun, a student nine years his senior, in the orchestra. "Spaun had originally formed the [Convict] orchestra and still played in it."[13] Spaun's contacts in Vienna as a lawyer later allowed him to introduce Schubert to artists, writers, and singers of the

day.[14] He also aided Franz financially numerous times in his later years.

Page 38: Schubert (like Mozart) was a very quick composer, able to conceive a work in his head and write it down, often without a piano to test the composition. If he ran out of music paper, he recorded his ideas on anything handy—a tablecloth or the back of a menu for instance.

Page 46: The friends dancing to Franz's tune were his lifelong friends from the Convict. Albert Stadler, who was three years older than Franz, lived into his nineties.[15] During the later years of their friendship, Stadler took it upon himself to make copies of many of Franz's works, which is why so many have survived to today.[16] Johann Senn was a poet friend who later spent fourteen months in prison and was exiled from Vienna because he allegedly spoke "rebellious thoughts."[17] Anton Holzapfel was five years older than Franz.

The Music of Schubert

Franz Schubert was the happiest when he was composing. Sometimes he even had a hard time concentrating because of the music that played in his mind. His greatest joy was to entertain his friends with his musical compositions. Throughout his lifetime, Schubert wrote many different styles of music. He wrote marches, lullabies, religious songs, rondos, dance music, ballet, sonatas, symphonies, and even tried his hand at opera. He was a very diverse and talented composer.

Some interesting details about the music discussed in *Franz Schubert and His Merry Friends*:

♫ A waltz is a dance written in triple time with the accent on the first beat of each measure. Waltzes were becoming the fashionable music style of the early nineteenth century.[18] (p. 43)

♫ An ecossaise is a Scotch dancing tune usually danced in 2/4 time. (p. 66)

♫ Schubert attempted to write an opera seventeen times in his lifetime, but with no great success. Vogl sang the lead in the opera *The Twin Brothers* (from 1820). As with all of Franz's operas, it enjoyed very minimal success. *Rosamunde* was one of Franz's final attempts at writing opera, and it was written near the end of his life (1824). (pp. 75, 116)

♫ Franz dedicated his First Symphony (completed October 28, 1813) to director Dr. Lang. Director Lang was a "theologian who was regarded as severe and rather gloomy by the boys but loved music and appears to have been remarkably encouraging to pupils and staff in their musical pursuits."[19] (p. 77)

♫ Franz excelled at writing lieder (from lied, or song, in German). Lieder was a Romantic form of music that was dependent upon a poem or a song to give the music its theme. So Franz's songs linked the meaning of the words of a literary work to the piano accompaniment and melody. He became a master of this form of musical composition. Many critics consider him one of the supreme creators of melody and among the greatest writers of songs.[20] Much of what we know about Franz Schubert comes from remembrances by his friends, and from his over six hundred lieder, or lyric songs. (p. 100)

"Where others keep a diary in which they record their momentary feelings, Schubert confided his passing moods to music paper; his soul, musical through and through, wrote notes where others resort to words."[21]

Robert Schumann, fellow composer

Using the *All About Lieder* lapbook pages, follow the directions to cut out and assemble the pieces. Adhere this activity vertically to section #7 in your Schubert lapbook.

Word Search

```
R  Y  N  O  H  P  M  Y  S  G  O  F
C  E  R  C  O  N  C  E  R  T  R  A
M  U  T  C  I  S  U  M  M  R  C  Y
E  M  N  S  W  A  L  T  Z  V  H  T
L  O  E  A  A  S  I  U  I  R  E  R
O  Z  V  I  N  M  R  O  Z  C  S  E
D  A  O  E  S  N  L  D  P  O  T  B
Y  R  H  O  U  I  E  O  H  B  R  U
E  T  T  T  N  V  C  I  O  R  A  H
E  Z  E  N  S  L  S  P  V  H  I  C
T  A  E  O  N  A  I  P  M  W  C  S
E  A  B  S  C  H  U  M  A  N  N  S
```

Find the following hidden words:

BEETHOVEN	SCHOOLMASTER
CONCERT	SCHUBERT
MELODY	SCHUMANN
MOZART	SYMPHONY
MUSIC	VIENNA
ORCHESTRA	VIOLIN
PIANO	WALTZ

Music Throughout the Ages

Music has changed and developed throughout the centuries. Each new era has produced its own unique style of music. It is valuable to study each musical period in order to have a better understanding of music's development.

Although Franz Schubert lived from 1797–1828, he is viewed as one of the leading composers of the Romantic Period.

Schubert's Place in Musical History

Middle Ages	450 – 1450
Renaissance	1450 – 1600
Baroque	1600 – 1750
Classical	1750 – 1820
Romantic	**1820 – 1900**
20th Century or Modern Music	1900 – Present

Using the *Music Throughout the Ages* lapbook pages, follow the directions to cut out and assemble the pieces. Adhere this activity to sections #11 & 12 in your Schubert lapbook.

An Introduction to Music Theory, Part 2

(Vocabulary and Symbols)

There are many words and symbols used in written music that occur over and over again. It is helpful to learn the meanings of these terms and symbols.

Vocabulary	Definition[22]
Meter	the pattern of beats that combines to form musical rhythm
Tonality	how the notes of a song create a central note or harmony as the main sound
Staff	a set of five horizontal lines, and the four spaces between them where the notes of music are written
Harmony	a combination of notes that are sung or played at the same time as the melody; harmony provides momentum and richness to the melody
Measure	divided sections on the staff that organizes music; measures are indicated by bar lines which are the vertical lines on the staff (The time signature determines how many beats can be in a measure.)
Chord	two or more musical notes played or sung at the same time
Scale	an ascending or descending series of notes

Symbol	Meaning
al Fine *al Fine*	means to the end: a note to the performer to continue to the end of a repeated section
Da Capo *D.C.*	means repeat from the beginning (D.C. al fine=repeat from the beginning and end with the word Fine; D.C. al coda=repeat from the beginning and end with the coda symbol)
Dal segno 𝄋	means repeat from the sign
Double Bar ‖	Indicates the end of a piece of music or the end of its principal sections
Repeat	a symbol that means to play a portion of music again; a recurring musical passage

Symbol	Meaning
Fermata (hold)	a symbol appearing above or below a note or rest signaling that it can be prolonged beyond its prescribed time
Coda	the final section of a musical piece: often adds dramatic energy to the work as a whole
Accent	a symbol meaning to stress specific notes in a piece of music
Staccato	a symbol that means to play the notes crisply; detached or separated from the others

Study these terms and symbols. Quiz yourself by covering up the vocabulary/symbol side of the chart and give the correct definition or meaning. Can you cover the opposite side of the chart and still give the correct answer?

Music Vocabulary Scavenger Hunt:
Turn to pages 102-103 in *Franz Schubert and his Merry Friends*. Can you find these symbols or musical parts in the song *Moment Musicale*? Check them off as you see each one.

- ☐ The staff
- ☐ Harmony notes
- ☐ A measure
- ☐ A chord
- ☐ A double bar
- ☐ The repeat sign
- ☐ An accent symbol
- ☐ Staccato markings

Extra Challenge: Find a fermata symbol in another one of Schubert's songs. What page did you find it on? _____

4ᵗʰ-6ᵗʰ grade:
Write a short paragraph discussing how musical terms and symbols can help an instrumentalist communicate emotion while playing a song. (Refer to dynamics and the terms and symbols above.)

Schubert

Chapter Three Comprehension Questions

1. As this chapter began, what special honors did Franz receive in the school orchestra? _____

_____

_____

2. What did Franz do to prove he was a committed conductor of the orchestra? (There are several

   possible answers.) _____

   _____

   _____

   _____

3. What famous Viennese musician encouraged Franz in his composing? _____

   _____

4. After five years at the Convict, what happened that made Franz realize his need to move on with

   life? _____

   _____

5. Franz passed his exams to enter a training school. For what was he being trained, and what was

   Theodore's (Franz's father's) response to that training? _____

   _____

   _____

Character Qualities

Uncomplaining (*pp. 55, 77*) – Franz expressed his hunger in his letter to his brother, but his humor in the note seems to show Schubert's attempts to "get by" without complaint. He demonstrated this amiable nature even more when his voice changed and his career in the choir came to an end. Franz agreed to leave the Convict and enter a training school for teachers so he could earn a living, though music was still his passion.

Ambitious (*pp. 56, 64, 65, 74, 75*) – Franz made rapid progress in his music and was moved to first chair for the violin, the highest place of honor. He also earned the right to conduct the orchestra when Herr Ruzicka was away—even teaching himself to play all the different instruments. Moreover, Franz worked hard to improve his grades to please his father. And at the suggestion of master musician Salieri, Franz wrote an opera in a matter of weeks.

Confident (*pp. 64, 74, 75*) – Franz was confident that he could lead the orchestra and quickly proved himself as a conductor. Though he repeatedly went over difficult portions of the music, his orchestra members trusted him and cheered for him. Franz also had confidence to show his compositions to Salieri, and took on the challenge of writing an opera without a moment's hesitation.

Tidbits of Interest

Page 55: Franz's mother died in May of 1812, so Franz wrote his brother about needing extra food and money. Ferdinand, Franz's brother who was three years older than the musician, was a constant help and source of friendship to Franz. He even cared for Franz in Vienna during his final days by allowing Franz to live in his home.[23]

Page 57: Antonio Salieri was the court Kapellmeister (or music director) for the royal family in Vienna—a position he held for forty years. Salieri was considered the most important musician in Vienna.[24] Besides Schubert, Salieri had also taught students such as Ludwig van Beethoven and Franz Liszt. Some sources throughout history tell us of a great rivalry between Salieri and Mozart.

Page 67: Josef Kenner was another long-time friend of Franz's who became one of the "groupies" who gathered informally in the evenings to hear Schubert play his works. These evenings were called "Schubertiads" and the listeners were "Schubertiaden" (or "Schubertians"). Even as a youth, Franz found no greater joy than in writing music. He once told a friend, "I have come into the world for no purpose but to compose."[25]

Page 75: The full name of this opera is *Rosamunde, Princess of Cyprus*. The music has become quite popular since Schubert's death. The complete musical score is almost an hour long, but only portions are typically played.

Apple Fun

Franz spent much of his time hungry while at the Convict. In a letter to his brother (p. 55) he talks about how satisfying a roll and a couple of apples can be when one is so hungry.

Did you know there are over 600 varieties of apples? You can research the various kinds online. Try slicing a couple of apples to enjoy while you read this chapter.

Using the *Apple Fun* lapbook pages, follow the directions to cut out and assemble the pieces. Adhere this activity to sections #5 & 6 in your Schubert lapbook.

Here are several options to continue your apple explorations:

1. Cut out the different apple cards on the four pages and use them to create apple patterns.
2. Print the named apple cards on card stock and use the cards to play a memory match game. (Print two copies of each page and create a somewhat more difficult memory match game.)
3. Use the named apple cards in an alphabetizing game.
4. Choose several of the apple variety cards to paste onto a research journal page. Research your chosen apple variety, writing down information like color, region, taste, season, etc. (Several types of journal pages are provided for this option.)
5. Draw a picture of each of your favorite apple varieties.
6. Go to the grocery store and buy one of each kind of apple that you can find. DO NOT remove the stickers from the apples until you record their names on individual cards. Wash each apple separately. After drying the apple, place it on the correct card. (Be careful not to mix up the apples or your results will be wrong.) Taste each apple and write your observations on the card. Is it sweet? Is it crispy or soft? Do you like it? What color is it? Is it large, medium, or small? After you have tasted each apple, choose your favorite kind.

Music Chairs

Franz was ecstatic when he was made first chair violinist of the school orchestra (p. 56).

What *is* so important about the post of first chair violin? A violinist is a violinist is a violinist, right? Actually, there are some very important responsibilities that go along with the post of first chair violin.

This is a leadership role in the orchestra, second in importance only to the conductor, and is sometimes called the concertmaster. The first chair violin is to work with the principal players in the string sections (first chair in the second violin, viola, cello and bass sections) so that they can form a sort of string quartet surrounding the conductor. Those first chairs in strings then work with the first chairs in the wind, brass, and percussion sections to lead the rest of the orchestra. Furthermore, any violin solo in an orchestral work is typically played by the concertmaster. Many times the first violin is given charge of leading the orchestra in tuning the instruments before rehearsals and concerts, as well.

Using the *Musical Chairs* lapbook pages, follow the directions to cut out and assemble the pieces. Adhere this activity to sections #15 in your Schubert lapbook.

"Places, Everyone!" (Orchestra Review)

Using the *"Places, Everyone!"* lapbook pages, follow the directions to cut out and assemble the pieces. Adhere this activity to sections #13 & 14 in your Schubert lapbook.

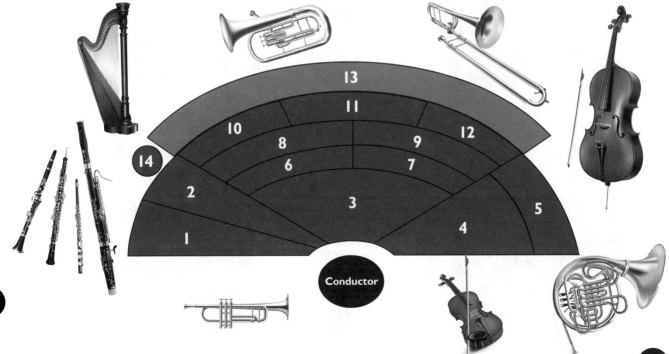

Schubert

Franz Schubert, Teacher

In the summer of 1812, Franz's voice began to change, and the fifteen-year-old scrawled on a copy of a mass the choir was presenting, "Schubert, Franz, crowed for the last time, July 26, 1812."[26] Franz wished to compose music for a living, but the political uncertainty of the Napoleonic invasions made life difficult for musicians in Vienna. The once-wealthy Viennese patrons of the arts were rapidly disappearing, so Franz studied at St. Anna's College for teacher training during the 1813–1814 academic year. Father Theodore Schubert considered teaching an "acceptable" profession, but Franz had tried everything to avoid it. Franz actually tried to join the military first; however, he was turned down because he was too short.[27]

Finally on August 19, 1814 (at age seventeen), Franz joined the staff at his father's school, which had grown to over 300 pupils and six assistant teachers in the five years Franz was at the Convict. Franz taught the lowest age in his father's school (1814–1818). In fact, Franz often composed during his six-year-old students' lesson times—without his father's knowledge—and the worst offense a young pupil could commit would be to interrupt the teacher composer while he was writing a musical idea.

When Franz left his father's school, after teaching (so to speak) for three years, Father Theodore feared the influence that his many artistic and poetic friends would have on Franz.[28] One friend, Franz Schober, convinced Franz to give up teaching and stay at his mother's house where Franz could compose in peace and spaciousness. This invitation was extended from late 1816 until August of 1817 when he had to leave the Schober's home and return to teaching at his father's school.

Using the *Franz Schubert, Teacher* lapbook pages, follow the directions to cut out and assemble the pieces. Adhere this activity to sections #3 & 4 in your Schubert lapbook.

(Musical Notes and Rests)

> "Let's start at the very beginning,
> A very good place to start
> When you read you begin with ABC
> When you sing you begin with
> Do Re Mi..."
> (Taken from *Do-Re-Mi*)

Just like stories are made up of letters, music is made up of notes. There are six main types of notes. When these notes are combined together they create songs. In this lesson, you will learn about note values and rests. You will also practice recognizing the different types of notes and rests. (NOTE: These note and rest values are for 4/4 time or common time.)

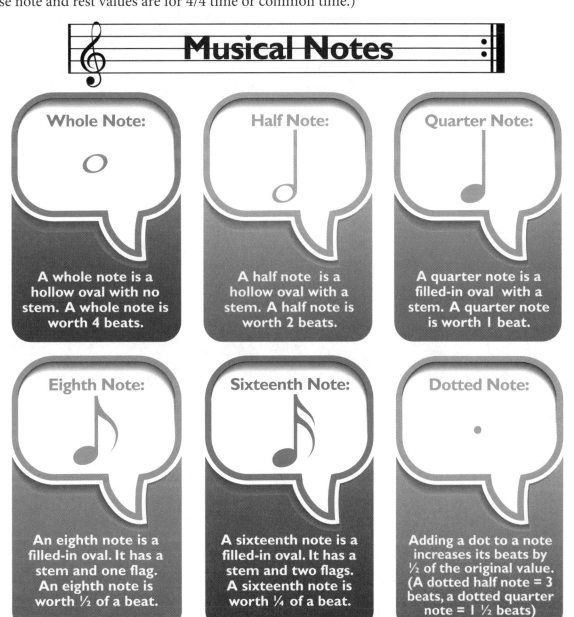

Musical Notes

Whole Note:
A whole note is a hollow oval with no stem. A whole note is worth 4 beats.

Half Note:
A half note is a hollow oval with a stem. A half note is worth 2 beats.

Quarter Note:
A quarter note is a filled-in oval with a stem. A quarter note is worth 1 beat.

Eighth Note:
An eighth note is a filled-in oval. It has a stem and one flag. An eighth note is worth ½ of a beat.

Sixteenth Note:
A sixteenth note is a filled-in oval. It has a stem and two flags. A sixteenth note is worth ¼ of a beat.

Dotted Note:
Adding a dot to a note increases its beats by ½ of the original value. (A dotted half note = 3 beats, a dotted quarter note = 1 ½ beats)

Schubert

Musical Rests

A rest is a pause between musical notes. Each rest has its own beat value. Whenever you see a rest in music, do not play or sing for that number of beats.

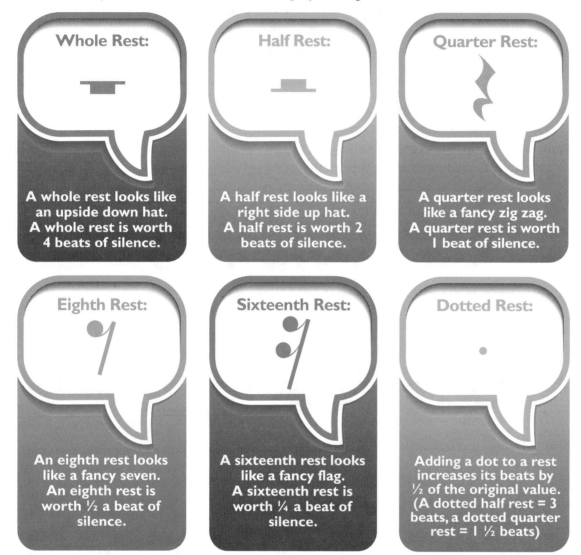

Whole Rest:
A whole rest looks like an upside down hat. A whole rest is worth 4 beats of silence.

Half Rest:
A half rest looks like a right side up hat. A half rest is worth 2 beats of silence.

Quarter Rest:
A quarter rest looks like a fancy zig zag. A quarter rest is worth 1 beat of silence.

Eighth Rest:
An eighth rest looks like a fancy seven. An eighth rest is worth ½ a beat of silence.

Sixteenth Rest:
A sixteenth rest looks like a fancy flag. A sixteenth rest is worth ¼ a beat of silence.

Dotted Rest:
Adding a dot to a rest increases its beats by ½ of the original value. (A dotted half rest = 3 beats, a dotted quarter rest = 1 ½ beats)

Practice: Do the following activities to help you learn the notes and rests.

Activity #1 Search and Find:
Turn to pages 40-41 in *Franz Schubert and his Merry Friends* book. Find the notes and rests listed below in *Cradle Song*.

Circle these items as you find them.

Half note	Quarter note	Eighth note	Sixteenth note
Whole rest	Quarter rest	Dotted note	

Can you find the same items in other songs by Franz Schubert? What about the other notes and rests that you have learned?

Activity #2 Note and Rest Identification

Circle the notes and rests with these colors:

red = whole notes and whole rests
blue = half notes and half rests
green = quarter notes and quarter rests
orange = eighth notes and eighth rests
purple = sixteenth notes and sixteenth rests
brown = dotted notes and dotted rests

Activity #3 Note and Rest Match

Match the note with its corresponding rest.

Activity #4 Note and Rest Flashcards

Using the pictures at the beginning of this lesson, draw the correct note or rest in each box (based on 4/4 time). Cut out the sets of cards, **being sure to leave the corresponding note and rest together.** Adhere the cards to sections #17-20 in your Schubert lapbook. (six cards on each side)

Whole Note:
A whole note is a hollow oval with no stem. A whole note is worth 4 beats.

Whole Rest:
A whole rest looks like an upside down hat. A whole rest is worth 4 beats of silence.

Eighth Note:
An eighth note is a filled-in oval. It has a stem and one flag. An eighth note is worth ½ of a beat.

Eighth Rest:
An eighth rest looks like a fancy seven. An eighth rest is worth ½ a beat of silence.

Half Note:
A half note is a hollow oval with a stem. A half note is worth 2 beats.

Half Rest:
A half rest looks like a right side up hat. A half rest is worth 2 beats of silence.

Sixteenth Note:
A sixteenth note is a filled-in oval. It has a stem and two flags. A sixteenth note is worth ¼ of a beat.

Sixteenth Rest:
A sixteenth rest looks like a fancy flag. A sixteenth rest is worth ¼ a beat of silence

Quarter Note:
A quarter note is a filled-in oval with a stem. A quarter note is worth 1 beat.

Quarter Rest:
A quarter rest looks like a fancy zig zag. A quarter rest is worth 1 beat of silence.

Dotted Note:
Adding a dot to a note increases its beats by ½ of the original value. (A dotted half note = 3 beats, a dotted quarter note = 1 ½ beats)

Dotted Rest:
Adding a dot to a rest increases its beats by ½ of the original value. (A dotted half rest = 3 beats, a dotted quarter rest = 1 ½ beats)

Schubert

Chapter Four Comprehension Questions

Comprehension

1. In Goethe's poem "The Erlking," a father rides on a black horse in search of help for his sick child. How did Franz convey that story musically in his composition? _____

_____

_____

2. Why did Franz find busywork for his students in his morning classes? _____

_____

_____

3. Can you supply two ways that Franz's friends encouraged or supported him in his music? (There are many possible answers.) _____

_____

_____

_____

_____

4. For what royal family did Franz work? _____

5. What "kind" of people tended to be Franz's dearest friends? (That is, what were their occupations or interests, typically?) _____

_____

_____

6. For which composer did Franz have the highest regard (even leaving music for him to critique)?

_____

Schubert

Character Qualities

Imaginative *(pp. 84, 86, 87, 90, 108, 109, 121)* –
Franz used poetry quite frequently as inspiration for his compositions—conveying musically the theme of a poem's words. He was also able to withdraw into himself in his imagination and write music practically anywhere. He could be in a stuffy classroom with students, in a crowded coffeehouse with friends, or locked in a room by his friends and still write music effortlessly.

Productive *(pp. 84, 87, 104, 119)* – Schubert was able to write compositions quickly, sometimes within the hour of getting an idea. In one year, he composed over one hundred fifty songs! He was so eager to compose that he would wear his glasses to bed so he didn't have to waste time looking for them in the morning, although it made for rather bent frames.

Character Qualities Review

Take the Character Challenge!

Directions:

1. Cut out each page. (book pages and badges)
2. Color each of the badges and store them away.
3. Stack the book pages on top of one another and staple them together at the top. (Staple at the line on the title page.)
4. Ask an adult you respect to help you fill out the *Character Challenge Chart.*
5. As you complete each Character Challenge, adhere the corresponding badge to your *Character Challenge Chart.* (Definitions are from Encarta® World English Dictionary.[29])

Admirable Attributes
Of
Franz Schubert

My Little Book about
Good Character

Schubert

keen
"quick to understand things"

Franz was a quick learner and had a keen ability for music. He rapidly learned the violin, piano, and voice.

Character Challenge #1
What topic interests you?
Pursue 3 different ways of learning more about that subject.

purposeful
"determined, having a definite purpose or aim"

Schubert appeared to be motivated by music, even as a child. He developed his own piano exercises, played the factory pianos, and was unfazed by teasing.

Character Challenge #2
Set a goal to improve one skill. Practice that skill one time every day for 5 days. Have you improved? (More practice will make you even better!)

goodwill
"a friendly disposition"

Franz's jolly nature and kindliness made him a young person of whom his masters and his friends were very fond.

Character Challenge #3
Choose one person to do something kind for today.
(Be creative in what you do!)
Remember—a character trait is something for which you are known Are you known as a kind person?

uncomplaining
"patient, tolerant"

Schubert demonstrated a desire to get by without complaint, even when he was hungry or teaching.

Character Challenge #4
Make a list of 5 things for which you are thankful. When you feel like complaining about something, stop and read your list instead.

#1
Character Challenge
keen

#2
Character Challenge
purposeful

#3
Character Challenge
goodwill

#4
Character Challenge
uncomplaining

Schubert

Schubert—Week 4 Activity Pages

ambitious

"having a strong desire for success"

Franz made rapid progress in his music. He even taught himself to play all the different instruments.

Character Challenge #5
What do you want to be when you grow up? Choose: 1. Role play that job and describe what you like about it OR 2. Write a biographical paragraph about someone who is already in that position.

confident

"certain of having the ability and resources needed to succeed"

Franz was confident that he could lead the orchestra and proved himself as a conductor. He had the confidence to show his music to Salieri.

Character Challenge #6
Choose something you are good at doing. Use that ability to encourage someone else.

imaginative

"the ability to form ideas in the mind; to think of new things"

Schubert often conveyed poems musically. He could write creatively practically anywhere.

Character Challenge #7
Create a picture or story from your imagination. Tell at least one other person about the story or picture.

productive

"producing something abundantly and efficiently"

Franz was able to write music quickly. In one year, he composed over 150 songs!

Character Challenge #8
Ask an adult for an extra job that can be done. Time yourself as you do the job on three different days. Try to beat your time each day! (Make sure you do the job correctly!)

#5
Character Challenge
ambitious

#6
Character Challenge
confident

#7
Character Challenge
imaginative

#8
Character Challenge
productive

Schubert

Character Challenge Chart

Challenge #1: My favorite topic is _____. I will do these three things to learn more about it.

    1. _____

    2. _____

    3. _____

Challenge #2: My goal is _____.

    I practiced   Day #1   Day #2   Day #3

Challenge #3: I will show kindness to _____ by _____

_____

_____

Challenge #4: Five things for which I am thankful:

    1. _____

    2. _____

    3. _____

    4. _____

    5. _____

Challenge #5: I want to be a _____ when I am older.

    Option #1 I like this job because _____

_____

_____

    Option # 2 I will write a biographical paragraph about _____

Challenge #6: I will encourage _____ by _____

_____

Challenge #7: (Circle One) I will   write a story   OR   draw a picture.

    I will show it to _____

Challenge #8: The job I will do is_____

    My time on Day # 1: _____

    My time on Day # 2: _____

    My time on Day # 3: _____

Adhere your badge to the appropriate circle as you complete each challenge.

Character Challenge #1   Character Challenge #2   Character Challenge #3   Character Challenge #4

Character Challenge #5   Character Challenge #6   Character Challenge #7   Character Challenge #8

Schubert

Tidbits of Interest

Page 90: 1815 was a very productive year musically for Schubert. In that one year he composed some 21,850 bars of music, which amounts to 420 bars of music each week.[30] Given that most pages of music have four bars per page, Franz was composing over 100 pages of music each week. All in all, Schubert composed over six hundred songs in his short lifetime.

Page 118: A friend of Franz' once described his habits during composing just as Wheeler did in this chapter: he could write regardless of noise and movement around him, seldom used a piano, bit his pen, and drummed his fingers while thinking.[31]

Page 119: The Unfinished Symphony was retrieved from his friend Anselm Hüttenbrenner in 1865, almost forty years after Franz's death. Some biographers claim that it was illness (not a picnic invitation) that caused the symphony to be unfinished.

Page 124: Wheeler wrote that Franz wondered what he would ever do without his friends. His final five or six years were tumultuous and difficult—not only because of the disease he was battling physically, but also because his circle of friends started to scatter (due to job changes and marriages), causing him to become somewhat detached and casual in his relationships.

Schubert and Beethoven

Franz was thirteen when he started composing music; this was also the age at which he first conducted the orchestra at the school. It is appears that the orchestra began rehearsing a composition by Beethoven, who was Franz's musical hero. Franz once asked a friend, "Who can do anything after Beethoven?"[32]

Franz's musical hero was Beethoven. And this hero-worship continued throughout Franz's life. He attended Beethoven's concerts whenever he could afford to go, once even selling books to buy a ticket.[33] It is said that Franz frequently ate at the same restaurant as the older master, but he never approached the deaf composer.[34] Apparently, on March 19, 1827, Schubert finally visited Beethoven's home, leaving sixty songs for the ailing composer to review on his deathbed.[35] Beethoven's proclamation upon looking at Franz's music was, "Truly in Schubert dwells a divine spark!"[36] Beethoven died within the week; Schubert served as a torchbearer at his hero's funeral.

Franz Schubert

Ludwig van Beethoven

Using the *Schubert and Beethoven* lapbook pages, follow the directions to cut out and assemble the pieces. Adhere this activity to sections #10 in your Schubert lapbook.

Composers Scramble

Wheeler notes that Franz was introduced to the music of Joseph Haydn while he was in the orchestra. Haydn was an old man dwelling in Vienna at this point, defiantly opposing Napoleon's invasion of Austria. Vienna was invaded twice during the Napoleonic Wars of 1805–1815, and in 1809 (when Franz was twelve), the city was attacked by cannon fire as the proud Austrians tried to defend their chief city. On May 11th, in fact, the seminary building was pierced by a howitzer shell during the bombardment before Napoleon took up residence at Schönbrunn, the royal family's palace.[37] Joseph Haydn was a firm Austrian loyalist and had openly defied the French by daily playing the Austrian national anthem (a text called "God Save the Emperor Franz," which you may recognize better as the hymn "Glorious Things of Thee Are Spoken"). Napoleon had ordered a guard posted outside the invalid composer's home, rather than arresting the honored musician, so Haydn could be as comfortable as possible during the French occupation of the city. Haydn died on May 31, 1809, at the age of 77.

Nicolò Paganini

Franz Liszt

Joseph Haydn

Robert Schumann

In 1828, Franz Schubert, who was quite sickly, gave a concert, that provided him with some decent money but was not well publicized. Little was printed about his concert, because the press was more interested in the musical sensation and visiting Italian violin virtuoso, Nicolò Paganini.[38]

It took almost forty years for the world to realize Schubert's musical genius. This recognition began in 1838 when Robert Schumann visited Schubert's grave and stopped by Ferdinand Schubert's home, rediscovering Franz's Ninth Symphony in C Major.

Schubert's subjective approach to music, and his abilities as a "lyric poet of music" influenced numerous other composers, including Schumann, Liszt, Brahms, Dvořák, and Mahler.[39] Franz Liszt praised him as "the most poetic musician who ever lived."[40]

Unscramble the following letters to properly spell the names of famous composers.

1. EHTEVEOBN _____
2. HBMSRA _____
3. NADYH _____
4. HSAUNMNC _____
5. TILZS _____
6. HESCRUBT _____
7. GAINPAIN _____

Schubert

Writing Poetry

Franz enjoyed German Romantic poetry, which emphasized the beauty of nature and the sorrows and joys of love. Franz's lyrical inspiration for his songs ranged from works by German poets like Schiller, Heine, Goethe, and Mayrhofer, to words by Shakespeare and Sir Walter Scott. "Hark! Hark! the Lark" actually comes from Shakespeare's comedy *Cymbeline*. Johann Mayrhofer was a poet who claimed his poems only came to life when Franz set them to music.[41] In fact, Franz composed music for forty-seven of Mayrhofer's works.[42] These poets inspired some of Franz's greatest works.[43]

When Franz was impressed by or attracted to a poem, he immediately wanted to express it musically, as he did with "The Erlking" (also written as The Erl King).[44] The poem was written by Johann Wolfgang von Goethe, one of Germany's greatest poets and playwrights (best known for his play *Faust*). In 1815, Franz wrote the accompaniment for this legend from Danish folklore in less than a day, and several sources say even less than one hour! The accompaniment for *The Erlking* was so difficult because of the repeated triplets that even Franz was unable to play them when he presented the piece. When his friends asked him why he omitted the triplets in his performance, Franz replied, "They are too difficult for me, but a virtuoso would be able to play them!"[45]

In 1821, a number of Franz's friends collected funds to publish *The Erlking* since no publisher would risk his own money on Franz's music. Publisher Leopold von Sonnleithner, Josef Hüttenbrenner (brother of Franz's friend, Anselm, from the Convict days), and other friends printed the music, which became quite popular immediately.

Poetry and music are similar in many ways. Both forms of art communicate emotion and engage the audience. They are beautiful in rhythm and flow. It has been said that "Poetry is plucking at the heartstrings, and making music with them.[46]"

Poetry Writing Activity #1: Sausage Poems

These poems are lighthearted and fun. They may seem simple at first, but can become quite challenging. The rule for writing these poems is that each word must start with the same letter that the previous word ended with. This is why they are called sausage poems-- the words are <u>linked</u> together. Any group of words that are connected by common letters makes a sausage poem.
Example:

> *Bob better remember Rachel's special ladybug.*
>
> *Lions stalk king-size elands.*
>
> *The enormous stopwatch has seven new wires.*

Note: A thesaurus may be helpful.

Poetry Writing Activity #2: Word Tile Poems

Directions:
1. Cut out the word tiles below.
2. Use the word tiles to create descriptive poetry. (The poems do not have to rhyme. Focus on rhythm and how the words sound together.)

fall	try	walk	a	special	with	slow
red	the	pretend	before	corner	you	time
think	I	on	whisper	run	brown	she
up	summer	black	star	talk	father	dog
door	house	if	new	an	year	stay
by	below	winter	through	dream	their	wind
far	to	sun	white	around	is	was
that	a	big	what	only	think	little
snow	turn	hands	an	beautiful	think	smile
makes	bear	flowers	night	write	may	horse
he	bring	the	sad	who	rose	tree
thoughtful	when	say	sight	sing	takes	day

Did You Know?

Intriguing Facts about Schwammerl

Schubert would often compose for six to seven hours a day.[47] He never slowed in his enthusiasm for composing, even though he spent much of his life destitute and in need. "When one piece is finished, I begin another," he once stated.[48]

Franz was somewhat shy and introverted. He was nicknamed Schwammerl (which means "Little Mushroom") by some of his friends.

Franz slept with his glasses on so he could begin working as soon as he awoke.

Franz Schubert and Johann Vogal made a short concert tour through Austria in 1825.

Franz Schubert and Franz Schober wrote many works together and called themselves "Schobert."

Schubert suffered from terrible headaches and often took walks to relieve the pain.[49]

The farthest from home that Schubert ever travelled was to the summer chateau of Count Esterhàzy.[50] (It was 300 miles north of Vienna.)

Schubert

1822 was a year of tragedy in many respects for Franz Schubert. Not only did his opera, *Alfonso and Estrella* fail, but he was also diagnosed with an incurable disease that would attack his body with hepatitis, meningitis, and later typhoid fever.

By September of 1828, Franz's health required him to move to his brother Ferdinand's country home. The next month he walked with his brother and a couple of friends to Eisenstadt to visit Joseph Haydn's grave, but the walk weakened him. The following weeks he stayed in, requesting books to read—especially enjoying James Fenimore Cooper's *The Last of the Mohicans*.[51]

By November 16, 1828, he was diagnosed with typhoid fever. Typhoid fever is transmitted by ingesting food or drink contaminated by an infected person or flying insects spreading the bacterium. Therefore, typhoid was considered a "slum" disease in cities because it readily passed from person to person or building to building in crowded neighborhoods. Though this is not a problem we would expect to see in major cities anymore, it is still quite common in developing parts of the world. In fact, the CDC web site tells us that of the approximate 400 cases of typhoid fever the United States sees every year, about 300 of those cases are contracted while people are traveling outside of the country.

Using the *Typhoid Fever* lapbook pages, follow the directions to cut out and assemble the pieces. Adhere this activity to sections #16 in your Schubert lapbook.

Franz Schubert died three days later, whispering to his brother, "Here is my end."[52]

Franz Schubert
1797-1828
"Music has here buried a rich treasure . . .
Franz Schubert lies here."

In keeping with Schubert's earlier request, he was buried near Beethoven, at Vienna's central cemetery, Währing Cemetery.

Ultimately, many of Schubert's six hundred poetic melodies that continue to bring joy to our world were produced, preserved, printed, and performed because of Schubert's band of merry friends!

Timeline Fan

Materials Needed:

- 1 - 8 ½ x 11 sheet of paper
- Ruler
- Pencil

Directions:

1. Turn an 8 ½ x 11 sheet of paper horizontally.
2. Using a ruler, divide the paper into eleven one-inch sections as shown below.
3. Accordion fold the paper along the one-inch lines.
4. In the first column write the title of your timeline-- "A Timeline of Franz Schubert's Life"
5. Use the provided timeline information to write a year at the top of each column. (You will need to use the front and back of your fan.)
6. In each column, write one fact from the timeline information about Franz Schubert and one fact about another event in world history during that year.
7. Refold your fan. Use it to keep cool and to review the life and times of Franz Schubert.

Example:

A Timeline of Franz Schubert's Life	1797	1807	1808	1809	1810	1812	1813	1814	1815	1816

Schubert

Timeline Information:

1797
Franz Peter Schubert is born on January 31. John Adams is inaugurated as President of the United States. Samuel T. Coleridge writes "Kubla Khan." German poet Heinrich Heine is born. Joseph Haydn composes the "Emperor" Quartet.

1807
Schubert begins lessons with Michael Holzer at Lichtental parish. Napoleon suppresses the Tribunate, guaranteeing his dictatorship of France. Charles and Mary Lamb write *Tales from Shakespeare*. Robert Fulton's paddleboat steamer, *Clermont*, navigates the Hudson River. England prohibits slave trade.

1808
Schubert joins the court choir and school in Vienna, known as the Convict. The United States bans the importation of African slaves. Napoleon and his army invade Spain and occupy Rome. Goethe's *Faust* is published. Goethe and Napoleon meet at the Congress of Erfurt. Ships' anchor chains of iron are patented.

1809
Schubert plays violin at Stadtkonvikt, and is referred to as "a musical talent." Schubert is attending school in Vienna when Napoleon attacks the city. Haydn dies in May. Napoleon divorces Josephine. Abraham Lincoln, Felix Mendelssohn, Charles Darwin, Edgar A. Poe, and Louis Braille are born.

1810
The earliest surviving compositions by Schubert are written. This was the year of Napoleon's height of power. German composer Robert Schumann is born. Francois Appert develops techniques for canning foods.

1812
Schubert's mother dies in May. In July, Schubert realizes his voice is changing and he has "crowed" for the last time at the Convict. Napoleon invades Russia, but retreats after losing 95% of his army. U.S. declares war on Britain. Poet Robert Browning is born. The Brothers Grimm publish their *Grimm's Fairy Tales*.

1813
Schubert completes his first symphony, dedicated to the Convict's director, Dr. Lang. He also leaves the court choir and school to attend St. Anna's College for teacher training. Prussia and Austria declare war on France. Simon Bolivar becomes dictator of Venezuela. Mexico declares its independence from Spain. Scottish explorer and missionary David Livingstone is born. The waltz becomes the rage in European ballrooms.

1814
Schubert joins his father's school as an assistant teacher on August 19. Napoleon abdicates and is banished to the island of Elba. Beethoven's *Fidelio* is presented. Francis Scott Key writes the poem that later becomes the U.S. national anthem.

1815
Schubert writes *The Erlking*. He has a very productive year musically, though he is still teaching at his father's school. Schubert meets Franz Schober, who will influence his life and music dramatically. The Congress of Vienna meets to redraw the European map and create a peace that lasts forty years. America defeats Britain at the Battle of New Orleans.

1816
Schubert moves into Schober's mother's home to devote himself to composing music. Argentina declares its independence. Jane Austen's *Emma* is published.

1817
Schubert returns temporarily to his father's school to teach. James Monroe is inaugurated as the fifth U.S. President. Jane Austen dies. Construction of the Erie Canal begins.

1818

Schubert becomes the music teacher for the Esterházys. Chile proclaims its independence. The border between Canada and the U.S. is agreed upon (the 49th parallel). Karl Marx is born.

1819

Schäfers Klage is the first public performance of one of Schubert's songs[53]. The first bicycles in the United States are introduced in New York City. The *Savannah* becomes the first steamship to cross the Atlantic.[54]

1820

The Twin Brothers, Schubert's opera with Vogl as the lead, is presented in Vienna. The "Missouri Compromise" is passed, with Maine entering the Union as a free state and Missouri entering as a slave state (in 1821).

1821

Schubert's friends pay for the publication of *The Erlking*. Michael Faraday discovers the fundamentals of electromagnetic rotation.

1822

Schubert tries to write an opera with Schober. Symphony No. 8 in B Minor (The "Unfinished" Symphony) is started. Louis Pasteur and Ulysses S. Grant are born. Franz Liszt makes his piano debut in Vienna (at age eleven).

1824

Schubert returns to teach at the Esterházy summer estate. Simon Bolivar is proclaimed Emperor of Peru. The Erie Canal is completed.

1825

Schubert moves in with artist Moritz von Schwind in Vienna. He takes a short concert tour of Austria with singer Johann Michael Vogl. John Quincy Adams is inaugurated as the sixth U.S. President. Composer and music director Antonio Salieri dies. Waltz composer Johann Strauss is born.

1826

Schubert is denied the post of Assistant Kapellmeister to the court in Vienna. Thomas Jefferson dies. Russia declares war on Persia.

1827

Ludwig van Beethoven receives musical pieces from Schubert for his consideration. Beethoven dies and Schubert is a torchbearer at his funeral.

1828

Construction begins on the B&O Railroad, the first passenger line in the U.S. Schubert gives first and final concert in Vienna. As his illness worsens, he moves to his brother's home. He dies of typhoid fever on November 19.

Schubert

An Introduction to Music Theory, Part 4

Remember the definition of a staff? It is a set of five horizontal lines, and the four spaces between them are where the notes of music are written.[55]

Notes are written on the staff in a specific order. When the instrumentalist plays the notes in that order, he is playing a song. It is not just the notes that indicate how to play music however. There are other symbols that show how a song should be played.

What clef are the notes in?

 The Treble Clef (also called the G clef): The notes written in this clef should be played above middle C, usually with the right hand on keyboard instruments; it is used for soprano and alto voices, and high-pitched instruments.

The Bass Clef: the notes written in this clef should be played below middle C with the left hand on keyboard instruments; it is used for tenor, baritone, and bass voices and low-pitched instruments.

Look at the music in *Franz Schubert and His Merry Friends*. Can you find the treble clef and the bass clef? Look at the notes in the staff besides the clef symbols. See the notes written there? Answer the following questions about those notes.

Which hand would you use to play the notes in the treble clef line? _____

Would these notes sound high or low? _____

Which hand would you use to play the notes in the bass clef line? _____

Would these notes sound high or low? _____

How fast should you play the notes?

Tempo is the speed at which a musical composition or passage is performed. The time (or meter) signature helps us know how fast or slow we should play the written notes. It determines how long a measure is and the beat value of the notes.

Do you remember the definition of a measure? It is the divided sections on the staff that organizes music. Measures are indicated by bar lines which are the vertical lines on the staff. The top note of the time signature tells you how many beats should be in each measure. The bottom note tells you what kind of note gets one beat. For example, in ¾ time each measure gets three beats and each quarter note is worth one beat.

The time signature is found right after the clef sign and key signature on the staff. Several time signatures are used in music, but the most common one is 4/4 time.

$\frac{4}{4}$ = Each measure gets four beats and each quarter note is worth one beat.

$\frac{3}{4}$ = Each measure gets three beats and each quarter note is worth one beat.

$\frac{2}{4}$ = Each measure gets two beats and each quarter note is worth one beat.

$\frac{6}{8}$ = Each measure gets six beats and each eighth note is worth one beat. The dotted half note is worth six beats, half notes are worth three beats, and the quarter note is worth two beats.

Note: 4/4 time is often referred to as "common time" and can also be shown with this symbol: **C**. (See page 36 in *Franz Schubert and His Merry Friends*.)

You can practice counting notes by clapping the following rhythms. Check the time signature to see how many notes should be in each measure. Then use your note and rest flashcards to remember how many beats each note and rest is worth. Keep the rhythm even as you count out the note and rest values.

Clap the rhythms while you count aloud.

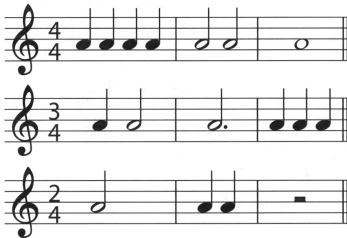

Schubert

Now clap the rhythm of this song while you count the notes aloud.

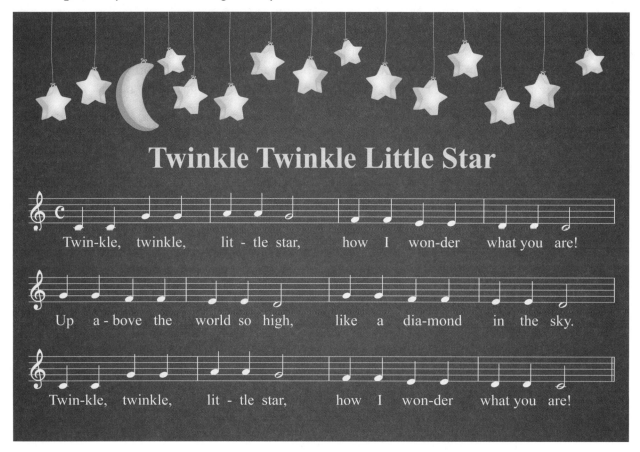

Using the *Make Your Own Music Paper* lapbook pages, follow the directions to cut out and assemble the pieces. Label the parts of music that you have learned. Enjoy making your own music paper!

Franz Schubert and His Merry Friends Quiz

Name: _____ Date: _____

Multiple Choice
Circle the correct answer.

1. In what country was Franz Schubert born and where did he spend most his life?
   a. Germany
   b. England
   c. Austria
   d. Italy

2. In which famous choir did Schubert sing as a young boy?
   a. Copenhagen Boys' Choir
   b. Aurelius Boys' Choir
   c. Sofia Boys' Choir
   d. Vienna Boys' Choir

3. Who was Franz Schubert's hero?
   a. Beethoven
   b. Mozart
   c. Bach
   d. Haydn

4. How many lyric songs (lieder) did Schubert write?
   a. only 50
   b. less than 320
   c. over 600
   d. more than 900

5. How did Franz Schubert die?
   a. typhoid fever
   b. pneumonia
   c. stomach ulcers
   d. none of the above

Fill in the Blank
What do these dynamics markings mean? Complete the sentences.

1. *pp* means _____.

2. *p* means _____.

3. *mp* means _____.

4. *mf* means _____.

5. *f* means _____.

6. *ff* means _____.

Matching

Match the note with its corresponding rest.

Week One: Chapter One Comprehension Questions

1. Administrator and teacher of a school, p. 9.
2. A piano factory, p.13.
3. Wheeler tells us outright that Schoolmaster Schubert earned little money teaching, p.9. Father wanted Franz to go to the court choir school so he had one less in the house for whom to provide, p. 20. Franz went to his musical tryout for the court choir in ragged clothes, p. 21.
4. He had to demonstrate his knowledge of music by answering difficult questions, and he had to sing for the choirmasters, p. 23.
5. His brother Ignaz, p. 18; his church choir-master, Michael Holzer, p. 19; even his father introduced him to music by playing it frequently, p. 11.

Week One: An Introduction to Music Theory

1. *pp* (p. 52)
2. *p* ➔ *f* ➔ *p* (pp. 102-103)
3. *p* ➔ *pp* ➔ *f* (pp. 110-113)
4. *p* ➔ *mf* ➔ *p* ➔ *pp* ➔ *p* (pp. 122-123)

Week Two: Chapter Two Comprehension Questions

1. He played second violin, got the music ready for rehearsals, prepared the candles in their holders, and tuned the instruments, p. 32.
2. Spaun was an older student in the Convict who played in the orchestra and took an interest in Franz, p. 33. He even volunteered to buy music paper for Franz's compositions, p. 39. Spaun later left the Convict to earn a living in Vienna and be trained as a lawyer, pp. 49, 50.
3. He used a white tablecloth, p. 38.
4. He prefers writing and learning music, pp. 33, 44.
5. He refused to let Franz visit home until his grades improved, p. 51.
6.

Week Two: Word Search

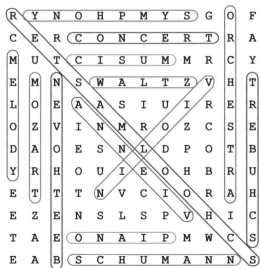

Schubert

Week Two: An Introduction to Music Theory, Part 2 (Vocabulary and Symbols)

Extra Challenge Answer: p. 89, p. 110

Short Paragraph (answers may vary)

Musical terms and symbols help an instrumentalist communicate emotion by providing directions concerning the sound of the song. As an instrument is being played, many different moods can be expressed by the loudness or softness of the music, by accents being placed on particular notes, or by playing some notes detached. The musical symbols and terms tell the instrumentalist how to play a piece of music so that a particular feeling is expressed to the audience. Music would all sound very similar if there were not distinctive markings for each song. It is important for an instrumentalist to recognize and understand the terms and symbols within a song so that a suitable emotion is portrayed.

Week Three: Chapter Three Comprehension Questions

1. He was moved to first chair violin, and Herr Ruziczka asked him to conduct the orchestra, p. 56.
2. He studied the music early, and he went over the difficult parts numerous times during rehearsals, p. 64. He also taught himself to play all the different instruments so he could take an absent boy's place, p. 65.
3. Master Salieri encourages Franz, pp. 60, 75.
4. His voice changed, essentially ending his career in the choir, p. 77.
5. Theodore was happy because Franz was training to become a schoolmaster "like all the Schuberts," p. 77.

Note and Rest Identification

Note and Rest Match

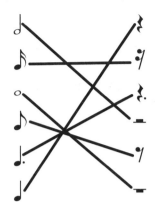

Note and Rest Flashcards

Whole Note: A whole note is a hollow oval with no stem. A whole note is worth 4 beats.	**Eighth Note:** An eighth note is a filled-in oval. It has a stem and one flag. An eighth note is worth ½ of a beat.
Whole Rest: A whole rest looks like an upside down hat. A whole rest is worth 4 beats of silence.	**Eighth Rest:** An eighth rest looks like a fancy seven. An eighth rest is worth ½ a beat of silence.
Half Note: A half note is a hollow oval with a stem. A half note is worth 2 beats.	**Sixteenth Note:** A sixteenth note is a filled-in oval. It has a stem and two flags. A sixteenth note is worth ¼ of a beat.
Half Rest: A half rest looks like a right side up hat. A half rest is worth 2 beats of silence.	**Sixteenth Rest:** A sixteenth rest looks like a fancy flag. A sixteenth rest is worth ¼ a beat of silence
Quarter Note: A quarter note is a filled-in oval with a stem. A quarter note is worth 1 beat.	**Dotted Note:** Adding a dot to a note increases its beats by ½ of the original value. (A dotted half note = 3 beats, a dotted quarter note = 1 ½ beats)
Quarter Rest: A quarter rest looks like a fancy zig zag. A quarter rest is worth 1 beat of silence.	**Dotted Rest:** Adding a dot to a rest increases its beats by ½ of the original value. (A dotted half rest = 3 beats, a dotted quarter rest = 1 ½ beats)

Week Four: Chapter Four Comprehension Questions

1. You can hear the sound of a horse's hoofs in the accompaniment, p. 85.
2. He wanted to write melodies, p. 87.
3. They brought him poems to inspire his compositions, p. 92. They exhorted him to follow his dream of composing full time, p. 93. They invited him to live in their apartments, pp. 94, 100. They supplied him with food and music paper, pp. 94, 95. His friends shared their clothes with him, pp. 100, 108. They showcased his music in concerts, p. 106. His friends took him on refreshing vacations, p. 106. They paid to have some of his pieces printed, p.115. And his friends purchased a new piano for him, p. 120.
4. He taught music to Count Esterházy's children, pp. 95, 96.
5. Artists, writers, and musicians are his dearest friends, p. 108.
6. Franz respects Ludwig van Beethoven, pp. 114, 115.

Week Four: Composers Scramble

1. Beethoven
2. Brahms
3. Haydn
4. Schumann
5. Liszt
6. Schubert
7. Paganini

Franz Schubert and His Merry Friends Quiz

Multiple Choice:

1. c.
2. d.
3. a.
4. c.
5. a.

Fill in the Blank

1. *pp* means very soft.
2. *p* means soft.
3. *mp* means moderately soft.
4. *mf* means moderately loud.
5. *f* means loud.
6. *ff* means very loud.

Matching

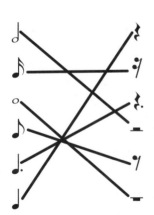

Endnotes

Sebastian Bach, The Boy from Thuringia

[1] Henry Thomas and Dana Lee Thomas, Living Biographies of Great Composers (Garden City, NY: Nelson Doubleday, Inc., 1940), 5.

[2] Patrick Kavanaugh, Spiritual Lives of the Great Composers (Grand Rapids, MI: Zondervan, 1996), 19.

[3] Jane Stuart Smith and Betty Carlson, The Gift of Music: Great Composers and Their Influence (Wheaton, IL: Crossway Books, 1995), 33.

[4] Kathleen Krull, Lives of the Musicians: Good Times, Bad Times (San Diego, CA: Harcourt, Inc., 2002), 15.

[5] Ibid., 16.

[6] Krull, Lives of the Musicians, 15.

[7] Kavanaugh, Spiritual Lives of the Great Composers, 19.

[8] Smith and Carlson, The Gift of Music, 32.

[9] Samuel Nisenson and William DeWitt, Illustrated Minute Biographies (New York, NY: Grosset & Dunlap, 1953), 19.

[10] Thomas and Thomas, Living Biographies of Great Composers, 5.

[11] Ibid., 8.

[12] Krull, Lives of the Musicians, 17.

[13] Cynthia Millar, Great Masters: Bach and His World (Morristown, NJ: Silver Burdett Company, 1980), 13.

[14] Hans T. David and Arthur Mendel, The Bach Reader: A Life of Johann Sebastian Bach in Letters & Documents (New York, NY: W.W. Norton & Company, Inc., 1945), 288.

[15] Jeanette Winter, Sebastian: A Book about Bach (San Diego, CA: Harcourt Brace & Company, 1999), 14.

[16] Smith and Carlson, The Gift of Music, 33.

[17] David and Mendel, The Bach Reader, 24. (An idea repeated in Smith and Carlson, The Gift of Music, 32.)

[18] Roland Vernon, Introducing Bach (Parsippany, NJ: Simon & Schuster, 1996), 31.

[19] Kavanaugh, Spiritual Lives of Great Composers, 17–18.

[20] Vernon, Introducing Bach, 5.

[21] Thomas and Thomas, Living Biographies of Great Composers, 9.

[22] Douglas Cowling, Mr. Bach Comes to Call (Ontario, Canada: The Children's Group, Inc., 1988), Track 12.

[23] Thomas and Thomas, Living Biographies of Great Composers, 4.

[24] David and Mendel, The Bach Reader, 287.

[25] Hendrik W. Van Loon, The Life and Times of Johann Sebastian Bach (London: George G. Harrap & Co. Ltd., 1942), no page number available.

[26] Vernon, Introducing Bach, 17.

[27] Krull, Lives of the Musicians, 15.

[28] Smith and Carlson, The Gift of Music, 33–34.

[29] Thomas and Thomas, Living Biographies of Great Composers, 4.

[30] Smith and Carlson, The Gift of Music, 35.

[31] David and Mendel, The Bach Reader, 222.

[32] Ibid., 125.

[33] Nisenson and DeWitt, Illustrated Minute Biographies, 19.

[34] Smith and Carlson, The Gift of Music, 36.

[35] Smith and Carlson, The Gift of Music, 34.

[36] Vernon, Introducing Bach, 30.

Handel at the Court of Kings

[1] Herbert Weinstock, Handel (New York: Alfred A. Knopf, 1959), 7.

[2] Jane Stuart Smith and Betty Carlson, The Gift of Music: Great Composers and Their Influence (Wheaton, IL: Crossway Books, 1995), 39.

[3] Henry Thomas and Dana Lee Thomas, Living Biographies of Great Composers (Garden City, NY: Nelson Doubleday, Inc., 1940), 19.

[4] Smith and Carlson, The Gift of Music, 41.

[5] Weinstock, Handel, 14.

[6] Ibid., 17.

[7] Louis Elson, Great Composers and Their Work (Boston: L.C. Page and Company, 1898), 59.

[8] Weinstock, Handel, 21.

[9] Thomas and Thomas, Living Biographies of Great Composers, 23.

[10] Elson, Great Composers and Their Work, 58.

[11] Thomas and Thomas, Living Biographies of Great Composers, 22.

[12] Elson, Great Composers and Their Work, 60.

[13] Smith and Carlson, The Gift of Music, 40.

[14] Weinstock, Handel, 32.

[15] Ibid, 252.

[16] Opal Wheeler, Handel at the Court of Kings (Zeezok Publishing, LLC, 2006), 124.

[17] Thomas and Thomas, Living Biographies of Great Composers, 30.

[18] Ibid, 23.

[19] Weinstock, Handel, 56.

[20] Smith and Carlson, The Gift of Music, 42.

[21] Thomas and Thomas, Living Biographies of Great Composers, 30.

[22] Ibid, 31.

[23] Weinstock, Handel, 240.

[24] Smith and Carlson, The Gift of Music, 42.

[25] Weinstock, Handel, 83.

[26] Ibid., 86.

[27] Ibid., 45.

[28] Ibid., 77.

[29] Thomas and Thomas, Living Biographies of Great Composers, 29.

[30] Smith and Carlson, The Gift of Music, 43.

[31] Kavanaugh, Spiritual Lives of the Great Composers, 33.

[32] Smith and Carlson, The Gift of Music, 44.

[33] Ibid, 45.

[34] Weinstock, Handel, 294.

[35] Ibid.

[36] Smith and Carlson, The Gift of Music, 45.

[38] Patrick Kavanaugh, Spiritual Lives of the Great Composers (Grand Rapids, MI: Zondervan, 1996), 30.

[39] Smith and Carlson, The Gift of Music, 45.

[40] Weinstock, Handel, 252.

[41] Smith and Carlson, The Gift of Music, 45.

[42] Ibid.

[1] Neil Butterworth, Haydn: His Life and Times (Neptune City, NJ: Paganin-iana Publications, Inc., 1980), 9.

[2] Butterworth, *Haydn: His Life and Times*, 12.

[3] Ibid.

[4] Karl Geiringer, Haydn: A Creative Life in Music (New York: W.W. Norton & Company, Inc., 1946), 24.

[5] Butterworth, Haydn: His Life and Times, 12.

[6] Geiringer, Haydn: A Creative Life in Music, 28 (quoting from Giuseppe Carpani's biography of the composer).

[7] Ibid., 28.

[8] Jane Stuart Smith and Betty Carlson, The Gift of Music: Great Composers and Their Influence (Wheaton, IL: Crossway Books, 1995), 48.

[9] Patrick Kavanaugh, Spiritual Lives of the Great Composers (Grand Rapids, MI: Zondervan, 1996), 38.

[10] Geiringer, Haydn: A Creative Life in Music, 23.

[11] Geiringer, Haydn: A Creative Life in Music, 21.

[12] Joan E. Haines and Linda L. Gerber, Leading Young Children to Music (Columbus, Ohio: Prentice-Hall, 2000), 11, 196.

[13] Butterworth, *Haydn*: His Life and Times, 15.

[14] Smith and Carlson, The Gift of Music, 48.

[15] Geiringer, Haydn: A Creative Life in Music, 35.

[16] Smith and Carlson, The Gift of Music, 50.

[17] Kavanaugh, Spiritual Lives of the Great Composers, 40.

[18] Butterworth, Haydn: His Life and Times, 21.

[19] Butterworth, Haydn: His Life and Times, 15.

[20] Geiringer, Haydn: A Creative Life in Music, 40.

[21] Ibid.

[22] Butterworth, Haydn: His Life and Times, 24.

[23] Ibid.

[24] "violin." Encarta® World English Dictionary[North American Edition]. http://www.bing.com/Dictionary/search?q=define+violin&go=&form=QB. (June 2011).

"viola." Encarta® World English Dictionary[North American Edition]. http://www.bing.com/Dictionary/search?q=define+viola&go=&form=QB. (June 2011).

"cello." Encarta® World English Dictionary[North American Edition]. http://www.bing.com/Dictionary/search?q=define+cello&go=&form=QB. (June 2011).

"double bass." Encarta® World English Dictionary[North American Edition]. http://www.bing.com/Dictionary/search?q=define+double+bass&go=&form=QB. (June 2011).

"harp." Encarta® World English Dictionary[North American Edition]. http://www.bing.com/Dictionary/search?q=define+harp&go=&form=QB. (June 2011).

"oboe." Encarta® World English Dictionary[North American Edition]. http://www.bing.com/Dictionary/search?q=define+oboe&go=&form=QB. (June 2011).

"bassoon." Encarta® World English Dictionary[North American Edition]. http://www.bing.com/Dictionary/search?q=define+bassoon&go=&form=QB. (June 2011).

"flute." Encarta® World English Dictionary[North American Edition]. http://www.bing.com/Dictionary/search?q=define+flute&go=&form=QB. (June 2011).

"piccolo." Encarta® World English Dictionary[North American Edition]. http://www.bing.com/Dictionary/search?q=define+piccolo&go=&form=QB. (June 2011).

"clarinet." Encarta® World English Dictionary[North American Edition]. http://www.bing.com/Dictionary/search?q=define+clarinet&go=&form=QB. (June 2011).

"french horn." Encarta® World English Dictionary[North American Edition]. http://www.bing.com/Dictionary/search?q=define+french horn&go=&form=QB. (June 2011).

"trombone." Encarta® World English Dictionary[North American Edition]. http://www.bing.com/Dictionary/search?q=define+trombone&go=&form=QB. (June 2011).

"trumpet." Encarta® World English Dictionary[North American Edition]. http://www.bing.com/Dictionary/search?q=define+trumpet&go=&form=QB. (June 2011).

"tuba." Encarta® World English Dictionary[North American Edition]. http://www.bing.com/Dictionary/search?q=define+tuba&go=&form=QB. (June 2011).

"cymbals." Encarta® World English Dictionary[North American Edition]. http://www.bing.com/Dictionary/search?q=define+cymbals&go=&form=QB. (June 2011).

"snare drum." Encarta® World English Dictionary[North American Edition]. http://www.bing.com/Dictionary/search?q=define+snaredrum&go=&form=QB. (June 2011).

[25] Geiringer, Haydn: A Creative Life in Music, 79.

[76] Kavanaugh, Spiritual Lives of the Great Composers, 39.

[27] Butterworth, Haydn: His Life and Times, 79.

[28] Smith and Carlson, The Gift of Music, 49.

[29] Butterworth, Haydn: His Life and Times, 67.

[30] Leopold Mozart, Personal letter dated February 16, 1785.

[31] Brockway and Weinstock, Men of Music, 113.

[32] Butterworth, Haydn: His Life and Times, 70.

[33] Butterworth, Haydn: His Life and Times, 135.

[34] "electric instrument" en.wikipedia.org/wiki/Electric_instrument (June 2011).

[35] "synthesizer." Encarta® World English Dictionary[North American Edition]2009 Microsoft http://www.bing.com/Dictionary/search?q=define+synthesizer&go=&form=QB (June 2011).

[36] Butterworth, Haydn: His Life and Times, 81.

[37] Brockway and Weinstock, Men of Music, 116.

[38] Butterworth, Haydn: His Life and Times, 121.

[39] Kavanaugh, Spiritual Lives of the Great Composers, 40.

[40] Geiringer, Haydn: A Creative Life in Music, 170.

[41] Kavanaugh, Spiritual Lives of the Great Composers, 42.

[42] Kavanaugh, Spiritual Lives of the Great Composers, 41.

[43] Smith and Carlson, The Gift of Music, 50.

Mozart, The Wonder Boy

[1] Roland Vernon, *Introducing Mozart* (London: Belitha Press Limited, 1996), 6.

[2] Patrick Kavanaugh, *The Spiritual Lives of the Great Composers* (Grand Rapids, MI: Zondervan, 1996), 47.

[3] Alfred Einstein, *Mozart, His Character, His Work* (London: Oxford University Press, 1945), 78.

[4] Kathleen Krull, *Lives of the Musicians: Good Times, Bad Times* (San Diego, CA: Harcourt, Inc., 2002), 20.

[5] Louis Biancolli, *The Mozart Handbook* (Cleveland, OH: The World Publishing Company, 1954), 12.

[6] Einstein, *Mozart*, 25.

[7] Einstein, *Mozart*, 151.

[8] Lady Wallace, *The Letters of Wolfgang Amadeus Mozart* (Boston: Oliver Ditson & Co., no date given but sometime before 1877), 81.

[9] Catherine Brighton, *Mozart* (New York: Doubleday, 1990), 24.

[10] Peggy Woodford, *Mozart* (London: Omnibus Press, 1990), 11.

[11] Einstein, *Mozart*, 13.

[12] Smith and Carlson, *The Gift of Music*, 53.

[13] Rachel Isadora, *Young Mozart* (New York: Viking, 1997), 29.

[14] "genius." http://dictionary.kids.net.au/word/genius. (May 2011)

[15] Jane Stuart Smith and Betty Carlson, *The Gift of Music: Great Composers and Their Influence* (Wheaton: IL: Crossway Books, 1995), 52.

[16] Kavanaugh, *The Spiritual Lives of the Great Composers*, 46.

[17] Krull, *Lives of the Musicians*, 21.

[18] Smith and Carlson, *The Gift of Music*, 52.

[19] Ibid., 55.

[20] Ibid., 53.

[21] Biancolli, *The Mozart Handbook*, 13.

[22] Einstein, *Mozart*, 28.

[23] Biancolli, *The Mozart Handbook*, 36.

[24] Krull, *Lives of the Musicians*, 20.

[25] Kavanaugh, *The Spiritual Lives of the Great Composers*, 46.

[26] Biancolli, *The Mozart Handbook*, 49.

[27] Smith and Carlson, *The Gift of Music*, 53.

[28] Einstein, *Mozart*, 55.

[29] Krull, *Lives of the Musicians*, 23.

[30] Smith and Carlson, *The Gift of Music*, 54.

[31] Krull, *Lives of the Musicians*, 20.

[32] Einstein, *Mozart*, 89.

[33] Catherine Brighton, *Mozart* (New York: Doubleday, 1990), 18.

[34] Henry Thomas and Dana Lee Thomas, *Living Biographies of Great Composers* (Garden City, NY: Nelson Doubleday, Inc., 1940), 53.

[35] Kavanaugh, *The Spiritual Lives of the Great Composers*, 46.

[36] Ordentliche Wochenliche Franckfurter Frag-und Anzeigungs-Nachrichten, August 16, 1763. (Quoted from The Mozart Project website on November 21, 2004.)

[37] Samuel Nisenson and William DeWitt, *Illustrated Minute Biographies* (New York: Grosset & Dunlap, 1953), 113.

[38] Kavanaugh, *The Spiritual Lives of the Great Composers*, 52.

[39] Smith and Carlson, *The Gift of Music*, 56.

[40] Negrospirituals.com. Accessed May 2011. Available from http://www.negrospirituals.com.

[41] Negrospirituals.com. Accessed May 2011. Available from http://www.negrospirituals.com.

[42] Tyson, J. History of Native American Drums. Demand Media. Accessed May 2011. Available from http://www.ehow.com/about_5166077_history-native-american-drums.html.

[43] Nickson, C. Roma (Gypsy) Music. National Geographic Society. Accessed May 2011. Available from http://worldmusic.national-geographic.com

[44] "culture." Encarta® World English Dictionary[North American Edition]2009 Microsoft http://www.bing.com/Dictionary/search?q=define+culture&go=&form=QB (May 2011).

[45] Kavanaugh, *The Spiritual Lives of the Great Composers*, 45.

[46] Krull, *Lives of the Musicians*, 19.

[47] Vernon, *Introducing Mozart*, 18.

[48] Biancolli, *The Mozart Handbook*, 31.

[49] Smith and Carlson, *The Gift of Music*, 57.

[50] Krull, *Lives of the Musicians*, 23.

[51] Thomas and Thomas, *Living Biographies of Great Composers*, 69.

[52] Einstein, *Mozart*, 126.

[53] Smith and Carlson, *The Gift of Music*, 57.

[54] Opal Wheeler and Sybil Deucher, *Joseph Haydn: The Merry Little Peasant* (Zeezok Publishing, LLC, Elyria, OH, 2005), 86.

[55] Kavanaugh, *The Spiritual Lives of the Great Composers*, 47.

[56] Vernon, *Introducing Mozart*, 11.

[57] Lady Wallace, *The Letters of Wolfgang Amadeus Mozart*, 218.

[58] Kavanaugh, *The Spiritual Lives of the Great Composers*, 52.

[59] Krull, *Lives of the Musicians*, 21.

[60] Kavanaugh, *The Spiritual Lives of the Great Composers*, 49.

[61] Opera and American Music Theatre, Grade Five. Ohio Department of Education. Accessed September 2011. Available from http://dnet01.ode.state.oh.us/IMS.ItemDetails/LessonDetail.aspx?id=0907f84c805316b7

[62] Thomas and Thomas, *Living Biographies of Great Composers*, 62.

1 Patrick Kavanaugh, *Spiritual Lives of the Great Composers* (Grand Rapids, MI: Zondervan, 1996), 60.

2 Ibid., 58.

3 H.C. Robbins Landon, *Beethoven: A Documentary Study* (New York: Macmillan Publishing Co., Inc., 1974),23.

4 Ibid., 26.

5 Maynard Solomon, *Beethoven* (New York: Schirmer Books, 1977), 17.

6 Kathleen Krull, *Lives of the Musicians: Good Times, Bad Times* (San Diego,CA: Harcourt, Inc., 1993), 25.

7 Landon, *Beethoven: A Documentary Study*, 29.

8 Solomon, *Beethoven*, 18.

9 Pam Brown, *The World's Greatest Composers: Ludwig van Beethoven*, United Kingdom: Exley Publications Ltd., 1993), 18.

10 Ibid, 17.

11 Ibid., 57.

12 Landon, *Beethoven: A Documentary Study*, 29.

13 "time." Encarta® World English Dictionary[North American Edition] 2009 http://www.bing.com/Dictionary/search?q=define+time&go=&form=QB (August 2011).

"location." Encarta® World English Dictionary[North American Edition] 2009 http://www.bing.com/Dictionary/search?q=define+location&go=&form=QB (August 2011).

"culture." Encarta® World English Dictionary[North American Edition] 2009 http://www.bing.com/Dictionary/search?q=define+culture&go=&form=QB (August 2011).

"current events." Encarta® World English Dictionary[North American Edition] 2009 http://www.bing.com/Dictionary/search?q=define+current+events&go=&form=QB (August 2011)

"social climate." *Merriam Webster.com. 2011.* http://www.merriam-webster.com/dictionary/(social) climate. (August 2011).

"political climate." *Merriam Webster.com. 2011.* http://www.merriam-webster.com/dictionary/(politicall) climate. (August 2011).

14 *Battle Cry of Freedom.* Wikipedia. Accessed August 2011. Available from http://en.wikipedia.org/wiki/Battle_Cry_of_Freedom

15 Sabatella, M. *Ballad of America.* Accessed August 2011. Available from http://www.balladofamerica.com/music/indexes/songs/battlecryoffreedom

16 Jane Stuart Smith and Betty Carlson, *The Gift of Music: Great Composers and Their Influence* (Wheaton, IL: Crossway Books, 1995), 61.

17 Ibid., 63.

18 Brown, *The World's Greatest Composers: Ludwig van Beethoven*, 24.

19 Kavanaugh, *Spiritual Lives of the Great Composers*, 58.

20 Brown, *The World's Greatest Composers: Ludwig van Beethoven*, 12.

21 O.G. Sonneck, *Beethoven: Impressions by His Contemporaries* (New York: Dover Publications, Inc., 1967), 10.

22 Krull, *Lives of the Musicians: Good Times, Bad Times*, 27.

23 Barbara Nichol, *Beethoven Lives Upstairs* (Ontario, Canada: Classical Kids Recordings, 1989), CD insert notes.

24 Brown, *The World's Greatest Composers: Ludwig van Beethoven*, 15.

25 Roland Vernon, *Introducing Beethoven* (Parsippany, NJ: Silver Burdett Press, 1996), 15.

26 Ates Orga, *Beethoven: His Life and Times* (Neptune City, NJ: Paganiniana Publications, Inc., 1980), 45.

27 Landon, *Beethoven: A Documentary Study*, 37, 39.

28 Ibid., 37.

29 Ibid., 39.

30 Samuel Nisenson and William DeWitt, *Illustrated Minute Biographies* (New York: Grosset & Dunlap, 1953), 22.

31 Brown, *The World's Greatest Composers: Ludwig van Beethoven*, 12.

32 Krull, *Lives of the Musicians: Good Times, Bad Times*, 27.

33 Kavanaugh, *Spiritual Lives of the Great Composers*, 56.

34 Brown, *The World's Greatest Composers: Ludwig van Beethoven*, 53.

35 Krull, *Lives of the Musicians: Good Times, Bad Times*, 28.

36 Brown, *The World's Greatest Composers: Ludwig van Beethoven*, 53.

37 Vernon, *Introducing Beethoven*,15.

38 Nichol, *Beethoven Lives Upstairs*, CD insert notes..

39 Prabhat. April 15, 2010. *Difference Between Piano and Harpsichord.* Difference Between.net, Accessed August 2011. Available from http://www.differencebetween.net/object/difference-between-piano-and-harpsichord

40 Brown, *The World's Greatest Composers: Ludwig van Beethoven*,26.

41 Nichol, *Beethoven Lives Upstairs*, CD insert notes.

42 Kavanaugh, *Spiritual Lives of the Great Composers*, 57.

43 Solomon, *Beethoven*, 218.

44 Ibid, 114.

45 Brown, *The World's Greatest Composers: Ludwig van Beethoven*, 36.

46 Smith and Carlson, *The Gift of Music*, 65.

47 Nichol, *Beethoven Lives Upstairs*, CD insert notes.

48 Brown, *The World's Greatest Composers: Ludwig van Beethoven*, 42.

49 Krull, *Lives of the Musicians: Good Times, Bad Times*, 28.

50 Mitchell, R. September 25, 2005. *How Many Deaf People Are There in the United States?*
Estimates From the Survey of Income and Program Participation. Deaf Studies and Deaf Education. Accessed August 2011. Available from http://jdsde.oxfordjournals.org/content/11/1/112.full.pdf+html.

51 James Wierzbicki, "The Beethoven Sketchbooks," *St. Louis Post-Dispatch*, Jan. 5, 1986.

52 Dr. Gerhard von Breuning, *From the Schwarzspanier House: My Boyhood Memories of Beethoven* (Vienna: L. Rosner, 1874), 37.

53 Krull, *Lives of the Musicians: Good Times, Bad Times*, 28.

54 Vernon, *Introducing Beethoven*, 31

55 Smith and Carlson, *The Gift of Music*, 65.

56 Landon, *Beethoven: A Documentary Study*, 115.

57 Krull, *Lives of the Musicians: Good Times, Bad Times*, 27.

58 Nichol, *Beethoven Lives Upstairs*, CD insert notes.

59 Smith and Carlson, *The Gift of Music*, 64.

60 "revolution." *Merriam Webster.com. 2011.* http://www.merriam-webster.com/dictionary/revolution. (August 2011).

61 Vernon, *Introducing Beethoven*,12.

62 Ibid, 23.

63 Landon, *Beethoven: A Documentary Study*, 131.

64 Brown, *The World's Greatest Composers: Ludwig van Beethoven*, 60.

65 Vernon, *Introducing Beethoven*, 29.

66 Krull, *Lives of the Musicians: Good Times, Bad Times*, 29.

67 Kavanaugh, *Spiritual Lives of the Great Composers*, 61.

Paganini, Master of Strings

1 *Spaghetti Soup*. AllRecipies.com. Accessed August 2011. Available from http://allrecipes.com/recipe/spaghetti-soup/detail.aspx.

2 Opal Wheeler, *Paganini Master of Strings*, (New York, NY: E.P. Dutton & Company, 1950), 129

3 "criteria." *Merriam Webster.com. 2011.* http://www.merriam-webster.com/dictionary/criteria. (August 2011).

4 *Niccolo Paganini, Biography*. Last.fm. Accessed August 2011. Available from http://www.last.fm/music/Niccol%C3%B2+Paganini/+wiki.

5 John Sugden. *Nicolo Paganini: Supreme Violinist or Devil's Fiddler?*. (Tunbridge Wells, Kent: Midas Books, 1980), 22.

6 Robert Flodin, *The Meaning of Paganini*, (San Francisco, CA: Morgan Printing Company, 1953), 4.

7 Aaron Frisch and Gary Kelley, *Dark Fiddler: The Life and Legend of Nicolo Paganini*, (Mankato, MN: Creative Editions, 2008), 27.

8 Flodin, *The Meaning of Paganini*, 4.

9 Frisch and Kelley, *Dark Fiddler: The Life and Legend of Nicolo Paganini*, 27.

10 Ibid., 7.

11 McLamore, A. n.d. Music Vocabulary. San Luis Obispo, CA. Accessed August 2011. Available from.http://cla.calpoly.edu/~amclamor/315/vocabulary/vocabac.html.

12 Sugden. *Nicolo Paganini: Supreme Violinist or Devil's Fiddler*, 24.

13 Goodrich, F. 1875. *At the Court of Napoleon*. J.B. Lippincott & Co. Philadelphia. Accessed August 2011. Available from http://napoleonichistoricalsociety.com/articles/Elisa.htm.

14 *Order of the Golden Spur*. Wikipedia. Accessed August 2011. Available from http://en.wikipedia.org/wiki/Order_of_the_Golden_Spur.

15 Flodin, *The Meaning of Paganini*, 3.

16 Wheeler, *Paganini Master of Strings*, 33.

17 Flodin, *The Meaning of Paganini*, 17.

18 Wheeler, *Paganini Master of Strings*, 129.

19 Flodin, *The Meaning of Paganini*, 3.

20 Earls, J. n.d. *The World's Greatest Violinist*. Life in Italy.com. Accessed August 2011. Available from http://www.lifeinitaly.com/music/niccolo-paganini.asp.

21 *Nicola Paganini and the Viola*. Viola in Music.com. Accessed August 2011. Available from http://www.viola-in-music.com/nicolo-paganini.html.

22 "*Jokes: big list of kids music jokes*." Nov. 2011. *Ducksters*. Technological Solutions, Inc. (TSI). Accessed August 2011. Available from http://www.ducksters.com/jokesforkids/music.php.

23 Shah, S. n.d. *Universal Language of Music*. Buzzle.com. Accessed August 2011. Available from http://www.buzzle.com/editorials/1-24-2005-64674.asp.

24 "affect." *Merriam Webster Learner's Dictionary. 2011.* http://www.learnersdictionary.com/search/affect. (August 2011).

25 "experiences." *Merriam Webster Learner's Dictionary. 2011.* http://www.learnersdictionary.com/search/experience. (August 2011).

26 Ibid., 2.

27 Flodin, *The Meaning of Paganini*, 4.

Franz Schubert and His Merry Friends

1 Barrie Carson Turner, *The World's Greatest Composers: Franz Schubert* (Watford, United Kingdom: Exley Publications Litd., 1995), 8.

2 Jane Stuart Smith and Betty Carlson, *The Gift of Music: Great Composers and Their Influence* (Wheaton, IL: Crossway Books, 1995), 74.

3 Turner, *The World's Greatest Composers: Franz Schubert*, 11.

4 Charles Osborne, *Schubert and His Vienna* (New York: Alfred A. Knopf, 1985), 5.

5 Patrick Kavanaugh, *Spiritual Lives of the Great Composers* (Grand Rapids, MI: Zondervan, 1996), 66.

6 Ibid.

7 "dynamics." Encarta® World English Dictionary[North American Edition]2009 Microsoft http://www.bing.com/Dictionary/search?q=define+dynamics&go=&form=QB (August 2011).
   "rhythm." Encarta® World English Dictionary[North American Edition]2009 Microsoft http://www.bing.com/Dictionary/search?q=define+rhythm&go=&form=QB (August 2011).
   "melody." Encarta® World English Dictionary[North American Edition]2009 Microsoft http://www.bing.com/Dictionary/search?q=define+melody&go=&form=QB (August 2011).
   "solfege." Encarta® World English Dictionary[North American Edition]2009 Microsoft http://www.bing.com/Dictionary/search?q=define+solfege&go=&form=QB (August 2011).

8 *Maria and the Children, Do-Re-Mi*. ST Lyrics. Accessed August 2011. Available from http://www.stlyrics.com/lyrics/thesoundofmusic/do-re-mi.htm

9 Schonberg, *The Lives of the Great Composers*,127.

10 Smith and Carlson, *The Gift of Music: Great Composers and Their Influence*, 74.

11 Ibid.

12 Turner,*The World's Greatest Composers: Franz Schubert*, 14.

13 Ibid., 13.

14 Ibid., 26.

15 Osborne, *Schubert and His Vienna*, 10.

16 Turner, *The World's Greatest Composers: Franz Schubert*, 27.

17 Ibid., 39.

18 Harold Schonberg, *The Lives of the Great Composers* (New York: W.W. Norton & Company, Inc., 1997),126.

19 Brian Newbould, *Schubert: The Music and the Man* (Berkeley: University of California Press, 1997), 21.

20 Smith and Carlson, *The Gift of Music: Great Composers and Their Influence*, 78.

21 Turner, *The World's Greatest Composers: Franz Schubert*, 43, 44.

22 "meter." Encarta® World English Dictionary[North American Edition]2009 Microsoft http://www.bing.com/Dictionary/search?q=define+meter&go=&form=QB (August 2011).
   "tonality." Encarta® World English Dictionary[North American Edition]2009 Microsoft http://www.bing.com/Dictionary/search?q=define+tonality&go=&form=QB (August 2011).
   "staff." Encarta® World English Dictionary[North American Edition]2009 Microsoft http://www.bing.com/Dictionary/search?q=define+staff&go=&form=QB (August 2011).
   "chord." Encarta® World English Dictionary[North American Edition]2009 Microsoft http://www.bing.com/Dictionary/search?q=define+chord&go=&form=QB (August 2011).
   "da capo." Encarta® World English Dictionary[North American Edition]2009 Microsoft http://www.bing.com/Dictionary/search?q=define+da+capo&go=&form=QB (August 2011).
   "repeat." Encarta® World English Dictionary[North American Edition]2009 Microsoft http://www.bing.com/Dictionary/search?q=define+repeat&go=&form=QB (August 2011).
   "coda." Encarta® World English Dictionary[North American Edition]2009 Microsoft http://www.bing.com/Dictionary/search?q=define+coda&go=&form=QB (August 2011).
   "accent." Encarta® World English Dictionary[North American Edition]2009 Microsoft http://www.bing.com/Dictionary/search?q=define+accent&go=&form=QB (August 2011).
   "staccato." Encarta® World English Dictionary[North American Edition]2009 Microsoft http://www.bing.com/Dictionary/search?q=define+staccato&go=&form=QB (August 2011).
   Benjamin Hollis, *The Method Behind the Music*. Accessed August

2011. Available from http://method-behind-the-music.com/
theory/notation.

Musical Scale- Definition. Wordiq.com. Accessed August 2011.
Available from http://www.wordiq.com/definition/Musical_scale.

Dal Segno. Wikipedia. Accessed August 2011. Available from
http://en.wikipedia.org/wiki/Dal_Segno.

[23] Ibid., 55.

[24] Ibid, 11.

[25] Schonberg, *The Lives of the Great Composers*, 124.

[26] Turner, *The World's Greatest Composers: Franz Schubert*, 18.

[27] Ibid., 22.

[28] Ibid., 26.

[29] "keen." Encarta® World English Dictionary[North American Edition]2009 Microsoft http://www.bing.com/Dictionary/search?q=define+keen&go=&form=QB (August 2011).

"purposeful." Encarta® World English Dictionary[North American Edition]2009 Microsoft http://www.bing.com/Dictionary/search?q=define+purposeful&go=&form=QB (August 2011).

"goodwill." Encarta® World English Dictionary[North American Edition]2009 Microsoft http://www.bing.com/Dictionary/search?q=define+goodwill&go=&form=QB (August 2011).

"uncomplaining." *Merriam Webster.com. 2011.* http://www.merriam-webster.com/dictionary/uncomplaining. (August 2011).

"ambitious." Encarta® World English Dictionary[North American Edition]2009 Microsoft http://www.bing.com/Dictionary/search?q=define+ambitious&go=&form=QB (August 2011).

"confident." Encarta® World English Dictionary[North American Edition]2009 Microsoft http://www.bing.com/Dictionary/search?q=define+confident&go=&form=QB (August 2011).

"imaginative." Encarta® World English Dictionary[North American Edition]2009 Microsoft http://www.bing.com/Dictionary/search?q=define+imaginative&go=&form=QB (August 2011).

"productive." Encarta® World English Dictionary[North American Edition]2009 Microsoft http://www.bing.com/Dictionary/search?q=define+productive&go=&form=QB (August 2011).

[30] Newbould, *Schubert: The Music and the Man*, 40.

[31] Turner, *The World's Greatest Composers: Franz Schubert*, 23.

[32] Smith and Carlson, *The Gift of Music: Great Composers and Their Influence*, 79.

[33] Turner, *The World's Greatest Composers: Franz Schubert*, 31.

[34] Smith and Carlson, *The Gift of Music: Great Composers and Their Influence*, 79.

[35] Ibid., 79.

[36] Kavanaugh, *Spiritual Lives of the Great Composers*, 67.

[37] Osborne, *Schubert and His Vienna*, 6.

[38] Turner, *The World's Greatest Composers: Franz Schubert*, 54.

[39] Newbould, *Schubert: The Music and the Man*, 137.

[40] Smith and Carlson, *The Gift of Music: Great Composers and Their Influence*, 78.

[41] Turner, *The World's Greatest Composers: Franz Schubert*, 25.

[42] Ibid., 39.

[43] Henrietta Atkin, *Famous Composers and Their Music* (Pittsburgh, PA: Hayes School Publishing Co., Inc., 2001), 30

[44] Turner, *The World's Greatest Composers: Franz Schubert*, 24.

[45] Ibid., 29.

[46] Dennis Garbor, Brainy Quote. Book Rags Media Network. Accessed August 2011. Available from http://www.brainyquote.com/quotes/quotes/d/dennisgabo107282.html.

[47] Smith and Carlson,*The Gift of Music: Great Composers and Their Influence*, 77.

[48] Osborne, *Schubert and His Vienna*, 46.

[49] Smith and Carlson, *The Gift of Music: Great Composers and Their Influence*, 78.

[50] Turner,*The World's Greatest Composers: Franz Schubert*, 35.

[51] Ibid., 57.

[52] Ibid., 58.

[53] *Schubert Chronology.* The Schubert Institute (UK). Accessed August 2011. Available from http://www.franzschubert.org.uk/life/time.html.

[54] *Historical Events for Year 1819.* HistoryOrb.comAccessed August 2011. Available from http://www.historyorb.com/events/date/1819.

[55] "staff." Encarta® World English Dictionary[North American Edition]2009 Microsoft http://www.bing.com/Dictionary/search?q=define+staff&go=&form=QB (August 2011).